J. Henry Harris

Robert Raikes

The Man And His Work

J. Henry Harris

Robert Raikes
The Man And His Work

ISBN/EAN: 9783744677622

Printed in Europe, USA, Canada, Australia, Japan

Cover: Foto ©Thomas Meinert / pixelio.de

More available books at **www.hansebooks.com**

ROBERT RAIKES.

THE MAN AND HIS WORK.

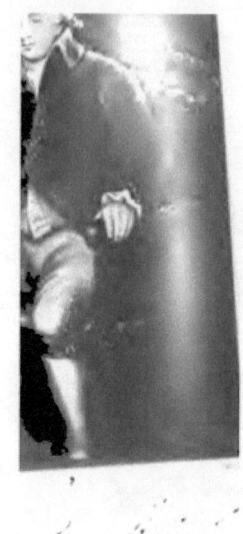

ROBERT RAIKES.

The Man and His Work.

Biographical Notes collected by JOSIAH HARRIS.
Unpublished Letters by Robert Raikes.
Letters from the Raikes Family.

OPINIONS ON INFLUENCE OF SUNDAY SCHOOLS.
(SPECIALLY CONTRIBUTED.)

EDITED BY
J. HENRY HARRIS.

INTRODUCTION BY DEAN FARRAR, D.D.

Illustrated Edition.

NEW YORK
E. P. DUTTON & COMPANY
BRISTOL, ENGLAND, J. W. ARROWSMITH
1899

CONTENTS.

	Page
INTRODUCTION BY DEAN FARRAR, D.D.	xiii
THE EDITOR'S NOTE	xxi

CHAPTER I.

WHY THESE MATERIALS WERE GATHERED . . . 1

    Some Early Influences of Sunday Schools—The Author's Visits to Gloucester in 1862-3—Robert Raikes's Sunday School—Interviews with Teachers—The Rev. Thomas Stock's Sunday School: Its Condition—State of Public Opinion in Gloucester on the Raikes Traditions—Effect on Author.

CHAPTER II.

HUMAN DOCUMENTS 13

    The Line of Inquiry—Rival Claims—Statements of Aged Persons: Arabella Herbert, John Oakley Packer, Sarah Packer, Caroline Watkins, Charles Cox, Priscilla Kirby, —— Eycott, and Anne Hannam—Some Results of Evidence of First Scholars and Teachers in Sunday Schools.

CHAPTER III.

WHOM NO MAN CARED FOR 36

    Why Raikes Interfered—Some First Scholars—Punishments in Sunday Schools—Statements by William Brick, ——-Cooksey, Samuel Pitt and —— Bourne, Respecting Condition and Behaviour of Children at School and in Church—Some "Terrible Bad" Boys—Language of the Children of the Lower Orders in Raikes's Day.

vi   CONTENTS.

CHAPTER IV.

AS SEEN OF MEN . . . .   Page
                                     48

 Robert Raikes Described—His Business and Places of Residence — Opinions Respecting Him by Paul Hawkins Fisher, of Stroud, and John J. Powell, Q.C., M.P. for Gloucester—Raikes a Vain and Benevolent Man, but not Actuated by Religious Motives — Further Investigation Necessary.

CHAPTER V.

AT WORK   57

 Raikes's Experiment Commenced 1780 — Some Social Conditions amongst Working Population — Experiment Successful—Allegations that Raikes "Borrowed" his Idea—Some Influences of Newspaper Press—Co-operation of Rev. Thomas Stock and Rev. Richard Raikes—Raikes's First Announcement in *Gloucester Journal*, November 3rd, 1783—Advocacy of the *Gentleman's Magazine*—The True Founder of Modern Sunday Schools—First Rules—The *Sunday Scholar's Companion*—Necessary Admonitions against Cursing—Mrs. Trimmer's Experiences.

CHAPTER VI.

THE NEW LIFE   71

 Raikes in Advance of his Time—The Slow Evolution of his Ideas—Studies from the *Gloucester Journal*—His Letter in the *Gentleman's Magazine*, 1785—Testimonies in Favour of the "Scheme" from Various Quarters—Raikes's Letters to Rev. William Lewelyn, Leominster: Anecdotes and Experiences—A Sunday School Lesson with the Magnet—He Complains that he is Allowed to "Walk Alone"—Signs of the New Life.

CHAPTER VII.

OPPOSING FORCES   86

 First Sunday School Board of Management—Sunday Schools Conceived as "Charity" Schools and Conducted as such—Sermons Preached, Large Sums Collected, and Donations Given for their Support—Reaction Against Sunday Schools—Hannah More's Experiences—What People Said Against Educating Lower Orders—Philippic in *Gentleman's Magazine* Against Sunday Schools and their Founder—The Bishop of Rochester Defends Himself—Anecdote by Raikes—His Love for the Psalms of David—Opposition in Scotland—The Rev. Thomas Burns's Sermon, 1798: Fears Sunday Schools will Destroy all Family Religion.

CHAPTER VIII.

WHERE RAIKES WAS TAUGHT 99

The Institution not an Inspiration—Raikes Twenty-five Years at Work on Social and Prison Reforms before Commencing Sunday Schools in 1780—His One Object to Prevent Criminals Being Made—Learnt His Lesson First from His Own Father—Robert Raikes the Elder—Prison Reforms: Extracts from *Gloucester Journal*—Raikes Forestalled Howard, but Worked with Him—Mastiffs Kept to Hunt Down Escaped Prisoners—Special Letters from Convicts to Botany Bay—Pages from a Closed History of England—Raikes a Student in Moral Pathology and a Practical Worker.

CHAPTER IX.

MR. RAIKES THE SABBATH-BREAKER 113

Prejudices Against Raikes in Gloucester—Printed the *Journal* on Sundays—The Whole Question Stated—Evidence of William Whitehead and James Whitehead, two Office Boys—Public Opinion with Reference to Sunday Work and Trading, End of Last Century—Note by Dr. Charles Cooke.

CHAPTER X.

FIFTY YEARS IN THE VINEYARD 126

Some Results of Mr. Raikes's Labours—Grand Moral and Social Reforms in Ten Years—Mr. Raikes's Own View of Himself—His Interview with Queen Charlotte at Windsor—Two of his Daughters Sunday School Teachers—The Duke of Gloucester Visits Him—The Empress Catherine Invites Him to Russia—Elected Honorary Member of Sunday School Society—Copy of Minute, June 11th, 1787—Raikes a Temperance Advocate; He Anticipates Hoyle—*Gloucester Journal* an Advanced Temperance Paper from 1757—Sunday Schools Unsectarian and Voluntary—Work of Sunday School Society in Ten Years—Raikes Lived to See Success of Sunday School System.

CHAPTER XI.

SOME PIONEERS 138

The Rev. John Marks Moffatt, Nailsworth, Established Sunday School about 1772—Biographical Notice—Miss

Page

Moffatt's Statement to the Author in 1863—Mr. Raikes's Letter to Mr. Moffatt in 1784—Mrs. Bradburn, *née* Sophia Cooke—Samuel Webb—William King, of Dursley—Adam Crompton, Little Lever—Catechising in Churches—Duty of Clergy Laid Down in Constitutions and Canons Ecclesiastical, 1603—Cardinal Borromeo's Schools—Differences Between Raikes and All Who Preceded Him.

CHAPTER XII.

THE PLACE OF MR. STOCK 161

His Claims to be Placed Before, or Bracketed with, Robert Raikes Considered—His History and Qualifications in 1780—Differences Between Raikes and Stock—Biographical Notes.

CHAPTER XIII.

SUNDAY SCHOOLS IN GREAT BRITAIN 170

Article Specially Contributed on Wales by Rev. David Charles—Sunday Schools in Scotland, Ireland, and the Channel Islands—Victor Hugo's Weekly Festival of Poor Little Children.

CHAPTER XIV.

MR. RAIKES AT HOME 185

The Domestic Instinct Strong—His Love of Family—His Will—The House in Bell Lane—Domestic Appointments—Statements by Servants, James Whitehead, William Whitehead, and William Redding, as to his Character and Habits—His Daughters' Marriages—Elected, with Dr. Jenner, Vice-President of Gloucestershire Society—His Religious Views Given in his Own Letters, from 1790 to 1794—His Politics—Fined £50 for Inserting an Advertisement: Story Told by Himself.

CHAPTER XV.

MRS. WELLER-LADBROKE'S LETTERS . . . 203

The Youngest and Last Surviving Daughter of Robert Raikes Tells the Story of her Father's Life.—Her Appreciation of his Character; His Habits and Studies—His Sudden Death—The Rev. Mr. Read's Appreciation of Mrs. Ladbroke.

CONTENTS.

CHAPTER XVI.

THE MOVEMENT WEIGHED 215

The Growth of Sunday Schools in England and Wales—Present Number of Schools, Teachers and Scholars in Great Britain and America—Letters from Elihu Burritt, Richard Cobden, M.P., Dr. H. Clay Trumbull, and Bishop Vincent on American Sunday Schools — Letters from Rev. Morley Punshon, the Right Hon. Sir John Packington, M.P., Rev. C. H. Spurgeon, Dr. John Cumming, and the Rev. Hugh Price Hughes on Raikes and Sunday Schools—The Opinions of Anglican Prelates on Some Influences of Sunday Schools, including: Dr. Tait (Archbishop of Canterbury), the Bishops of London, Exeter, Bath and Wells, Chester, Carlisle, Ripon, Down, Meath, Tuam, Quebec, and Adelaide, all written in 1870. Dr. Barry, formerly Primate of Australia, and Dr. Ellicott, Bishop of Gloucester, written in 1898.

CHAPTER XVII.

THE RAIKES FAMILY 240

Yorkshire Roots. History of the Family from 1507—The Gloucester Branch—Robert Raikes the Elder—Three Times Married—His Business Career—Robert Raikes the Younger—His Birth and Education—Correspondence with University Officials—His Trade and "Composing Stick"—The *Gloucester Journal* under His Editorship—His Marriage —Removal from Blackfriars to Southgate Street—His Family—Received Honorary Freedom of City of Gloucester, 1804—His Sudden Death and Funeral—Mrs. Raikes: Some Personal Recollections of Her—Early Popular Street Ballad on Raikes—Rev. Richard Raikes, Scholar and Christian.

CHAPTER XVIII.

LAST WORDS 286

True Birth of Modern Sunday Schools, 1783—Raikes's Methods Slowly Matured—Their Universal Application—"Very First" Sunday Schools Numerous in Gloucester—Absence of Reliable Testimony — Many Legends — Mrs. Critchley and Mrs. King's Schools—Illustrious Visitors to Raikes's Own School, Gray Fryars—Decadence of Raikes's and Stock's Historical Sunday Schools—Improved Condition of Things in 1898 — Unsympathetic Gloucester—Weakness of the Raikes Tradition since Centenary—Removal of Robert Raikes's Mural Tablet in St. Mary de Crypt Church—Pilgrims to the Raikes Tomb Deceived—Mr. Taylor's Opinion of a Simonical Transaction — The Raikes Memorial Hall and Tower—Reliability of Testimony of Aged Witnesses—The Editor's Sole Aim: to Make this History as Truthful and Profitable as Possible.

APPENDIX.

		Page
A.	RAIKES'S OWN STORY TOLD IN THE PRESS	303
B.	SUNDAY SCHOOLS IN FRANCE	327
C.	THE "SUNDAY SCHOLAR'S COMPANION"	329
D.	BREACHES OF PRIVILEGE OF PARLIAMENT	331
E.	A ROYAL ANECDOTE	333
F.	SIR THOMAS B. THOMPSON	334

ILLUSTRATIONS.

ROBERT RAIKES'S PORTRAIT   *Frontispiece*

                                                    Page

MRS. SARAH PACKER   19

MR. CHARLES COX   24

MISS PRISCILLA KIRBY   26

MR. WILLIAM KING   149

THE REV. THOMAS STOCK   161

MRS. SUSAN PERROT   181

FACSIMILE OF ROBERT RAIKES'S MARRIAGE
      CERTIFICATE   267

THE REV. RICHARD RAIKES   280

JAMES KING'S HOUSE   289

ROBERT RAIKES'S "OWN" SUNDAY SCHOOL   292

MEMORIAL TOWER TABLET   298

FACSIMILE OF LETTER WRITTEN BY MR. RAIKES
     IN 1784. (*Bound up in the Volume.*)

INTRODUCTION.

I HAVE been asked to say a few words by way of Preface to these new inquiries respecting the life and work of Robert Raikes, who is regarded, and justly regarded, as the main founder of the system of Sunday schools. Some very interesting records and reminiscences of his work will be found in the following pages; and the life of a man who was so kind, so good, and so richly blessed by the fruitfulness of his endeavours on behalf of his fellow-men cannot but contain valuable lessons.

The son of a Gloucester printer, and editor of the Gloucester paper, Robert Raikes inherited the position and trade of his father. The station which he occupied was, therefore, a comparatively obscure and humble one. But he had, nevertheless, been "anointed by the hands of invisible consecration" to achieve a great and blessed result, of which the effects have been fruitful throughout the whole world. Many might say, with the St. Paul of the modern poet:—

> "This is God's will: He takes, and He refuses,
> Finds Him ambassadors whom men deny.
> Wise ones nor mighty for this work He chooses?
> No; such as John, or Gideon, or I."

It is remarkable in how many instances those who have profoundly influenced the whole Church of God have been men who would otherwise have been utterly unnoticed in the world's annals. They listened to the Divine Voice which summoned them to a service of which they could neither estimate the importance nor measure the result. That voice of summons perhaps comes to thousands, and remains unheeded. Is not the biography of a simple citizen like Robert Raikes, and the fact that his life's work has produced an effect throughout the whole Christian world, at once an incentive to every one of us to neglect no duty to which we are called, and an encouragement also to believe that the simplest seedcorn of duty thus cast into the furrows of the world, may spring up in harvests of blessing more immense than we could have conceived to be possible? Just as one bad man may do incalculable mischief, so one good man may profoundly influence a whole generation—if not in his single person, yet by the combination of his work with that of others like-minded with himself.

> "The healing of the world
> Is in God's nameless saints. A single star
> May seem to give faint light; but countless stars
> Break up the night, and make it beautiful."

Any who work in Christ's vineyard for Christ's sake

may be influenced by numberless examples to work with the certainty that their efforts can never be in vain.

Let me give one or two instances, analagous to that furnished by the success of Robert Raikes, of the vast extension given, by God's blessing, to small and, apparently, humble efforts.

Take for instance the abolition of the slave trade.

The conscience of Christian England was amazingly dead to the enormous iniquity of buying or stealing men from their native country, and transporting them, often under circumstances of revolting cruelty, to toil as unpaid slaves in distant climates. The stirrings of doubt in men's minds upon this subject were stilled by various plausible sophistries of self-interest; and, most of all, because it is the tendency of custom to lie upon us

> " With a weight
> Heavy as frost, and deep almost as Life."

Familiarity with wrong deadens and paralyses the activities of conscience. In the year 1785, a young man, named Thomas Clarkson, had gained the Members' Prize for a Latin essay in the University of Cambridge. The subject of the essay had been "Is involuntary servitude justifiable?" The question was then regarded as an open one, so that either side might be advocated by the competitors. Clarkson, in his prize essay, had argued that the slave trade was morally unlawful. He recited his essay in the Senate house, and as he rode back to London his mind was agitated by the question: "If the slave trade be an iniquity, is it not my duty to fight against it?" Many would have been tempted to dismiss the thought as a chimæra. They might have contented themselves with the answer: "Here is a whole nation involved in the sanction of this trade, and of what possible use can it be for an unknown youth of the middle classes, like myself, to combat it?" But Clarkson was not content with this, and at last got off his horse near a little country inn, and sat down by the roadside to argue out the question with himself and his own conscience until the end. When he rose from his seat he had decided that, since he had a small independent fortune and was not called upon to follow a profession, it *was* his distinct duty to obey the call of God, and to devote the efforts of his life to put an end to this national iniquity. He did so; others joined him, especially Granville Sharpe, William Wilberforce, and Zachary Macaulay. Before their lives were over they had the high blessing of knowing that they had extended a nation's mercy to the most miserable and helpless of mankind, and had been enabled to save England from "the guilt of using the arm of freedom to rivet the fetters of the slave." Upon the spot where he alighted from his horse and sat down to think, has been erected a deeply interesting little monument commemorative of the event.

Or, take the case of John Howard. He was a private gentleman of quite humble rank, and a dissenter. "God's unseen Providence, by men nicknamed 'Chance,'" had brought him into a position which forced upon his notice the intolerable cruelty of the system maintained in our gaols. His sympathies were aroused. "The sorrowful sighing of the prisoners" which was ever entering into the ears of the Lord God of Sabaoth, stirred his inmost compassion. He did not say, "I am a mere nobody, and can do no good in this national matter." He simply devoted himself to the work of amelioration, leaving the results in the hand of God. What was the result? The foul prisons, not only of England but of all Europe, were purified. The tears of the rescued, which fell on his outstretched hand, were to him as jewels which were worth an Empire's ransom. And it was said of him at last: "For departed kings there are appointed honours, and the wealthy have their gorgeous obsequies. It was his nobler destiny to clothe a nation in spontaneous mourning, and to go down to the grave amid the benedictions of the poor."

I will take but one more instance: Antony Ashley-Cooper, Earl of Shaftesbury, might, had he so chosen, have spent his life in ease, luxury, and amusement, as thousands of other young noblemen have done. But while he was yet a boy at Harrow, he was witness of the brutal levity with which two drunken peasants were conducting a pauper's funeral; and then and there he vowed his life to the amelioration of the lot of the poor. Ere he died he had become the strongest living link of sympathy and unity between the rich and the destitute. Thousands of factory children, thousands of poor little "climbing boys," myriads of the neglected waifs and strays who thronged the ragged schools, the costermongers, the lunatics, and almost every class of the "sons and daughters of misery, and the multitude ready to perish," had reason to bless and perpetuate his name. His statue stands at the western door of Westminster Abbey, in marble not whiter than was his humane and noble life, and the two monosyllables carved upon the pediment—LOVE, SERVE—are a national lesson to which his example may help to give an eternal validity.

Such, too, was the characteristic of the life-work of Robert Raikes. He saw the little, dirty, neglected children—with the pitiable "slum-born" look written on their faces—singing lewd or brutal songs, and rioting in vice and ignorance, on Sundays, in the streets of the Cathedral City. Was he to be content with the faithless acquiescent plea that "What is everybody's duty is nobody's duty?" On the contrary, he asked himself, "Can nothing be done?" A voice within him said, "Try." "I did try," he says, "and see what God has wrought!" An experiment which now looks so simple and so humble as that of trying to lure these ragged children of wretchedness to the Cathedral service, and paying some poor women a shilling a day to teach them, resulted not only in a marked improvement in morals among the children of Gloucester, and a general amendment of the condition of the city, but in the gradual imitation of his example in thousands of other places, and in the founding of Sunday schools throughout this and many other countries.

It is no exaggeration at all to say that, through the organisation commenced by this simple citizen of Gloucester, hundreds of thousands of Christ's little ones have been reached, and have been influenced for their temporal and eternal good. One of the most brilliant of our judges—the late Mr. Justice Denman—once said to me that his experiences as a Sunday school teacher had been richer to him in interesting events and reminiscences than even his experiences as a Judge. And it is a remarkable fact that four, at least, of those eminent lawyers who have held the lofty position of Lord Chancellor—Lord Hatherley, Lord Cairns, Lord Selborne, and Lord Herschell—have been Sunday school teachers. Lord Hatherley continued his faithful labours in Sunday schools for forty years of his life. Such a work is indeed approved of God!

> "What, though around His throne of fire
> The everlasting chant
> Be wafted by the Seraph Choir,
> In glory jubilant?
>
> "Yet is He near us to survey
> These bright and ordered files,
> Like spring flowers in their best array,
> All silence and all smiles.
>
> "Save that each little voice in turn
> Some glorious truth proclaims;
> What Sages would have died to learn
> Now taught by cottage dames."

F. W. FARRAR.

EDITOR'S NOTE.

THE late Josiah Harris paid visits to the city of Gloucester and made "Notes" with the intention of writing a Biography of Robert Raikes, "The Man of Gloucester," as he was often called during and after the Jubilee Year of 1831. These visits were made in 1862-3, and there were then obtainable some fugitive magazine articles, and small volumes on Robert Raikes and the origin of Sunday schools. Inquiry led him to the conclusion that there existed in various forms a great deal of apparently unknown, certainly unworked, deposits of the richest character for biographical purposes.

The subject grew upon him, and his design broadened until his aim was to write the History of Sunday schools in all the counties of Great Britain and Ireland, and throughout the whole of the civilised world. This labour of love my father was unable to accomplish. He never lost sight of his object, but died in 1880 leaving behind him an immense quantity of notes, documents, and correspondence. It is only quite recently that I have had the leisure to give the whole mass careful examination.

After putting on one side all that might be considered as common knowledge about Robert Raikes and the first

Sunday schools in Gloucester, I found that there remained a precious residuum—all the more precious now because of the utter impossibility of re-collecting the narratives and opinions of persons long since silent.

It remained with me to determine whether I would destroy the notes and documents and letters, contributed often with love and in confidence of their being in some form published; or, whether I would produce a small volume by omitting the proposed History of Sunday schools throughout the world. I decided on the latter course, and it only remains to say that my work has been mainly editorial. I accept the responsibility for the form of the narrative, and only ask it to be believed that I have tried to present ROBERT RAIKES, THE THINKER AND WORKER, as he appeared in life to men.

After so long an interval I dare not use the language of compliment and thanks to the hundreds of ministers, Sunday school superintendents, chaplains of prisons and others, who contributed by letter or by word of mouth towards the completion of the volume as *originally* designed. Many, too many, I now know have passed away with the Author; but in all cases I have been careful to quote the authority for statements of fact; and, when possible and desirable, have given sufficient means for identification, so that survivors may be assured that no attempt has been made to deprive them of the best acknowledgment in my power for service rendered.

One exception, however, I may make; namely, in mentioning collectively the members of the Raikes family, to whom my late father was under the most precious of all obligations in matters of this kind—a friendly desire to help, and a generous toleration for delayed performance.

The volume, as it stands, is composed almost entirely of original documents, or documents derived from original sources. What has already appeared, when quoted at length, will be found in the Appendix.

The portrait of Robert Raikes is from an oil painting which in 1862 was in the possession of Mr. Warner, Gloucester, and is now in the possession of Mrs. Holloway, the Hill, Stroud; that of his brother, the Rev. Richard Raikes, is from a drawing by Charbonnier, now very rare; and the miniature likeness of the Rev. Thomas Stock is from the original, copied by Mr. John Jennings, Gloucester. The portraits of the old scholars and teachers were taken by photography in 1863—the youngest then being 75, and the oldest 87. I am able to give a tracing of Mr. Raikes's marriage certificate in 1767, and the facsimile of a letter written by him in 1784 to a gentleman who had anticipated him in establishing Sunday schools by about eight years.

In all about sixty autograph letters were placed at the Author's disposal. Some were on business matters, relating to the proof sheets of books passing through the press, to accounts, &c.; but some of them referred to Sunday schools, to his own position in regard to them, and his opinions respecting people and things social, religious, and political. Extracts from these letters will be found in various parts of the volume.

EDITOR'S NOTE.

The Editor recently paid a visit to the city of Gloucester, and had placed at his disposal a most valuable collection of documents, &c., relating to Robert Raikes, the Rev. Thomas Stock, and some Gloucesterhire Worthies, whose names can never be dissociated from the *origines* of Sunday schools. The collection of Mr. H. Y. J. Taylor, although more modern than that of the Author's, has been of much value to the Editor for supplemental and illustrative purposes; and sometimes it threw quite new light upon the older documents, obtained in many instances over thirty years previously.

ROBERT RAIKES.

CHAPTER I.

WHY THESE MATERIALS WERE GATHERED.

"Before I close this letter, I must assure you how thoroughly I appreciate your indefatigable efforts to make the history of my dearest father's life as truthful and profitable as possible."—Mrs. LADBROKE *to the Author.*

ROBERT RAIKES was born in the Cathedral City of Gloucester, in 1736. In 1780 he collected a few poor children and gave them instruction on Sundays. He died in 1811. His name, already on the lips and in the hearts of men, spread throughout the world.

More than eighty years after the germ of Sunday schools was planted and nursed into active life, Josiah Harris, who had been a Sunday school boy and then teacher in an antiquated but obscure fishing village on the south coast of Cornwall, visited the ancient and prosperous city of Gloucester. In his early youth he had sailed to Gloucester in one of his father's small coasting ships, and he had then fresh in his mind the part which he had taken in the Sunday school Jubilee, when the whole religious atmosphere in which he was born was charged with the magic of a name—the name of Robert Raikes.

The people of Cornwall in those days were very primitive, and susceptible to lasting religious influences. In 1831 the masses thrilled at the mere recollection of the Wesleys. A spiritual magnetism vibrated within, and there was for them a perpetual feast of love in the bare rooms and barns and whitewashed chapels. They were "believers" in its primitive and apostolic sense, and often fancied that Jesus was in very truth amongst them, and listened to them, and adopted them as "heirs to the inheritance" in the skies. But for this belief in a spiritual inheritance these people were very poor.

When Josiah Harris went to Sunday school, he had for teachers men in whom the Spirit of God seemed to dwell bodily. They were poor men, richly endowed with the faculty of drawing the young to them in the bonds of love; and as Robert Raikes and John Wesley were to them as two wings of the Seraph at the Throne of the Eternal, they imprinted on the souls of the young reverence for these men akin to worship.

In 1862 Mr. Harris contemplated his second visit to the city of Gloucester, with something of the spirit of a pilgrim visiting a holy shrine. For him it was "holy" in the sense in which a man who has suffered much may make holy a recollection, a place, a name associated with the happiest years of his youth.

A pardonable exaltation possessed him, so that he carried with him ideal notions of what he would hear and see in Gloucester, the birthplace and cradle of Sunday schools. Perhaps he expected too much, for he was certainly grievously disappointed. He thought he would find in the city wherein Robert Raikes was born and laboured and died, at least that reverential regard—worship almost—to which he had been accustomed in his youth; and further, he thought he would find the Sunday school system in flourishing perfection.

He found neither.

It was, however, reserved for the third visit, in January, 1863, to completely disillusionise him. The Editor of these pages was with him, and well remembers the visit paid to "Robert Raikes's Sunday school," in St. Mary de Crypt Church, on the afternoon of the 11th January. He stood upright in the chancel as one paralysed!

Then he busied himself with inquiries commenced the year previous, and it seemed as though in the City of Raikes the Raikes tradition had lost its charm and was rapidly dying out. After his visit in the previous year, he had read up what little had been preserved, and opened up correspondences which yielded much rich biographical matter; but he now wished to account to himself for the singular want of genuine interest shown in the very place where he expected to find it most ardent. He thought that there surely must be some glowing ashes yet to be found, to show that this was the place where the central fire once burned so luminously bright. He searched and found them, but for the most part amongst the poor and aged living in the narrow streets of the city.

The nearer he got to Raikes with the assistance of these tottering and poor men and women who had known him and been taught by him, the nearer he got to the secret of his success with children. Whatever else he lacked, he possessed the gift of enshrining himself in their hearts; and the nearer they approached the tomb, the deeper their love and the more certain they that " The Man of Gloucester " was deserving of all the praise which men spoke of him in every quarter of the world—except in his own city!

The reader is now prepared to make a pilgrimage of love through some of the narrow streets of Gloucester— never far from the shadow of the Cathedral, never far from St. Mary de Crypt Church, never far from Robert Raikes's dwellings. Before closing this book he will then have learnt all that, perhaps, it now is possible to learn of the character and habits and modes of thought and life's work of the man who, for more than a century, has set an impress upon the life of the world, without any regard to sect or creed. To classify the man he must be separated from his work, or, rather, from the results of it. With Luther or Wesley or Whitefield the man and his work seem one, so interdependent are they. If you separate them, you lose something of the man and something of the work; but it is not so with Raikes, and to see the man and know him as he was it is well to forget the results of his efforts, and see him through the eyes of those who knew him.

In 1863 this was possible, and those who knew Mr. Raikes knew him well, for, apparently, except when he married, he was never more than a few days absent from the city at any one time. The old population was very conservative in their habits—generation followed generation in the same houses, exercised the same trades, and handed on the old traditions. Of all the old people whom the Author interviewed, scarcely any had travelled far from the city in their lives, and not one had been long absent from it.

They knew Mr. Raikes, and, in very truth, were living guides. They remembered what he said and how he said it; where he went and when, what he did and what was said of it. Little details of every-day life impressed themselves on their memories, so that they could say what Mr. Raikes wore, and how he walked, and were careful to note when he had silver buckles in his shoes. They made careful note of his temper, and of his freedom in giving pennies to good boys and getting bad boys soundly thrashed. In all these and such manners the memories of these old people were "as perfect as acorns." In some other matters the infirmities of age made themselves felt; but with all drawbacks, we shall not be long with these "human documents" without getting a vivid presentment of the Man.

It is not probable that the Author would have taken the trouble which he did to unearth these old people, and to follow up the lines which they suggested, but for the fateful visit to the "Original" Sunday schools in Gloucester on the afternoon of the 11th January, 1863.

The following entries in the Author's diaries will now explain why these materials were gathered:—

VISIT TO ROBERT RAIKES'S SUNDAY SCHOOL.

"GLOUCESTER, *Sunday, January* 11*th*, 1863.

"Visited with my son the Sunday school established by Robert Raikes, in the Church of St. Mary de Crypt, this afternoon. When we entered the church we were fairly astonished to find in the 'boys' school,' on the right-hand side, where the remains of Mr. Raikes lie, a respectable-looking, steady man named Frederic Wakefield, 38 years of age, and only six or seven boys, apparently from 5 to 12 years of age. They were seated on one form, and the teacher sat on a stool in front of them.

"The children were orderly and clean. The teacher said they were very ignorant, and we found them to be so.

"We expressed surprise at so few being present. The teacher said he was very sorry, and the fault was not his. Usually more boys were present, but the schoolmistress [the superintendent] having left the previous week, the boys had heard of it and left too. He observed that when he induced boys to come, there were no teachers to look after them.

"He was a paid teacher. He was paid £4 per annum,

and said: 'I am fond of the work, and am willing to lend a hand under any circumstances.'

"*Q.* 'Do you know that this is Robert Raikes's Sunday school?'

"*A.* 'Yes, quite well.'

"*Q.* 'And what do you think the whole Sunday school world would say if they could see this pitiful sight?'

"*A.* 'I'm sure I do not know; but, sir, the fault is not mine.'

"The girls' school was on the other side, where there was a miniature Babel. There were about twenty scholars, apparently under the care of two females: one, Fanny Saunders, a steady-looking unmarried woman about 30, who had known and attended the school for twenty years; and the other, a young girl about 14, named Sarah Ann Cooper.

"Miss Saunders said the children were tolerably well up in reading the Bible; and they were intelligent-looking and clean. She attributed the ruin of the school to the systematic neglect which it had received, and gave me some particulars which shocked me. . . .

"I spoke to all three of them [Wakefield, Saunders, and Cooper] of the solemn importance of keeping up THIS school, as it was Robert Raikes's; and Miss Saunders seemed to be a little alive to it, Mr. Wakefield *very much so.*

"This 'school,' if such it may be called, seemed to me to represent ruin and decay—cold and cheerless and disorderly, right on the ashes of Raikes. Oh, the profanation! Is there no Inspiration!"

This visit to the St. Mary de Crypt Sunday School, to which was intrusted the great and distinguished privilege of carrying on the traditions of 1780, greatly distressed the visitor. His own ideals were shattered, and what added to a humiliation, which became to him something personal, was the rumour, often repeated, that the historical continuity of the "original" school had been broken, not once but twice, the first time being in the lifetime of Robert Raikes himself!

THE REV. THOMAS STOCK'S SCHOOL.

The narrative continues :

"I then went to Worcester Street and inspected the Sunday school. It was held in a schoolhouse devoted to day and Sunday schools. I saw there two respectable-looking, genteely-dressed and well-spoken females—one the governess of the day school, and the other an amateur friend.

"The governess said the boys' school in this building had been given up for some time, but there was a boys' school in St. John's parish. The girls' school had gradually dwindled away. She believed the reason was because none of the ladies in the congregation felt any interest in it. There were twenty girls present this afternoon, but usually there was a larger attendance—the holidays accounted for their absence.

"I asked the governess if she knew this was once the school that the Rev. Mr. Stock superintended and delighted in? She said yes, and there were banners on the premises about him now, one of which she shewed me. It was a neat banner bearing this inscription:

'FIRST SUNDAY SCHOOL ESTABLISHED IN GLOUCESTER, 1780, BY THE REV. THOMAS STOCK, RECTOR OF ST. JOHN'S.'

"The governess said that several persons had of late been there to see this banner—among others the Rev. Mr. Brown, the clergyman of the parish. She also said that she felt it irksome to have to attend church and school, Sundays, with the children, as well as [school] on other days, for she was tired with the scholastic duties of the other days; but she was told by Mr. Brown, when she engaged for the situation of teacher to the day school, where there were about fifty scholars, that she must attend to the Sunday school as well, for he had no one else to do it."

And then there follows this "note," which seems to have been wrung from the Author with anguish:

"By what fatality is it that here, in the very cradle of the Sunday school system, where the germ first budded so genially, the bloom burst so beautifully and fragrantly, and the fruits developed so healthily and so fair, that here it should be smitten with fatuity, and to be ready to die of inanition?

"How changed! While here, in the sacred spot where Raikes and Stock tried with such success the grand problem, the thing is all but dead, in America, as Elihu Burritt tells me in a letter just received, it is growing to a gigantic power, full of bloom and beauty! How is it that prophets can have no honour in their own country? Alas, alas, that it should be so. Oh, shades of Raikes and Stock, veil your faces as ye pass by St. Mary de Crypt and St. John's Schools!"

And these were the two Sunday schools about which the soul of the city was at that moment greatly disturbed by one of the periodical quarrels between the "Stockists" and "Raikists," as to whom the honour of the "First Founder" was due. This last quarrel had been unusually bitter and prolonged, and the Rev. Mr. Sayers, Rector of St. Mary de Crypt, had only a short time before concluded an angry newspaper correspondence with reference to Raikes's School under his charge. He indignantly denied that the school had ever been discontinued, and alleged, triumphantly, that in the boys' school the average attendance was 14 or 15, and in the girls' 19; total, 34!

In an interview with the Author he said:

"It is true that the Sunday school has been, and still is, greatly depressed; but there is no reason why it may not be raised again."

The Author had an interview with Mrs. Watkins, who had resigned her superintendence of the girls' school after twenty years. She was the grand-daughter of the Mrs. Mary Critchley who claimed to be the first schoolmistress, worthy of the name, appointed by Robert Raikes.

The note of the interview is as follows:

"'Is it true that Mr. Raikes's Sunday school was ever given up?'

"'No.'

"'How few children have you seen in the school at any one time?'

"'Perhaps a dozen.'

"'Enough to keep it alive?'

"'We kept school with them.'

"'Does anyone take a particular interest in this school *because* it is Robert Raikes's?'

"'I cannot speak outside my own family. We all do; but strangers think much more of Robert Raikes than the people of Gloucester do. My mother, Mrs. Sarah Packer, is alive; she is the daughter of Mrs. Mary Critchley. Yes, she is able to see you, and will be glad to tell you what she knows.'"

The reader will better follow the narratives in the next chapter, and understand the drift and purport of some of the questions, after reading these "notes" of a visit to the historical Sunday schools of Gloucester and the interviews set forth. In order more fully to understand the effect on the mind of the Author, a few interjectional sentences in his Journal may be quoted:

"I am daily astonished at the complete apathy amongst the people whom I talk to, at this miserable and disgraceful state of things." Again: "When I talk to well-to-do citizens earnestly, they seem surprised at my warmth and interest in the matter, and not a few seem to think that I am impertinently inquisitive. When, however, I tell them of what has been done, and is doing, elsewhere, and of the love and reverence in all parts of the world for Robert Raikes, 'The Man of Gloucester,' I notice a languid interest is excited." Again: " Some take the matter very philosophically, and say that 'Sunday schools have answered their purpose, and, like everything else, must decay, commencing, like some fruits, at the core'!"

This was the condition of things in Gloucester City in the beginning of 1863; and the effect upon the mind of the Author, to whom it was an astounding revelation, was to send him amongst those who composed and then helped to build up the first Sunday schools, and so find out for himself whether the love which had been infused into his own bosom when a child, and remained there, had reason for its claim or was simply one more delusion.

NOTE.—The improved condition of things in Gloucester City is referred to in the concluding chapter.

CHAPTER II.

HUMAN DOCUMENTS.

"Every heart that has beat strong and cheerfully has left a hopeful impulse behind it in the world, and bettered the condition of mankind."
—STEVENSON.

THE first line of inquiry was: Who is there now living in the city of Gloucester who knew Robert Raikes well, and can be relied upon to give their narratives honestly for the purposes of publication? In 1863, as already mentioned, the air was full of contradictions with regard to three points: 1. Who founded Sunday schools? 2. When they were founded. 3. Where the first Sunday school was held and by whom. It would be difficult for any one outside of the city to understand the heat which was engendered in discussions on the rival claims of the Rev. Thomas Stock, Rector of St. John the Baptist, and of Robert Raikes to the honour of being the First Founder of the Sunday School system. Much greater interest was taken in this purely Academic discussion than in the healthy working of the schools, and much care was necessary to avoid deception, because there were no written records in existence to which to refer. This is mentioned here partly to instruct the reader and partly by way of explanation of what follows.

It was, however, a matter of good fortune that in 1863 there were living in the city some aged persons of sound and vigorous intellect who were children when the first Sunday schools were founded by Mr. Raikes and Mr. Stock; persons who as they grew up continued a family connection with certain schools, and persons who were able to fix dates approximately by certain other events. The evidence of these persons was *firsthand and the best obtainable*.

It is the fact that the reminiscences of these old people had never been collected and published, and it is also the fact that the people who knew Raikes and Stock best in connection with the organisation and building up of Sunday schools were the poor. They always had been poor, and their original poverty in one way answered for their good faith, for had they not been poor and ignorant they would not have been taken into the first Sunday schools established in Gloucester. We know now that the collection of children on Sundays for instruction was at first an experiment pure and simple; that the experiment lasted nearly three years, and that the *real birth* of modern Sunday schools was not until November 3rd, 1783. From 1780 to 1783 their state was embryotic.

What doubt and confusion there is with regard to the first Founder and places and dates, exists also with reference to the three years of almost secret experiment. Apart from historical value, the evidence of the old people turned out to be of the greatest interest, as showing the social elements experimented upon and the modes of treatment. Sunday school flowers we have, but what were the seedlings?

Some of these old people were photographed. They were aged at the date of the Jubilee, they died long before the Centenary, and they speak now in print, and for the first time, of the Robert *Reekes*,* as they called him, whose memory for them was an inspiration. It should be stated that these old people were seen separately; their statements were taken down in shorthand, so as to spare them fatigue, and in consequence their narratives possess more freshness and vigour and picturesqueness than they otherwise might.

The following extracts are taken from the Author's notes:

Miss ARABELLA HERBERT, 40 Worcester Street, aged 72 next November (1863), in reply to my questions, said as follows:

"I am a native of Gloucester. I knew Robert Raikes by sight. I never was to his school. He used to be called 'Bobby Wild Goose,' because he was so active, I suppose. I have heard my mother call him so many times. She would say: 'There goes Bobby Wild Goose and his ragged regiment'—meaning the children he was taking to church after the morning school. Or, she would say: 'There goes Bobby Wild Goose to the Cathedral again.' Sometimes boys, ragged varments they were,

* In the old Gloucester dialect "a" is pronounced as "ee."

followed him or met him in the Palace Yard, because he was kind to them and gave them pennies and things. He used to go to early morning prayers in the Cathedral.

"Yes, I remember him well. He was a fair, well-looking man. He used to wear a brown wig with double curls [double rows of curls] to it, and he carried a stick. He had a school in Catherine Street, kept by Mrs. King, and then by her husband. I did not go to that school. Our family were 'Church Methodists.'

"I have heard say that Mr. Stock started the first school, but I do not know. There was one in the Northgate and another in the Eastgate Street, kept by a woman named Crowdy, and another in Cross Keys Lane. There were other schools, but I have no reason for remembering them. I don't know who founded them.

"I was at Mr. Raikes's funeral. A funeral dirge was sung to him, but I don't recollect the words.*

"I believe Mrs. Critchley—the man Critchley's wife —was Mr. Raikes's first regular schoolmistress, and she was an old woman when I was a young woman. The school was in the Southgate Street, close to and facing St. Mary de Crypt Church.

"The Reverend Richard Raikes, 'Pazun Reekes' he was mostly called, used to give the Wesleyan Schools 5s. every year; I am sure of this, because I used to know the young woman who used to go and collect it of him.

* Another witness, Anne Hannam, supplies the deficiency in part.

"When I was young we used to have a tea meeting* every year in honour of Robert Raikes.

"I recollect that the little girls who followed Mr. Raikes to his funeral wore white bonnets — muslin [?linen], I think—with black strings. The bonnets were formed of a pasteboard front and a kind of cap caul. They were not specially made. Mr. Raikes used to like to see the girls clean and neat, and bonnets were provided for them to wear on Sundays. This was not done for a long time after the starting of the schools—the girls had to be civilised first. They were worse than the boys, I have heard many people say.

"The girls were not taken into the schools until after the boys—I mean the first schools were for boys only, and when they succeeded, schools were formed for girls. I have always understood that this was so."

[NOTE.—This witness is a highly respectable woman; has an excellent memory, is very intelligent and affable in her manners.]

The next witness, Mr. John Oakley Packer, is the third generation of a family most intimately connected with Mr. Raikes's schools. His grandmother was the Mary Critchley who kept *the* Sunday school in Southgate Street which had the greatest amount of Robert Raikes's personal attention, after Mrs. Critchley's appointment. Although on his own initiative or in connection with others

---

* In 1880, the Centenary year, Mrs. Summerhill—an old scholar—stated that the first anniversary after Mr. Raikes's death the Crypt School children had a dinner of roast beef and plum pudding.

he started schools in Soot Alley, Catherine Street, and elsewhere, he abandoned some and drafted the scholars to Southgate Street. This school was held in an old-fashioned house, now (1899) occupied by Mr. Lapington, butcher, and may fairly be considered as Robert Raikes's own. Mrs. Critchley so considered it; so did her daughter (Mrs. Packer), the next witness in this group.*

Mr. JOHN OAKLEY PACKER says: "I live at 2 Bell Lane, am Registrar of Births and Deaths, and sexton to St. Mary de Crypt. I am 58 years of age. I knew Robert Raikes, and was six years old when he died. My grandmother, Mrs. Mary Critchley, was the first schoolmistress chosen by Robert Raikes."

Q. "Are you sure of that?"

A. "Yes, my mother is living, and can tell you."

Q. "Was not Mr. James King or his wife appointed before your grandmother?"

A. "For Sunday school children only, perhaps, yes; but they paid my grandmother to teach boys on week days as well. She was his regular schoolmistress, for she knew how to handle the boys, and a rough lot they were by all accounts."

Q. "Have you any letter or record of any sort of your grandmother's appointment?"

---

* Mr. J. Oakley Packer was the sexton of St. Mary de Crypt in 1863, and in 1880—the Centenary—made a statement to Mr. H. Y. J. Taylor, the Gloucester antiquarian. The Editor compared the later with the former statement, and found that it did not materially differ. It speaks well for the man's honesty that the Raikes' traditions had not grown upon him notwithstanding the local excitement during the Centenary, and *when he was the only surviving male Sunday school scholar who had a personal knowledge of Robert Raikes in the city of Gloucester.*

A. "None. I remember what I have heard. I can tell you about Mr. Raikes's funeral. The St. Mary de Crypt—Raikes's school children—walked in front of the coffin when it was carried from the house in Bell Lane into the church. They went through Crypt Alley. Mr. Raikes was buried in his father's vault, on the south side of the chancel. After his death Mr. Baylis took to the school, and then Mr. Montagu. *It never went down.* I went to the school in 1810. Mr. Raikes was a very benevolent, kind-hearted man. If a child pleased him he would sometimes give him a shilling—always something."

The next person whose testimony was taken was Mrs. SARAH PACKER, the mother of the preceding witness. She said: "I was 86 last December [1862]. My mother (Mary Critchley) was the very first person who kept Robert Raikes's Sunday school. At one time she kept a small public-house called the 'Trumpet Inn,' Littleworth; then she came and lived in Southgate Street, where Mr. Butt, the shoemaker, now lives.

Mrs. Sarah Packer.

[Mr. Lapington, the butcher's, in 1899.]

"Mr. Raikes came to my mother when she was living in Littleworth, and asked her if she would take care of some poor children, as it was a pity that they should run about on Sundays, and she said she would when she removed into Southgate Street. This she did. Her house was the corner of the Grey Fryars, facing the church."

Q. "There might have been other schools opened in the meantime?"

A. "I can't say. I only tell you what I know. I don't know the date, but I have heard it was in 1780. My mother remained schoolmistress up to her death, when I succeeded her. After me a Mrs. Alder officiated, and then a Mrs. Wilks. After her the Rev. Mr. Sayers [Rector of St. Mary de Crypt] came to my daughter, Mrs. Watkins, and asked her to take charge of the school. She did so. This was in the year 1844, as shown by an entry in a Bible given to my daughter by the Rector's wife.*

"General George Cooke came from America two years ago, and I gave him Robert Raikes's portrait. He was a native of Gloucester, and told me that he was a teacher in Mr. Raikes's Sunday school."

Q. "Did Robert Raikes's school ever go down?"

A. "No. It never died away. Robert Raikes was a very kind-hearted man, and so was his brother the parson. They used to go down on the quays and wharves

---

* The entry is as follows: "Caroline Watkins, from the Honourable L. S. Sayers, St. Mary de Crypt. Dec. 15, 1844."

and pick up the dirty boys, and sometimes have them clothed a bit."

Q. " Was he a rich man ? "

A. " He was not supposed to be very rich. He was a printer, and died in his house in Bell Lane. On the day of the funeral the children collected on the lawn, and received one shilling and a cake each."

[NOTE.—This old lady is rather feeble, but gave her testimony without wavering. She has a strong love for the memory of Raikes. She did not like any doubt being suggested even about his being the real Founder of Sunday Schools. She was wheeled to the photographer's, and I have an excellent likeness of her. She bears an irreproachable character, and so, I believe, all her family do.]

Mrs. CAROLINE WATKINS, daughter of the above, said:

" I am 50 years of age. I am sure the school—the original school I call it—never went down. I never heard of such a thing in my life. I and my family have always been connected with St. Mary de Crypt Church and with the school.

" I went to the school so soon as I was able to speak.

" My grandmother, Mary Critchley, kept Mr. Raikes's day school as well. My grandfather was the master of a Sunday school for boys, as well as clerk of the parish for a great many years. Mrs. Alder, who succeeded my grandmother, is dead, but Mrs. Wilks is still living.

"I will tell you the history of the school."

Q. "Robert Raikes's school?"

A. "Yes, Robert Raikes's *first and most important* school. It was first held in my grandmother's house, then in St. Mary de Crypt Church, then in the Crypt Grammar School adjoining the church, then at the Corn Exchange, on account of the increase of the number of children."

Q. "How long was it held in the Corn Exchange?"

A. "About twelve months, but being so cold 'they' came back to the church again, where the children still come to school.

"The greatest number of children I recollect ever attending the school is from 100 to 120—boys and girls—but at present the number is very much less. My connection with the school has, as you know, now ceased.

"When Mrs. Critchley died, she was followed to her grave by the Sunday school children—and she was the first schoolmistress of this, the first Sunday school. She died August 17th, 1822, aged 72 years. She lived, after my grandmother was born, at the 'Trumpet Inn,' Littleworth, in this city. My mother [Mrs. Packer] was quite young when she went to live in Southgate Street, just opposite Mr. Raikes's house, where the first school was held. It is likely that the school was opened shortly after they went to live in Southgate Street.

"The children who were brought there were of the very lowest kind that could be found."

Q. "You say 'brought,' did they not come of their own accord as children do now?"

A. "Some were certainly *brought*, and some were induced to come by promises of nice things to be given them if they would come regularly, and wash themselves and comb their hair tidy. I used to hear a rhyme when I was young. It was like this:

> 'Clean hands, clean face, and tidy combed hair,
> Are better than fine clothes to wear.' "

Q. "Of all the children who have passed through the schools, do you remember the names of any who have greatly distinguished themselves?"

A. "I know a great many who turned out to be respectable and fairly well-to-do citizens."

Q. "Do you recollect hearing of any great genius springing from Robert Raikes's school?"

A. "No, I never heard of any."

The next person who gave his testimony was, in many respects, a remarkable old man, and was a scholar in a school in Soot or Sooty Alley, opened by Mr. Raikes before Mrs. Critchley kept the Sunday and day* school in the Southgate Street. This Soot or Sooty Alley was in Littleworth, the slum of the city which Raikes most affected for getting choice specimens for his experiment in what he aptly called "botanizing in human nature."

* Mr. Raikes gave two shillings a week extra to one or more women to teach children at meal times or in the evenings; but this was not until he satisfied himself that Sunday teaching alone was insufficient. He himself says so.

Mr. CHARLES COX, Hare Lane, aged 87 next autumn (1863), and chapel keeper of the Baptist Chapel, said:

"I am a native of Gloucester. I was about five years of age when I went to a Sunday school opened by Mr. Raikes in Sooty Alley, opposite the City Prison. The place was called 'Sooty Alley' because the chimneysweeps lived there.

"This, I believe, was the first Sunday school opened in Gloucester. A woman named Meredith kept the school. There were twelve or fourteen boys there when I went there, and some of these boys afterwards went to the school in Southgate Street kept by Critchley."

Mr. Charles Cox.

Q. "Was it Mr. Raikes's or Mr. Stock's school in Sooty Alley?"

A. "Mr. Raikes's. After I attended the school for a short time, I was sent to a school opened by Mr. Stock in Dolphin Lane. A man named Bamford kept it. I was removed *because I belonged to Mr. Stock's parish*.

"I went to the school in Sooty Alley within a few weeks after it was opened. I feel certain that this was the first school opened in Gloucester by Mr. Raikes."

Q. "Or by Mr. Stock?"

A. "The school I was removed to was certainly opened by Mr. Stock afterwards, but not long—a few months may be."

[NOTE.—This old man's faculties are as keen as many men's twenty years younger. I asked him if he would go and have his likeness taken, and he said, "Yes, gladly." He walked to the photographer's and had his likeness taken.

I visited Sooty Alley. It is in a low part of the city. The house in which Cox says the school was held is still standing. It is a brick house—nearly 100 years old, I should think. A mason's labourer inhabits it now. I made inquiries, but no one in the neighbourhood had heard anything about a Sunday school having once been there.

It may be that Cox is the only man now living in the city who has any knowledge of a school held there as a makeshift before Mrs. Mary Critchley was ready to take the little ragamuffins into her house in Southgate Street—one of the principal thoroughfares in the city.]

Down to this point the Raikes traditions as to the origin of Sunday schools is pre-eminent; and now we come to the evidence of an aged spinster, of most sweet and gentle character, whose knowledge and sympathies were all in favour of the Rev. Thomas Stock.

Miss PRISCILLA KIRBY, Sweet Briar Street, said: " I am a native of Gloucester, and I am 75 years of age.

St. Catherine's Nap and St. Mary's Nap [meadow] were spaces of ground where children used to play. I knew the Rev. Thomas Stock. The first school I know anything about was kept in Hare Lane by a Mrs. Bretherton.

Miss Priscilla Kirby.

She was an old woman when I was a girl. Mr. Stock employed Mrs. Bretherton and her husband to keep that school. Mr. Stock established it; but I cannot say in what year. He had three schools: two in St. John's and one in St. Aldate's parish. A person named Tanner was the master of one of the St. John's schools, and a Mrs. Lea kept the school in St. Aldate's. They are all dead—many a long year ago.

"These schoolmistresses were paid £1 per quarter for each school by the Rev. Mr. Stock, who got the money by public subscription.

"The children used to go to school at ten o'clock on a Sunday morning. We used to go to school in the church in the afternoon, and after service in the afternoon Mr. Stock used to come to us. He used to explain the Scriptures to us.

"We used to learn reading, Catechisms and Answers —Mann's Catechism and Lewis's, I think. He used to stay until twelve o'clock. We went again at two o'clock in the afternoon, and every third Sunday Mr. Stock used to address us in public in the church.

"Mr. Robert Raikes and his brother [the Rev. Richard Raikes] used to come occasionally to visit us, and see how we progressed: he [R. Raikes] used to distribute a crown [piece] in small prizes.

"I think I can see Robert Raikes now saying to the boys: 'I can see what bad boys you have been.'

"Mr. Stock was a poor man when compared to Mr. Robert Raikes.

"When Robert Raikes was buried *the children in his parish followed him to his grave, but we did not.*

"Robert Raikes was considered by some [persons] as a very ostentatious sort of a man. I think he was a very good man; and I am sure the Rev. Mr. Stock was a very excellent man indeed. Mr. Stock was a very pious man, and was much abused for his goodness.

"My father followed Mr. Bretherton in the mastership of the school in Hare Lane—his name was Jacob Kirby.

"I was always in that school, and was for ten years the mistress (sole).

"After many years elapsed the Dissenters began to form Sunday schools, and as they advanced we declined. Another cause of our decline was because the Rev. Mr. Bayly, who succeeded Mr. Stock, did not attend to the school as Mr. Stock did. I was born in 1787. The school was finally given up about the year 1817. I think Mr. Stock died about the year 1803.

"St. John's School, I believe, has always been kept up. It is now in Worcester Street.*

"The ladies in my time used to think it below them, and that it was a degradation to them to assist as teachers in Sunday schools, but it is very different now.

"My mother always said that Mr. Stock was the Founder of Sunday schools.

"There was a Bible class when I was a child, and this was conducted by Mr. Stock.

"Robert Raikes was a very 'buckish' sort of a person when he was young, and there was always a great deal of 'style' with him.

"He used to go every morning with the children to the College prayers. After that he used to read the Bible to them. I know this, because I knew some of the boys who liked to go with him. He was very kind to them, and there was no one scarcely in those days to condescend to notice poor children like he did.

"I never knew there to be any unpleasantness between Robert Raikes and Thomas Stock.

"Mr. Stock was a very benevolent man and a very popular man, and was sent for from all parts of the city to come and visit poor sick people. At this the other clergymen grew displeased, and he would not afterwards go unless he had a written request.

"Mr. Stock was a great disciplinarian. I profited very much under him. He did me much good. He gave me

* Visited by the Author, January 11th, 1863. *See* preceding chapter.

kind instruction and sound advice, and I shall always feel grateful to him, and I should wish to see justice done to him in the matter respecting Sunday schools.

"A gentleman named Wintle [the Rev. Mr. Wintle], who knew Mr. Stock very well, once came to my house, and while there he read from a book published on Robert Raikes and Sunday schools, and when he came to a certain passage in it he said: 'Now this is what Mr. Stock has been reading to his wife and to me, and when he came here he said, "This is false!"'

"I do not remember the title of the book, but I think the passage was something stating that Robert Raikes was the Founder of something connected with Sunday schools, which he was not.

"I cannot say that Mr. Raikes did not first start Sunday schools, I can only say I don't believe he did."

Q. "And for what reason?"

A. "One reason is, he had not the time to devote to them that Mr. Stock had. He had a newspaper, and *every Sunday he was all day at work in printing it.* I know this to be the truth."*

[NOTE.—The above witness has an extraordinarily clear memory, never hesitates, and at times speaks with natural eloquence. She is said to have come from a very respectable family. She evidently was greatly predisposed towards Mr. Stock. When I expressed myself as at all doubtful of what she was saying, she would say: "This

---

* The editing and printing of the *Gloucester Journal* on Sundays is fully dealt with in Chapter IX.

is as true as if I were at the table of the Lord's Feast."
I subsequently had her likeness taken.*]

Mr. EYCOTT, furniture broker, &c., 62 next November, deposed: "I am a native of Gloucester. I was about six or seven years old when I first went to Robert Raikes's Sunday school in Southgate Street. The girls' school was kept by Mrs. Critchley, and the boys' school was in the next house to it, nearer the church. The only education I ever received was at Robert Raikes's school. I cannot write.

"Robert Raikes had a knack of touching the boys under their chins and saying: 'That is a nice little boy.' He used to take us sometimes into his garden, and whoever was the best boy in his examining of us, was the best rewarded by him.

"He was buried in the morning, and all the children assembled outside his house in the Crypt Alley, and each of them had a cake and one shilling before they started to the funeral.

"The schools were never dropped in my time. They ebbed and flowed-like [as to numbers], but never went down.

"I knew his brother, the Rev. Richard Raikes. He was a good man and humble. He used to take his lantern

---

* Those who knew her well described her in 1880 to Mr. Taylor, of Gloucester, as "a well educated and most intelligent woman." She was then long dead. She gave her nephew (a Mr. Goddard) a narrative which "he wrote out and put with other documents into a silk stocking!" These valuable records were, however, destroyed by fire.

and go out into the streets by night and bring in all the loose women he could find, and take care of them, and try to bring them into better ways. The good that man did no one can tell!"

The next interview took place in the old women's day ward in the Gloucester Union. There was a fire in the ward, and some of the old women wore white caps and blue check costumes, and some sate around the fire and listened to the conversation. Sometimes these old people nodded their approval, and sometimes they sighed and muttered to themselves, but took no part in the dialogue.

Miss ANNE HANNAM said: "I am 73 years of age. I was sent with other children to Mr. Raikes's school when I was quite little—five years old perhaps. My sister had been there two years before, she was older than I.

"Oh, yes, I was at the funeral, which took place on a Saturday* morning. I took charge of some of the younger children, and I got one shilling and a cake like the rest. What happened was like this. We went on to the Garden Green through Crypt Alley, and when they were bringing out the coffin we pitched singing. Then we went on in front, and the coffin was carried by bearers behind. There's only a wall separating the churchyard from the grounds of the house in which Mr. Raikes died.

"What did we sing? We sang five verses from the

---

* This is quite accurate. Mr. Raikes died on Friday, April 5th, and was buried eight days afterwards, namely, April 13th, 1811, as appears by the church register.

xvi., xc., and another Psalm; and we sang on until the service commenced.

"After the service we sang again 'till the body was lowered into the vault.

"The Rev. Mr. Baylis read the funeral service."

Q. "Was there an address?"

A. "Not then."

Q. "Was a funeral sermon preached about Mr. Raikes?"

A. "I do not know. The only person who preached at St. Mary de Crypt then was Mr. Baylis, so I suppose if there was any sermon preached he preached it."

Q. "Is your sister alive who went to the Sunday school with you?"

A. "I don't know. She left, and when poor people get divided they're lost to each other. It was so with us."

Q. "What books were used in the school?"

A. "The book which explained the meaning of the Fast Days, Collects, etc., a Reading-made-Easy* Book, Texts and Psalters.

"Sometimes we went in the week-day to Mr. Raikes's house and stood on the Green. He used to read a chapter to us, and explain the meaning of it. He had a very good way with children."

Q. "What do you mean by 'good way?'"

---

* The old people usually pronounced this as "Redinmadesy" in one word, and meant any elementary book. In this instance the *Sunday Scholars' Companion* was meant, printed and published by R. Raikes, in or before 1785.

A. "He had authority with him and yet they were not afraid; and he would pat them on the head and on the cheeks, and touch them under the chin and say they were good and nice and clean, if they were so. He liked to see boys' and girls' hair combed. Many children never saw a comb before he gave them one. Their hair was all matted, and it was not easy to use a comb at first. The children would use their fingers for a time."

Q. "Were there many scholars in your school?"

A. "I have known fifty or more girls together. I can give you a list of lady teachers in my time: Miss Elizabeth Montagu, the two Miss Edwards, Lady Thompson, and Mrs. Garrett, the two last were Raikes's own daughters. I was in the school twenty years."

Q. "Did Mr. Raikes's daughters show much interest in the children?"

A. "Well, they were ladies, and the children were not always so nice and clean as they should be. It was a rare thing for a real lady to teach vulgar children then."

Q. "But they taught?"

A. "Oh, yes! I fancy they came by way of encouragement to poor people's children to pick up nice ways by imitating them. I was in the school twenty years—quite five years after Mr. Raikes died."

Q. "During your time did the school ever go down?"

A. "No, certainly not. Mr. Raikes used to visit the prison if there was anyone there he knew. Oh, Mr. Raikes was a good man, he was!"

The reader will now be able to judge from these narratives something of the good faith and intelligence of those who made them. They differ on points, and these differences attest to their genuineness. After allowing for infirmities of memory, and the natural weakness of age to exaggerate sentiments of love and respect or their opposites, there remains a uniform testimony to large-hearted benevolence on the part of Raikes. After more than fifty years the impression left upon the minds of all these old people, who themselves were chafed by the friction of ill fortune, was that benevolence was the basis of his character.

He was a little "buckish" and "stylish" in his dress and manner, but he was BENEVOLENT.

Putting on one side the differences of opinion as to whether Mr. Raikes or Mr. Stock started the first schools in the city of Gloucester, we get, from the only person who could tell us, the fact that Mr. Raikes's *first* school was in Soot or Sooty Alley—a most suggestive name for the young ragamuffins on whom he was trying an experiment. The idea we gather is that Mr. Raikes got the woman Meredith, living in the sweeps' quarter, to try her hand until Mrs. Critchley was ready to take them; and that when she was ready the Soot Alley place was closed, and such children as could be induced to go to the new school were drafted there. This school in the Southgate Street and Grey Fryars did become Robert Raikes's school in preference to all others, and it is satisfactory to learn that, although it had been permitted to fall into a state

THE MAN AND HIS WORK. 35

of pitiable decay, its historical continuity has never been broken.*

It is only whilst the Sunday schools were in an embryo stage, and for local purposes, that the precedence of Stock over Raikes, or Raikes over Stock, is of the slightest consequence. As before said, the real birth of the Sunday school movement was November 3rd, 1783, and then the true Founder was Raikes and Raikes only, and we shall not travel far before understanding why this is so.

* The number of "first" and "very first" Sunday schools established in the city of Gloucester is a little confusing. After sifting the evidence it seems probable that Mr. Raikes's first school was in Soot Alley, but his *first permanent* school was in the Grey Fryars (Mrs. Critchley's) facing St. Mary de Crypt Church. Mr. Stock's first school was probably at 103 Northgate Street—Mrs. Roberts, mistress. The Rev. F. T. Bayly, writing in 1864, says he remembers the grocer living there heading his bills with a vignette of the house and this legend: "On these premises the first Sunday school in England was established." The house in Catherine Street, occupied by James King, for some years steward to "Madam" Pitt, may be regarded as the place where a school was established by the joint enterprise of Raikes and Stock. In the absence of documents these conclusions savour of the probable. July, 1780, has been fixed as the date when the first start was made, but direct evidence is wanting. It is founded on the gift of a Bible to Mr. King, with that date on the fly-leaf.

CHAPTER III.

WHOM NO MAN CARED FOR.

"Infant lips humming the hymns of hell."—MS.

"The streets of the city are full
Of poor little perishing souls."—American *Golden Apples*.

TO the question: What was the need for Robert Raikes to interfere with the existing order of things? sufficient answer will be given on becoming acquainted with the children who were constrained, induced, or enticed to put themselves under some sort of external control one day in seven. Fortunately it was possible to obtain descriptions in 1863 of what took place in 1780, and after.

These descriptions seem to put us back not merely a century in our own history, but behind the civilisations of the world which we call "Early." What actually took place in Sooty Alley is left pretty much to conjecture. Mr. Cox only remembered that he was there "instead of playing in the streets," and that he "would much rather have been playing about." He did not remember that anybody learnt anything there. They were "turrible bad boys," and he did not believe that they went to school in Sooty Alley from choice after the first time. There were no girls in the Sooty Alley school.

Mr. Raikes took a personal interest in poor children. He sometimes met them after early morning service in the Lady Chapel of the Cathedral,* and so was known by some as a kind man and a giver of pence before he engaged the woman Meredith in the sweeps' quarter to look after such children as he could bring to her.

Mr. Raikes had some of the popular notions of the day with regard to "obedience" and the right of those in authority to enforce it. As he was not above marching through the streets with his "ragged regiment" because they were ragged, he wished not to be put to shame on account of their ill-conduct. Whether he ever heard himself called "Bobby Wild Goose" is not certain. If he did, he took no notice of it. As for rags and dirt and ignorance, they were the three things which he sought for and paraded in the streets and in his *Journal*.

A certain amount of repression was necessary before the boys could be got under control; and corporal punishment once commenced became customary.

WILLIAM BRICK was a Sunday school scholar when Mr. Raikes died. He attended the funeral and received a cake and a shilling along with the rest. He says:

"I can remember Mr. Raikes well enough. I remember

---

* It has been denied that Mr. Raikes did systematically meet children at the Cathedral. In an hitherto unpublished letter, he says: "I am surrounded every morning at seven o'clock prayers at the Cathedral, especially on a Sunday morning." (*See* Chap. VI.) Long before starting what he was fond of calling his "seminaries," he used to give presents and instruction to children who would meet him in the Cathedral yard after divine service.

his caning me. I don't suppose I minded it much. He used to cane boys on the back of a chair.

"Some turrible bad chaps went to school when I first went."

Q. "Did things improve?"

A. "There were always bad 'uns coming in. I know the parents of one or two of them used to walk them to school with 14-lb. weights tied to their legs."

Q. "What for?"

A. "To keep them from running away. Sometimes boys would be sent to school with logs of wood tied to their ankles, just as though they were wild jackasses, which I suppose they were, only worse."

Q. "Did Mr. Raikes teach?"

A. "He mostly looked on or talked to the boys. When a boy was very bad he would take him out of the school, and march him home and get his parents to 'wallop' him. *He'd stop and see it done*, and then bring the young urchin back, rubbing his eyes and other places. Mr. Raikes was a terror to all evil doers and a praise to them that did well. Everyone in the city loved and feared him."

An old man named COOKSEY, 80 years of age, said:

"Mr. Raikes used to go to church—St. Mary de Crypt Church—with the boys. If they walked orderly and quietly and didn't fight each other on the way, he seemed quite proud. The boys would play tricks on each other and begin to fight in no time. I went to Mrs. Critchley's school, opposite the church. She made us mind her when we were there.

"When Mr. Raikes came she would sometimes make complaints. Sometimes he would hold his glass up to his eye [describing an old-fashioned reading-glass held in the hand] and, looking at the disobedient boy, sternly say: 'Ah, I can see you did not say your prayers this morning!'

"The boys believed he could see through stone walls with that glass; and *it magnified his eye*, so that they were sometimes frightened and told wonderful stories about what Mr. Raikes could do with this wonderful glass."

Mr. SAMUEL PITT,[*] Green Court, King Stanley, near Stroud, said:

"Mrs. Critchley used to visit my aunt, who lived with us at the 'Queen's Head,' Catherine Street. I have heard her speak in words of praise of Mr. Raikes, but the boys were sometimes too much even for his temper.

Q. "Did you ever hear of his chastising them?"

A. "Oh yes, what else could he do? They were varmints, most of them. They were the children of the worst anywhere in the city, some of them. Some were quiet enough. But some! . . ."

Q. "Did you ever see the children brought to school or marched to church with weights to their ankles?"

---

[*] This gentleman is referred to on another point, and in contradiction to the Rev. John Adey's statement that Robert Raikes's Sunday School at one time ceased to exist.

A. "No, but I've heard stories about the boys being 'strapped' all the way to school by their parents."

Q. "What do you mean by strapped?"

A. "The men used to wear leather belts, and when they took them off and laid them on the youngsters that was 'belting' or 'strapping.' It's called the same now; and down by the canal and in the worst parts of the city youngsters often get a taste of the strap. No one would take any notice of boys being punished in Sunday schools when they were first started, or during Mr. Raikes's lifetime. The only sense you could appeal to in the boys who were first got together was the sense of pain; I am sure of that. Some of 'em were so hard, it was difficult to find *where* they felt."

Another old scholar named BOURNE, who had preserved a copy of the edition of the *Sunday Scholars' Companion*, printed by R. Raikes, 1794, made the following statement with regard to punishment:

"I can speak as to what took place in 1800. The first Sunday I went a boy called 'Winkin' Jim' brought a young badger with him and turned it loose. You should have seen old Mother Critchley jump! I laugh now! I shall never forget my first Sunday, nor Winkin' Jim. He went to sea, and was rolled off the yard and drowned. I don't remember if Mr. Raikes was in the room when the badger was 'let fly.'

"No writing was taught in the school in my time. We used to learn [from a] 'Reading-made-Easy' Book, the Collects, Bible and Testament. That is those who could read. Some learnt their letters and A.B.'s.

"Mr. Raikes used always to come to school on Sundays and inquire what the children had learnt, and whether they had been 'good boys.' If there had been extra bad boys, or Mrs. Critchley was out of temper and put it on strong, then he would punish them himself."

Q. "How did he punish them?"

A. "The same way as boys were birched. An old chair was the birching stool or horse. The chair was laid on its two front legs, downwards so [describing with chair], and then the young 'un was put on so, kicking and swearing all the time, if he were pretty big and pretty new. Then Mr. Raikes would cane him. I knew a boy he could never draw a tear from—we used to say he couldn't feel. I don't know whether he could or no.

"One boy was a notorious liar. No, I don't remember his name for certain. He was sure to have a nickname, but I don't remember it. Mr. Raikes could do nothing with him, and one day he caught him by the hand and pressed the tips of his fingers on the bars of the stove or fireplace."

Q. "Was he burnt?"

A. "Blistered a bit. Mr. Raikes would take care that he was not much injured; but he did hate liars! Look at my book. This is what he printed for us to learn: 'A thief is better than a man who is accustomed to lie.' What I think hurt him most was to hear boys cursing and swearing at each other in church. We were at church one morning and a boy named Philpotts (we called him Mugs) stuck a big shawl-pin* into a boy who was nodding. He jumped up into the air with pain, and yelled and swore and flew at 'Mugs.' The beadles came and turned them out. I saw Mr. Raikes's face and I have never forgotten his look."

Q. " Did Mr. Raikes lecture the boys about swearing in church ? "

A. " He must have; it was the only language which some of them knew, and they meant nothing in particular when cursing. Mr. Raikes went down to 'Mugs's' father and had him 'well leathered.' We lived close by and I heard him. 'Mugs's' father told mine that he'd strapped Joe well, and didn't know what for except that Mr. Raikes told him he must. He seemed hurt about having to do it. My father said he would see Mr. Raikes —— first. He meant it; for he was a kind man, if rough, and I liked him all the better."

Q. " Did you receive any education except what you got in the Sunday school ? "

A. " Not until I grew up."

Q. " You are an old man and have had plenty of time for thought. What do you say has been the influence on you of Sunday school teaching ? "

A. " In every way it has been a great blessing to me."

---

* A piece of stout wire about three inches long and used to fasten coarse shawls and turnovers.

Q. "So you have a respect for the memory of Robert Raikes?"

A. "I love it."

These are statements made by old people who, as children, were experimented on for the purpose of seeing whether the children of the poor, when disciplined and instructed, would show the same evidences of human feelings and instincts as children more favourably situated.

There is a very close agreement between what these children lived to think and say of themselves and what Mr. Raikes at the time said of them.

The parents he found everywhere degraded, and either ripe or ripening for the gallows when to be guilty of felony was to be hanged, and of a very small felony, transported. This state of degradation he traced to ignorance of the most elementary principles of right and wrong, morality and immorality. For a quarter of a century before gathering a few children together in Sooty Alley he had been studying some social questions by the dim uncertain glare of prison lanterns. He had been actively engaged in attempting to make the condition of criminals, and of poor debtors who were treated as criminals, endurable. He attempted to improve the adult, and to reach the child through the parent. This very old plan failed in his case—the minds of the parents being embruted and then glazed against knowledge.

He found children whom he knew to be prison born*

* *See* Chapter VIII.

running in the streets, filthy and degraded, only waiting their turn to pass through the hands of the gaoler.

Then he did what a few had done before him, and were doing in various places at that moment: *he commenced with the children.*

It cannot fairly be said that he was sanguine of success. For three years, from 1780 to 1783, he worked quietly without giving much publicity to his plan. Apparently he wished to see whether in Littleworth, and elsewhere, he could tame the untamed, and bring to the surface something of the divine image believed to be somewhere imprinted on the soul of every human child. This three years of experiment has often been a stumbling-block to many, who have asked: "Why did not Robert Raikes give the public the benefit of his idea soon after he commenced working it?"

The answer is, that it was necessary for him to have some time in which to labour before he could say whether or no he would be justified in mentioning the matter at all. The descriptions and statements already given make us pause before calling the children first got together, and put into the hands of the woman Meredith in Sooty Alley, a "school" at all. The ragged robins were taken off the streets and pined for freedom. When they could help it, apparently they did not come a second time unless there was sufficient inducement. They were there chafing under restraint. "Terrible bad" boys they were. "Terrible bad" is the idiomatic equivalent for the superlative in Gloucester. Poor Mrs. Meredith was apparently not strong enough on the nerves for these wild untrained Arabs of the city, who had pet badgers and fought each other like demons. Mr. Charles Cox does not think that during the six months, or so, the children who came to Mrs. Meredith's learnt much. Certainly he did not, except, perhaps, to sit still, which the older boys found it hard to learn.

Then Mrs. Mary Critchley took them in hand. Mr. Raikes was close to her elbow in Southgate Street, and she had been the landlady of the "Trumpet Inn," in Littleworth, where the gaol was, and where the chimney-sweeps lived. Mrs. Critchley by association seemed well chosen for disciplining boys brought to "school" with logs of wood and iron weights tied to their legs—boys who had to be birched on the premises, or taken home to be "leathered," or have the tips of their fingers burnt for lying. With all her qualifications, Mrs. Critchley was more than two years at work before Mr. Raikes could venture to say to the public that he was right in principle, and that the salvation of the world must in very truth come through the young.

Superintendents and teachers in Sunday schools who now see children in all the holy beauty of childhood, think for a moment what that school in Sooty Alley must have been; and fancy what were the duties of the good woman Meredith! The children she had to take care of were no worse that the young Ishmaelites in the rest of the country—even in pastoral Buckingham. The poet Cowper wrote: "Heathenish parents can only bring up heathenish children, an assertion nowhere oftener or more clearly illustrated than at Olney, where *children of seven years of age infest the streets every evening with curses,* and with songs to which it would be unseemly to give their proper epithet. Such urchins as these could not be so diabolically accomplished unless by the connivance of their parents. It is well indeed if, in some instances, their parents be not their instructors. Judging by their proficiency, one can hardly suppose any other. It is therefore doubtless an act of the greatest charity to snatch them out of such hands before the inveterancy of the evil shall have made it desperate."

This was written five years after the opening of the schools in Gloucester. We may go in imagination with Robert Raikes to the schools in the Grey Fryars and Southgate Street, and see the restless, fighting, high-spirited children full of savage frolic, and lisping blasphemy as their only language; and we may then ask whether Raikes was not right in not being over-sanguine, but in waiting for three years before telling the world of a simple plan which to many (and Cowper among them) seemed like a second redemption necessary to complement and complete the first which had been made for all mankind.

The graphic descriptions in black and white of what took place in the first Sunday schools answers as fully as it can now be answered the question: "What need was there for Robert Raikes to interfere when he did, and as he did, on behalf of those for whom no man cared?"

NOTE.—The "lower classes," the "vulgar," and the "common people" were made to keep their distance, and to feel that they were of another race, even by those who wished them well, and wanted to obtain their confidence and win their affections. In 1786, Dr. Samuel Glasse, Rector of Wanstead, preached an oft-quoted sermon on Sunday schools, and published it. This is the title-page :

"The Piety, Wisdom, and Policy of Promoting Sunday Schools : A Sermon preached in the Parish Church of Painswick, in the County of Gloucester, on Sunday, September 24th, 1786, by Samuel Glasse, D.D., F.R.S., Rector of Wanstead, Essex, and Chaplain in Ordinary to His Majesty. 'To endeavour to influence the common people with such sentiments as are suited to their earthly condition, and calculated to promote their everlasting felicity, is the most honourable occupation of the most worthy citizen.'—Mr. Hanway. Published by the desire of the Minister and parishioners, &c. London : Printed for and sold by Mess. Rivington in St. Paul's Churchyard, and Mr. Gardner in the Strand, MDCCCLXXXVI. N.B.—The profits (if any) will be applied to the benefit of Sunday schools."

And this is not an exaggerated specimen of the art of building up a title-page on small occasions, and letting the common people know their places even when smiled on. This sermon was dedicated "To Mr. Robert Raikes, of the city of Gloucester, an instructor of the ignorant and a father to the poor : to whose piety and zeal, in the first institution and subsequent encouragement of Sunday schools, every friend to religion is indebted ; the following Discourse, preached at his request, is inscribed as a token of friendship, approbation, and esteem by the Author."

CHAPTER IV.

AS SEEN OF MEN.

" I have travelled in various counties of England, and examined scores of people and many places and documents, in order to trace the influence and view the ' Man of Gloucester ' from various standpoints."—THE AUTHOR.

ROBERT RAIKES was a prosperous man, and walked through the city with a certain air of proprietorship, which some of the poor called "Buckishness" and "style," but which was also called "swagger" and "pompousness." The dress of the period was decidedly showy, and in the case of a "Buck" or "Dandy," elaborate and expensive.

He used to wear a dark blue or claret coat, and white, buff, or fancy waistcoat with silver-gilt buttons, and a not too elaborate cambric frill and cuffs. His breeches were of nankeen in summer and cloth in winter, white stockings, and buckles in his shoes. He wore a wig and a three-cornered turned-up civilian's hat, which could be carried under his arm. In winter he dressed in the same fashion, only with gaiters and a "'Spencer' which came down around his waist." He did not carry a sword, only a cane; but after he had retired from business a man-servant accompanied him to and from church, and in the evenings carried a lantern before him.

He took snuff, and had a large massive gold box for dress occasions. Usually he carried a horn box, and was said "to snuff with elegance."

He was above the medium height and comfortably stout; and when he walked he drew attention to himself. The curate of his parish, St. Mary de Crypt, said of him in 1831: "An excessive vanity was a predominant feature in Mr. Raikes's character;" and he was supposed to have known him well, having dined at his table and read some of his correspondence.

He was a tradesman carrying on the craft and mystery of printing—about which in those days there was a great deal that was mysterious to the ordinary run of men,—but lived as a gentleman, and was always referred to as "respectable" or "eminently respectable," which in those days was even applied to persons of county rank. During the greater part of his business life he lived in a quaint old-fashioned oak-timbered house of the seventeenth century in the Southgate Street, where the book-printing and newspaper business was carried on, and he printed large books in quarto in big type and with fine margins for the Bishop of St. David's and the *literati*, for his was the only printing press for many years in many counties. Later in life he took a house in Bell Lane—a city house with green lawn around it, but near to the printing premises, and from one house to the other was a pathway, made and kept clean at his own expense.

He kept sufficient company of the "best sort," and

had a handsome service of plate.* The house in Southgate Street has historical interest, but is now a shop. When Mr. Raikes and his family lived in the Southgate Street he kept no shop. In a letter written in 1789 he says: "I keep no shop, and have no concern in the bookselling line." The printing office was connected with the house, and opened into Bolt Lane. Mr. Raikes had a little office for himself shut off from the composing room, but the window opened into Bolt Lane. When he was reading proofs and otherwise seriously engaged, he was "much annoyed by children playing under his very nose." An old compositor who got possession of Mr. Raikes's composing "stick" stated that he had heard the old compositors in the *Journal* office say that the children played hop-scotch, five-stones, and chuck, under the

* Mr. William Warner, gentleman, living in Brunswick Square, told the Author that he knew Mrs. Robert Raikes very well. In the course of conversation he said:

"After her death (which took place in 1828) all her furniture and effects were sold. I bought all the plate, including a handsome gold snuffbox which belonged to her husband. I also bought his lantern, which he used to go from his house in Bell Lane across the lawn and out through a narrow passage which led to St. Mary de Crypt Church."

Mr. Warner showed me the receipt for the plate, and I took a verbatim copy. It is as follows:

"Gloucester,
"17th April, 1828.

"Memorandum,
"I have received the sum of forty-nine pounds for 156 ounces and 9 pennyweights of plate agreeable to the enclosed.

"Robert Napier Raikes."

"This snuff-box was subsequently purchased from me by his daughter Caroline, the wife of General Ladbroke, then living at Worthing."

Mr. Warner showed me some of the plate, which was marked with the Raikes' crest—a griffin's head.

editorial sanctum, and that when they cursed and quarrelled Mr. Raikes was much annoyed, as well he might be. The windows on the ground floor of the Southgate Street dwelling were those of a private house, as when Judge Powell lived there.*

The house in Bell Lane—the lane wherein George Whitefield was born—in 1863 was in the possession of a solicitor who, when the author visited him, had a personal affection for Robert Raikes, and built a "Memorial Tower" † in one corner of the grounds over the spot which Raikes's coffin passed on its way to the church. The Author's note of his visit is as follows:

"Mr. Addison showed me a room which Robert Raikes had built expressly for himself. It looks out on a nice green lawn,—the lawn spoken of by the old people whom I have examined, as being the lawn where they were sometimes assembled by Robert Raikes, and on which they were drawn up and received their cakes and shillings on the day of the funeral.

"I found that Mr. Addison took a great interest in the St. Mary de Crypt Sunday School, *because* it was Mr. Raikes's. Some ladies of his own family taught in it. 'The school is nearly snuffed out now,' said he.

"Yes, there are various opinions about Mr. Raikes. He certainly did a lot towards carrying out prison reforms in this city. He was not paid for his labour, either with regard to prisons or Sunday schools, and if his vanity was a little bit tickled we may very well afford him that.

* In 1898 a wine merchant's office.   † *See* concluding chapter.

"I don't think the Raikeses have any property in the city, or indeed any particular connection with it now. His grandson, the Major, lives in the county. All Robert Raikes's daughters were well married."

Passing from the poor persons whose judgment, from want of larger experience of men, is certain to be governed by their affections, there is the opinion of a gentleman of education and position residing, in 1863, at the Castle, Stroud. This gentleman, Mr. Paul Hawkins Fisher, had practised as a solicitor. He was then 83 years of age, and was educated at the Gloucester Cathedral College. Mr. Fisher was born about the time that Mr. Raikes was experimenting with his "ragged regiment" in Soot Alley, in the Grey Fryars and elsewhere; and when Mr. Raikes died he was in the flush of early manhood, and a keen critic of men and things. His standards were entirely different from those of the poor people whose statements have already been given, and the following account of an interview is worth preserving, if only for this reason:

"Mr. PAUL HAWKINS FISHER told me that when he was a boy and went to the College School at Gloucester, he used to meet Mr. Raikes almost every morning going to early service in the Lady Chapel. He says Mr. Raikes invariably spoke to him, put his hand upon his head and said kindly: 'That is a fine boy,' or some such thing. He says Mr. Raikes had a very 'swaggering' walk with him.

"Mr. Fisher has his own views with regard to Robert

Raikes, and his estimate of him differs very much from that which I have hitherto heard expressed. He does not give him credit for being actuated by any *religious* motive in acting as he did. Mr. Fisher said to me:

"'Robert Raikes was a benevolent and emotional man by nature, and he was a respectable, prosperous, and shrewd man of business. You can tell that by the very judicious manner in which he conducted his newspaper in times of very great peril for newspaper conductors and printers.

"'He patted me on the head because he thought I was a nice little boy going to school, and then he continued to do so from habit. He had no particular interest in me.

"'His great friend was "Jimmy Wood," the banker, popularly known as "the miser," as "miser" he was. No one ever accused "Jimmy Wood" of being religious, and yet he and Raikes were regular attendants at early morning service at the Cathedral. "Jimmy Wood" was a spare, neat-figured man, and had a beautiful smile for everyone. He was a retiring little man in those days, and dressed in black—rusty black,—white neckerchief and knee breeches of course, worsted stockings, and shoes. By the side of Raikes, who affected the swagger of the well-to-do, he was quite refined.

"'Robert Raikes was a foil to the banker without knowing it, and greatly to his own disadvantage.'

"Q. 'Why should Raikes go regularly to early

morning service, if it were not from a deeply religious motive?'

"*A*. 'There was nothing particular in his doing that. He was not the only one; and you must remember that in a Cathedral city there is always a great deal of patronage for a printer. When we come to questions of motive, we are on rather delicate ground.'

"I was charmed with Mr. Fisher. He has a very fine collection of paintings and a magnificent library. At his age, a perfect wonder—vivacious and epigrammatic; an antiquarian, with a fine range of literary subjects. Mr. Fisher has kindly promised to see me again next week, and to give me any information in his power, and show me any documents in his possession which may be of service to me in writing my proposed work.

"I told him what I had done in Glo'ster, and repeated some of the evidence which I had taken down in shorthand from the lips of the old scholars and teachers.

"He said: 'These people seem to me to be the witnesses of truth as far as they know it.'"

Mr. JOHN J. POWELL, Q.C., and M.P. for the city of Gloucester in 1863, placed the Author under many obligations, and showed much interest in his effort to get really reliable information about Robert Raikes, the Man, apart altogether from Sunday schools, the Institution. Writing from Gloucester during the Long Vacation in 1863, he said:

"I am not, however, so surprised as you appear to be that so little should be known about Raikes and his efforts in establishing Sunday schools. You must remember he led the quiet life of a tradesman in a somewhat dull provincial city, and that such a life is seldom attended with incidents that are remembered, or that, indeed, are worth remembering; and, moreover, important as have been the results of the establishment of Sunday schools, it is probable that in Raikes's time the world in general thought little of them, and, possibly, Raikes himself never anticipated anything like the extent to which they have spread, or the good which has resulted from them.

"Having for the sake of local information gone painfully through very many of the volumes of the *Gloucester Journal*, while under Raikes's management, and observed the remarks on men and things inserted in them (and which I have no doubt were all written by Raikes himself), my opinion of him is that *he was a very steady, methodical man of business, and of a kindly and benevolent disposition; but I should doubt if he was a man of superior capability, or even, in the modern acceptation of the term, of Evangelical principles.*

"His paper was published on Monday mornings, and I believe there is no doubt that he and his workmen worked at it on Sunday evenings, which, in the days when Dr. Parr* kept the cricket score for his parishioners on Sunday afternoons, was not deemed inconsistent with the character of a religious person.

"*I also attribute his instituting Sunday schools rather to a*

* Dr. Samuel Parr is referred to.

benevolent than a religious motive. It is certain that the sight of pain, poverty, and depravity was very distressing to him, for his papers abound with representations of the vice and misery resulting from the overcrowding of the local gaols, and with benevolent appeals to the public for assistance for the poor prisoners—both debtors and criminals."

The reader has now before him some materials with which to form for himself a moral portrait of the "Man of Gloucester." What stands out prominently so far is, that he was A MAN OF ACTIVE BENEVOLENCE AND GREAT TENACITY OF PURPOSE.

With regard to motive and principle, the reader will be in a better position to form a sound judgment when he has stood by his side and seen him at work, breathed the atmosphere which he breathed, and followed the slow but logical workings of his mind towards the solution of the now simple, but then almost unheard-of, problem of "levelling up" the very dregs of society.

CHAPTER V.

AT WORK.

"Persons are mistaken who consider the lower orders of mankind incapable of improvement, and therefore think that an attempt to reclaim impracticable, or, at least, not worth the trouble."—R. RAIKES, MS.

"Teaching is a lifelong learning how to deal with human minds."—THRING.

MR. RAIKES arrived at the conclusion at the end of a three years experiment—commencing in Soot Alley—that an attempt to reclaim was practicable. During these three years of precious seedtime he had not been idle. Those who look upon the idea as a sudden inspiration and on the Sunday school system as of spontaneous generation may undeceive themselves.

There were at the time living in the county of Gloucester a few men who had arrived at a like conclusion, and, what is more, acted on it. They saw that the salvation of the future depended largely upon the education of young children. The county of Gloucester held a very different position then to its present, when compared with our great centres of industry. The city itself was the home of the pin industry and largely commercial. Whole portions of the city were devoted to "pinners" and child labour was largely employed.*

* Heading, drawing, pointing and sticking were the four processes in making a pin. Whole families worked at pin-making at home.

Stroud and the small towns and villages in the Golden Valley were busy with the hand loom and the manufacture of pins.

A pin passed through many hands and became a work of art when a coil of fine wire forming the "head" was fastened to the pointed stem. "Nine tailors to make a man, but four men to make a pin" became a proverb. The hand loom weavers worked at home, and the finest of cloths and velvets were made by them. Sometimes there was a "double loom" and the woman helped the man, and the household was neglected. Child labour was employed for all purposes whilst the adults worked. Even young children earned "good money" as compared with the standard of agricultural wage, which was low, although corn ruled high per bushel.

The children grew in Stroud and the Golden Valley as the flowers grew, but soon lost their beauty and fragrance in dirt and bad habits. Sunday was a saturnalia—the day for sports and drinking. Bull baiting, bear baiting, badger baiting, cock fighting, dog fighting, running and wrestling, were the principal pastimes. Children earning wages took a quasi-independent attitude towards their parents and became "independent" as soon as possible. A most deplorable state of affairs resulted, and individual efforts were made in many places to give these children some sense of religion, and sufficient education to enable them to read in the New Testament. Some of these efforts will never be known, but in some parts of the county of Gloucester, and notably in Painswick and Nailsworth, there were men who did gather children together on Sundays, pay men and women to teach them, and did (what Raikes did in Gloucester) visit the schools, speak kindly to the children and distribute coppers and little gifts as rewards for good conduct.

During the period of experiment in Gloucester Mr. Raikes made himself familiar with what had been done elsewhere, and in 1863 there were many aged people who said they remembered Mr. Raikes visiting certain schools; and in nearly every case it was said that "Mr. Raikes drove over in a chaise and pair." In addition there grew up the legend, which these old people always declared they had received on the best authority, that " Mr. Raikes borrowed his idea of Sunday schools from" a certain person, as for example, Mr. Samuel Webb, of the Hill, Painswick, once a wealthy cloth manufacturer, and descended from the De Webs; from William King, woollen card maker, of Dursley, or from William Twining, clothworker, Sheepscombe, in the parish of Painswick.

There is no sufficient reason for doubting the good faith of these old people. Robert Raikes did visit various schools and learn what had been the results of the experiment to reclaim the lower orders of mankind; and the only question worth discussing now is, whether in any proper sense he "borrowed" his own idea from anyone?

It is now certain that children were gathered together

and taught on Sundays in private houses, weavers' kitchens, and regularly catechised in churches, long before he himself was born; and it is also certain that no general system arose, or spread even into neighbouring parishes in England, from these individual and isolated efforts.

The triumph of Sunday schools as a system, apart from Robert Raikes, is the triumph of the Newspaper Press. In the city of Gloucester, where Mr. Raikes had, at all events, the loyal co-operation of the Rev. Thomas Stock, and of his own brother, the Rev. Richard Raikes, it seems probable that nothing permanent would have resulted but for the fortunate circumstance that Mr. Raikes was the proprietor and editor of the *Gloucester Journal*.

So great a social reformation had never before followed the efforts of the Newspaper Press. The religious education of poor children was one of the few subjects on which too sensitive Parliaments had left journalists a free hand. This was fortunate. In nearly every other department (except the purely Academic) the printer felt the pressure of thumb screws. On education he was at least free to say that people were improved by it.

It is only right to mention that another journalist, the eminent John Nichols—"Mr. Urban," of the *Gentleman's Magazine*,—shares largely with Mr. Raikes the gratitude of the world for the spread and organisation of Sunday schools after their usefulness had been demonstrated.

Reading now all that was published in the *Gentleman's Magazine*, one has the impression that Mr. Nichols was fully aware of Raikes's design, and the hopes he entertained, before any public references were made to Sunday schools. In Nichols and the *Gentleman's Magazine* we, in fact, get Raikes and the *Gloucester Journal* speaking from another centre and, at times, with even greater authority. When attacks were made on Sunday schools the judicious assistance of Nichols was of the first importance.

Mr. Raikes did not expose his little plan to public criticism before satisfying himself that if new manners were to prevail, and new conditions of society arise, the child, and not the adult, must be taken in hand in such a manner that the laity could form an efficient auxiliary to the church in its broadest sense. He had enlisted the sympathies of clergymen in several neighbouring parishes. John[*] and Charles Wesley and Whitefield were his personal friends, and Charles Wesley sometimes stayed at his house during the musical festival.[†] To say the least, it is probable that prior to November 3rd, 1783, Raikes had made known his scheme for reform to all men capable of assisting him with advice and sympathy.

[*] *See* Chapter XV., "Mrs. Ladbroke's Letters."

[†] Mrs. Arabella Herbert says: "Mr. Charles Wesley was in the habit of coming from Bristol to Gloucester to attend the musical festival, and on these occasions he used to put up at R. Raikes's house. Upon one of these occasions Mrs. Raikes was confined and Mr. Wesley had to go back to Bristol that same night."

John Wesley when he came to Gloucester generally put up at Mr. Kellow's, in St. Mary Square. Mr. Kellow was Mrs. Arabella Herbert's grandfather.

Reading only what has survived destruction, it seems probable that minds had been already prepared when the *Gloucester Journal* of November 3rd, 1783, appeared with the first printed reference to the new plan for evangelising the young.

The paragraph was written in the form of an "editorial," and in the only form in which "editorials" took in the *Journal*. It ran:

"Some of the clergy, in different parts of this county, bent upon attempting a reform among the children of the lower class, are establishing Sunday schools, for rendering the Lord's day subservient to the ends of instruction, which has hitherto been prostituted to bad purposes. Farmers, and other inhabitants of the towns and villages, complain that they receive more injury in their property on the Sabbath than all the week besides: this, in a great measure, proceeds from the lawless state of the younger class, who are allowed to run wild on that day, free from every restraint. To remedy this evil, persons duly qualified are employed to instruct those that cannot read: and those that may have learnt to read, are taught the Catechism and conducted to church. By thus keeping their minds engaged, the day passes profitably, and not disagreeably. In those parishes where the plan has been adopted, we are assured that the behaviour of the children is greatly civilized. The barbarous ignorance in which they had before lived, being in some degree dispelled, they begin to give proofs that those persons are mistaken who consider the lower orders of mankind incapable of improvement, and therefore think an attempt to reclaim them impracticable, or, at least, not worth the trouble."

This was Robert Raikes's Hegira. Had the undercurrent of sympathy known at that date to exist not been stimulated and strengthened, the movement would have remained in its experimental stage, and, perhaps, have died out—at all events for the time. It was at this critical period that the *Gentleman's Magazine*—a monthly periodical admirably conducted and of great influence—threw open its columns to the advocacy of the new idea, and obtained for it publicity and support. The publication of Mr. Raikes's letter to Colonel Townley, of Sheffield, in the *Gentleman's Magazine*,[*] in 1784, really, and for the first time, put the reading and thinking public of Great Britain in possession of his views and results; and the simplicity and effectiveness of the method took possession at once of the imagination of real workers, like Mrs. Hannah More, sighing for better days.

Mr. Raikes's correspondence during the following two or three years must have been very great. He was apparently a rapid and vigorous letter writer, but it is a very singular thing that with the exception of about half a dozen lengthy letters written for the express purpose of immediate publication, very few letters of his are known to exist. Mr. Raikes did not keep a diary, and there does not appear to have been any attempt to

[*] *See* Appendix A.

preserve letters and correspondence on the subject of Sunday schools. He may have destroyed his letters from time to time, after having used items of information in the newspaper. Items constantly appear about the schools and school children, anniversary services and special sermons preached on their behalf, and it does seem more than probable that the great mass of his correspondence was from time to time destroyed. It is also worth noting that Mr. Raikes, almost from the first, recognised the insufficiency of Sunday schools to meet the national requirements. He wanted a national system of education, and his own schools were weekday as well as Sunday schools so soon as he could get women capable of teaching. He also promoted schools of Industry, so that his negligence in preserving correspondence may be attributed to an idea that Sunday schools would disappear with the appearance of day schools, and the re-establishment of the old and salutary practice of catechising children in churches on Sundays.

The work done by Mr. Raikes and his friends becomes, in the most reliable sense, the early history of the Sunday school movement, after its passage through its experimental stage; and, regarding the movement as from November, 1783, Robert Raikes is its true Founder. After giving all credit to those who preceded him on very much the same lines, and those who walked by his side and worked with him from 1780 to 1783, we find that a start is given in 1783 of which he was the sole centre, and John Nichols from that time forth did more than any other to ensure that the living potential centre of the movement should not be wanting in attraction.

We are now in this position: we can see and appreciate the tiny rivulets trickling in the parishes of Stroud, Painswick, Dursley, Nailsworth, and outlying parishes in the county of Gloucester, forming that small but still sufficient stream for Raikes to direct the eyes of the public to. For three years it had trickled, and he was able to show Colonel Townley and the world that it was possible "to raise up amongst the lowest of the people a new race."

He had worked patiently and silently towards this end, and when he was able to point to success in this limited area the whole world took up the subject with the eagerness which, in later years, it would discuss "the conversion of slag and refuse into steel." The neglected children of the poor were then the slag and refuse of society.

The impression that from and after the hour that publicity was given to Sunday schools everything went gaily as a marriage bell, is a pleasing though popular error. Had Mr. Raikes not brought a good deal of calm common sense and sound business capacity to bear upon the movement, it seems, even now, more than probable that the nascent system would have died from want of proper organisation. So soon as people enamoured of the prospect of this birth of a new race among the lower orders were willing to work, Mr. Raikes was ready to assist them. The drawing up of rules for adoption by local committees was the first and most important thing, if there was to be a sufficient principle of cohesion.

These earliest rules show faintly what was the material to be worked on. The first rules provided for personal cleanliness, and *against cursing and swearing in church*. It was the business of the masters and mistresses and teachers to prevent fighting, and the introduction of live badgers into schoolrooms. Mr. Raikes knew what to expect, and in the first rules very little care is taken to provide against fine breaches of good conduct; but in the House of God he seemed always anxious that a spirit of reverence should prevail. That reverence in church was not innate, he was aware when the boys stuck pins into each other and had to be removed, cursing and fighting. The habit of blasphemy (although it means so little, is yet most revolting in the mouths of children) is one of the most difficult things to eradicate where the blasphemy forms an integral part of the currency of speech. In the *Sunday Scholars' Companion* there is an "Admonition against Swearing." It proceeds: "There is no excuse to be made to it. It has neither honour, pleasure, nor profit attending it. It is teaching *others*, especially *children*, the language of hell." This admonition was probably intended to influence adults and parents. There is a footnote in which it is said: "Thus a church is to be kept holy, that is to be used only when people meet together to worship and adore the Great Creator. Would it not shock the most profligate if a beast market were held in a church, and the floor and seats were seen as filthy as a stable; or if men were to be behave in the House of God as they do in an alehouse?"

The leading idea in the first work done towards the evolution of the new race was to instil a sense of *reverence*. If children could only be got to reverence something, there was hope for discipline, and orderly conduct, and industrial habits. We are not entitled on Mr. Raikes's written and published authority to go beyond this in his name, until he himself grew dissatisfied with the insufficiency of the plan of 1783. In his own mind the system was a living force and grew.

Those who acted with Mr. Raikes found it necessary to strive for years against the habits of irreverence which were engrained into the generation. In 1807 a pamphlet was published for "T. Smith, No. 19 Little Moorfields, Secretary to the General Sunday School Society," entitled, *Hints for the Formation and Establishment of Sunday Schools*. It is here recommended that corporal punishment should be avoided in Sunday schools *as much as possible*; and Rule 3 shows a very unsatisfactory state of things:

"If any scholars do not come clean, washed and combed, or be guilty of lying, swearing, pilfering, talking in an indecent manner," &c., then the scholars shall be excluded the school if "*he or she*" is still unreformed. The sexes were pretty much on a level at the commencement of the century.

On this subject of the conduct of children, there exists an earlier description, written by Mrs Trimmer, and published in 1787. Sunday schools had been established in Old Brentford, and Mrs. Trimmer, being a literary woman, looked at the whole matter with observant literary eyes. A want of reverence and entire disregard for personal cleanliness in both sexes, called for immediate observation. For instance, she would teach girls not to clatter into church with their pattens on; and she would have boys take off their caps—if they possessed any—on entering the church door. Then she wanted children to be taught that the singing of psalms was a solemn part of divine worship, and not a mere accomplishment for vulgar people in the streets. Some useful admonitions were put up in the schools at Old Brentford. A few may be given shortly:

"When you are in church, kneel."

"When the Clergyman enters arise from your seats."

"Pray for yourselves."

"Pray for others."

"Do not talk in church: do not eat apples or other things either there or in school; for you come to church and to school to serve God and to learn your duty, not to eat and drink."

"Do not spoil hassocks, or anything belonging to the house of God."

"Do not sing at improper times."

"Those among you who have coughs should take care not to give way to them, as the noise is very disturbing to other people."

Very useful admonitions these, and very much like Mrs. Trimmer!

Then for the evening there are more admonitions:

"Keep from swearing, stealing, and lying."

"Let no one tempt you to drink drams."

"Do not fight or quarrel, call nicknames, or tell tales."

"Do not take birds' nests, spin cockchafers, or do anything to torment dumb creatures."

"Bow to gentlemen and ladies whenever you meet them."

"Remember the Christian Covenant."

"Come to school early next Sunday."

"Come with your faces and hands clean, your hair combed, and your apparel neat."

"Go home quietly!"

There are a great many of these "admonitions," but the pith of those which are here given will suffice; and they serve, amongst other things, to show that the descriptions of the conduct of the young ragamuffins, whom Mr. Raikes tried to cultivate in Sooty Alley and Grey Fryars, only falls short of accuracy by not being sufficiently descriptive.

Another point on which Mrs. Trimmer comes into agreement with Mr. Raikes is, that at the end of a year the human soul becomes visible in the child. Speaking of the girls, she says that they came at first deplorably ragged and shamefully dirty. "Most of the scholars were so deficient as not even to know a single letter; and many, nay, even some of the bigger girls, were not able to tell who made them." With regard to the boys, she says: "In respect to religious knowledge and civility of manners, many of them were as untaught as the savages of America, and an arduous task it has been found to govern some of them." We may suppose that the gentle Mrs. Trimmer stops short here of descriptions of badger baiting, fighting and swearing among the boys, especially as she found *great improvement in all respects at the end of a single year.*

This was the grand secret of the early and continued and continuous success of Sunday schools—THEY WORKED WELL.

CHAPTER VI.

THE NEW LIFE.

"He who knows and does not teach is as a myrtle flowering in the desert."—*Talmud.*

"God begins His work in children."—JOHN WESLEY, 1784.

MR. RAIKES was "in advance of his time" when he relied on something so elementary and simple as the education of children for the production of "a new race"; and what became apparent to him sooner than to most persons was, that the new departure adapted itself to every circumstance and condition of society. How much he was in advance of the public is shown in this: whilst others were in their first or experimental stage, he was already dissatisfied with Sunday schools unless they were—as they in time became and now are—auxiliary to a more complete system of education.

The old files of the *Gloucester Journal** afford some most instructive reading when we are endeavouring to follow Mr. Raikes's views. As Editor, he had so many opportunities for expressing his own, or adopting those of others similar to his own, that the *Journal*—when

---

* The late Mr. Walker's great kindness in lending these most valuable files for leisurely inspection is only one of several acts of courtesy which I have much pleasure in acknowledging.—EDITOR.

we know how to read it—becomes a diary of the most valuable character.

Year by year we are able to trace the steady application of the following ideas:

"Ignorance is the root of the degradation everywhere around us."

"Idleness is a consequence of ignorance."

"Idleness begets vice, and vice leads to the gallows."

Another series of arguments is found in brief sentences leading to the following conclusions:

"Prevention is better than punishment."

"Religion must wait on improved education among the masses before we shall be able to make much advance; but religion and education may go together."

It was whilst he was labouring week after week to obtain permanent prison reform, anticipating Howard by many years in Gloucester, that he worked out this conclusion: With knowledge will come the upward tendency of man to spring towards the light.

By carefully reading the *Journal*, it will be seen that he was more than twenty years coming to this conclusion, and believing in it sufficiently to act on it. Popularly speaking, he was not a brilliant man like Canning, nor an enthusiast like Whitefield, but ideas once fixed in his mind slowly unfolded and developed.

In August, 1785, he had come to the conclusion that Sunday schools alone were not sufficient. A Sunday and day school had been opened at Mitcheldene, and then he writes: "*This school is an improvement on Sunday schools;* for not only do they have school on the Sunday but in the week, suitable to the capacities of poor children when they are out of work."

This was a marvellously frank confession of insufficiency, just at the moment when the whole civilised world was ringing with the praises of the new plan.* From the columns of the newspaper we see that Mr. Raikes kept his mind open and was willing himself to be instructed.

He believed that hungry children were easier handled and better taught by being fed, and said a word of approval of Lady Ducie's beef and plum-pudding dinners on Sundays. He also approved of persons sending to the Trustees of the Mitcheldene Sunday School "a sum of money sufficient to buy a 3d. loaf for each of the Sunday scholars." There is a note in the spirit of apology for this kind of bribery to be good, but he says "rewards serve to emulate the children"; and from the first he acted on this principle.

The brief paragraphs in the *Journal* stand out with almost pathetic simplicity because of their nakedness. For example: "October, 1785. Two hundred children of the lower class have been taught to read in the Painswick Sunday School, and that, *therefore*, they who were conspicuous for their brutality and profaneness have now become quiet, and have a sense of respect and subordination to their superiors."

Mr. Raikes's second important and acknowledged

* *See* Appendix B.

appeal to the public through the *Journal* appears on May 24th, 1784, and there is a quotation from the *London Chronicle* to the effect that in Leeds two thousand poor children had been admitted into Sunday schools.

The *Gentleman's Magazine* backed up Raikes's efforts in all directions. Under the head of "County News" [1784] there is a special reference to the Leeds schools. "This institution," it is said, "wears a most pleasing appearance, and were it to be adopted generally, would do more towards lessening the increase of felons than all the schemes that have been proposed. Strictness in keeping the Lord's Day gives an early bias in the mind to virtue, and establishes an abhorrence to vice. Scotland exhibits an example. There the Sabbath is strictly kept, and there the executions for felony are few, though the people are poor."

On the opening of a Sunday school at Chester, when 150 children were admitted, "Mr. Urban" says: "Their clean and decent appearance at church formed a most pleasing sight."

The Kendal [Westmorland] Sunday School Managers published their annual report, and "Mr. Urban" gives the following items: Scholars admitted 331; 47 "gone apprentices to service." Subscriptions amounted "only to £57 4s. 6d."

Then "Mr. Urban" gives his friend in Gloucester a little kindly encouragement, just when he wants it perhaps, for he was sometimes dispirited and needed a helping hand, as we shall see directly. Vol. lvii. [1787]

contains the following short article, which is evidently an excuse to enable Robert Raikes to speak in the pages of the *Gentleman's*:

"The truly benevolent Mr. Raikes, in a private letter to our printer, November 13th, 1787 (which his own good heart will pardon our thus divulging) after politely noticing the mention we have occasionally made of 'his project for civilizing the common people of this kingdom,' and observing that 'he has found the plan more widely dispersed by the *Gentleman's Magazine* than by any other publication,' adds: 'It is incredible with what rapidity this grain of mustard seed is extending its branches over the kingdom. The third of this month completes four [*] years since I first mentioned the expediency of Sunday schools in the *Gloucester Journal*, and by the best information I am assured that the number of poor children who were heretofore neglected as the wild asses' colt, but who are now taken to these little seminaries [†] of instruction, amounts to 250,000. In the town of Newcastle alone the seminaries contain 5,000.

"'It would delight you to observe the cheerfulness

---

[*] Mr. Raikes generally dates the movement from the 3rd November, 1783, when he stood committed to the plan by its publication. It seems as though he had up to then held himself free not to continue his schools started in 1780, unless satisfied with the results obtained. He never contested or challenged honours claimed by or on behalf of anyone prior to 1783, after which date he was the "Organiser" by universal consent.

[†] Mr. Raikes having once found a word or phrase to suit him, invariably made it his own. In going through the newspaper files one learns quickly to identify his work. "Seminaries" was a pet word of his, and "grain of mustard seed" and "wild asses' colt," favourite illustrations.

with which the children [in Gloucester] attend on the Sunday.*

"'A woman told me last Sunday that her boy enquires of her every night whether he has done anything in the day that will furnish a complaint against him on Sunday. You see, sir, to what care and vigilance this may lead.—Yours, &c., R. RAIKES.'"

In August, 1784, we find "the suppression of Sunday revels and wakes is becoming very general in this country." These Sunday revels, however, died hard in the West of England, and may still be heard of in Devon.

Then follows the announcement: "The establishment of Sunday schools, we also hear, is becoming very general. . . . The children of the poor, who were heretofore allowed to pass the Sunday in licentious idleness, are now engaged in acquiring a knowledge of their duty, and attending public worship."

Later in the year is the intelligence that in the parish of Nympsfield, where there has been great improvement in the morals and habits of the children, "Lady Ducie has recently given the school children a Sunday dinner of beef and pudding."† The effect was that: "The children

* A very different state of things to what at first prevailed.

† This, no doubt, was very pleasant news for poor, hungry little children, and showed Lady Ducie's good sense. But she had a forerunner in good Mrs. Catharine Boevey, of Flaxley Abbey, who died in 1726. This good lady used to have every Sunday to dine with her, by turns, six of the school children at Flaxley; and after they had dined she heard them say their Catechism. This must have been a popular Sunday school, but the children at Flaxley were limited. When good Mrs. Boevey died this very wholesome custom was discontinued.—*See* BALLARD'S *Memoirs of British Ladies, &c.*

used to go about begging on Sundays of any stranger that came into the village, and now they go to church and behave themselves well."

These buddings of the new life were very precious. Nor were testimonies wanting from almost every quarter, from those who were competent to speak, that the life was "New."

The Bishop of Salisbury wrote, 1785*: "I have established them [Sunday schools] in every parish where my property lies, and warmly recommended them in my Diocese. . . . From the experience I have already had of the benefits arising from these institutions to good order, morals and religion, amongst the lower ranks of the people, I feel the most earnest satisfaction at the prospect of their becoming general."

The Bishop of Llandaff, 1785,† says: "I have long thought favourably of Sunday schools, and that experience alone would be the sure test of their utility. I have taken some steps towards introducing them into the large towns in my Diocese."

The Dean of Lincoln, in his charge to the Clergy of the Archdeaconry of Nottingham (April, 1786), after referring to the late increase of capital crimes, owing to the universal depravity of the people, says: "The contemplation of this would be a gloomy office but for the establishment of Sunday schools." He then adds: "Having anxiously watched their infancy and attended to their progress, I have thought their principles the most

* Letter to Mr. Henry Thornton.   † *Ibid.*

unequivocal, their influences the most extensive, that can be employed in the cause of general reformation. . . . Nor will the benefit be solely confined to the children who partake of these benevolent aids; it will importantly affect the manners of families and even of the neighbourhood to which they belong."

The Rev. John Fletcher, who seemed to his contemporaries more of a saint than a man, commenced gathering children together for Sunday instruction, so soon as Mrs. Derby—a lady always ready to promote every good work—brought Sunday schools under his notice. The Rev. John Wesley, in his *Life of Fletcher*, bears testimony to the delight which Fletcher took in the schools, in which reading, writing, and the principles of religion were taught. He established six schools—three for boys and three for girls—at Madeley, Madeley Wood, and Coalbrook Dale. Says Wesley: "It was not long before he [Mr. Fletcher] observed that a general reformation had taken place in the parish, and it was not only an outward reformation, even of many that had been notorious for all manner of wickedness, but an inward also; many, both young and old, having learnt to worship God in spirit and in truth."

The feelings of respect and goodwill which Raikes had for Wesley were fully reciprocated. They respected each the other's work, and each the other for doing it. In the *Gloucester Journal* the veteran preacher was always spoken kindly of, and sometimes his future movements recorded. On the other hand, John Wesley finding Sunday schools springing up everywhere, preached them everywhere, and recommended them by letter to everyone. This man did nothing by halves. In 1784 he wrote: "Perhaps God may have a deeper end thereto than men are aware of. Who knows but what some of these schools may become nurseries for Christians!"

His intellectual vision was certainly not at fault, and his admiration for school children knew no bounds. At Bolton, 1788, he found that their voices could not be exceeded, except, perhaps, by "the singing of angels in our Father's house." Then their faces attracted him: "Both boys and girls had as beautiful faces as, I believe, England or Europe can afford; and when they sang, their melody was beyond that of any theatre!" When he wrote to his brother Charles, he said: "This is one of the best institutions which has been seen in Europe for many centuries." The child of to-day would be the adult of to-morrow; but he was most concerned with the adult of to-day and yesterday, perishing under his eyes and in his very grasp. These must be saved now, and this was his work. Raikes's he looked on as vastly important and supplemental to his own; so he incorporated it, and made the care of children a prominent feature in all his Societies.

The Dean of Lincoln's observation, that the teaching of children did and would have far-reaching and beneficial influences upon families and neighbourhoods, was carried still further by a correspondent of the *Gentleman's Magazine*, who said: "If these useful seminaries are supported, many thousands of children when adults, more than at any other period, will then have the capacity of contributing to the sciences; thousands for the want of the capacity to read—the introduction to all knowledge —take up the alternative of idle and unprofitable company at public-houses and the like. And if, besides this, with the increase of Book Clubs all over the country, *a number of farmers are now using their bacon racks in the double capacity of bookcases*, we may reasonably expect that ignorance and superstition will be driven from their latest retreats."

These shrewd and practical remarks are so entirely consistent with what we know Mr. Raikes often wrote, that it is quite probable that the communication came from, or was inspired by, him. The waste of intellect, simply because children were neglected, was an observation worthy of a man who had studied the subject, and we find the use of the word "seminaries" for Sunday schools, which was his own particular word for describing them.

In 1789 Mr. Raikes commenced a correspondence, which extended over a considerable period, with the Rev. William Lewelyn, of Leominster, and in letters which have been preserved occur some passages which give a remarkably clear insight into the operations of his mind. In one place he says: "I have two clergymen [*] engaged with me in an effort to raise up, among the

---

[*] It is generally supposed the Rev. Thomas Stock and the Rev. Richard Raikes are meant; Mr. Stock died in 1803, and Mr. Richard Raikes in 1823.

lowest of the people, a new race, taught at an early period the happiness of thinking on that which is good, and bringing those thoughts into action in the several duties that Christianity enjoyns. We consider it as an experiment how far it be practicable to lead mankind, by slow and gentle steps, to the comforts and peace that good morals supply, and thereby render those a blessing who have hitherto been a scandal to the community."

In 1792 Mr. Raikes writes:

"If the higher orders of society would seek this true and exalted pleasure, they would find it more readily in promoting the glory of their Creator, than in sacrificing to those idols that sensuality has set up. Let them go about doing good, as He whose example we ought to imitate. Let them visit the mansions of ignorance and vice, and hold forth light to men that sit in darkness, and lead them to the knowledge of Him that is invisible, but who may be plainly seen in the work of His hands and the dispensations of His providence."

Then follows his own account of a little address which he himself gave to children in a Sunday school:

"I had, some time ago, been exerting my feeble powers to convey some ideas of this kind to some poor children, at the opening of a Sunday school in a village in this neighbourhood [Gloucester], where, till then, the poor had been entirely neglected; and a little boy, who had listened attentively to my conversation, went home to his mother (as I was afterwards informed) and asked her whether that gentleman had not been at [sic] Heaven?

"The simplicity of the question diverted me very much when I heard it. It shewed, however, that the boy's mind had been strongly impressed."

In the next letter he writes:

"It would please me to show you my flock, and I think it would divert you to see *the pleasure we take in each other's company.* Instead of running out of church as though released from a situation of the most painful restraint, you will see them waiting for my leaving my seat, and then crowding around me as though I had loaves and fishes to distribute."

Mr. Raikes was fond of telling his correspondent about the little outcasts whom he now calls "My children." In March, 1792, he says:

"My children last Sunday told me that they were sorry when the time came that I was to leave them. The subject of my conversation with them was the History of Joseph. It occurred in the lesson for the day. I brought it down to a level with their conditions, with Joseph as a poor boy like one of them. You would have been agreably [sic] struck with the fixed attention of their little minds. I dare say many went home and told the story to their parents.

"What delightful sensations spring up in the mind,

when the faculties and powers are engaged in promoting the glory of Him that is invisible!"

The following lengthy extract shows Mr. Raikes in the capacity of a teacher, and the powers which he had to rivet the attention of the children and instruct them. It bears date Gloucester, November 8th, 1793.

"I have lately had a new flock of children [Sunday school] come about me from a singular circumstance. I was shewing my Sunday scholars a little time ago how possible it is for an invisible power to exist in bodies which shall act upon other bodies without our being able to perceive in what manner they act. This I prove to them by the powers of the magnet. They see the magnet draw the needle without touching it. Thus, I tell them, I wish to draw them to the paths of duty, and thus lead them to Heaven and happiness; and as they saw one needle, when it had touched the magnet then capable of drawing another needle, thus when they became good they would be made the instruments in the hands of God, very probably, of making other boys good.

"Upon this idea those children are now endeavouring to bring other children to meet me at church, and you would be diverted to see with what a groupe [sic] I am surrounded every morning at seven o'clock prayers, at the Cathedral, especially upon a Sunday morning, at which time I give books, or combs, or other encouragements. Sometimes they read to me a part of the Gospel for the day, which I explain in a manner suited and applied to their own situations and comprehensions. They were reading that verse in St. Luke, the other morning, where our Saviour says: 'The Kingdom of God cometh not with observation.'* 'The Kingdom of God is within you.' † Who can tell me, says [sic] I, what we are to understand by that expression—'The Kingdom of God is within you'? They were all silent for some minutes. At last the boy who was reading said: 'I believe it means when the Spirit of God is in our hearts.'

"Don't you think this is encouragement to cultivate the lower orders of the people? I could recount to you numberless incidents of this nature that occur to me, to render my scheme of botanizing in human nature pleasant and agreable. But I have been already too tedious and prolix.

"I wish you lived near me; I should receive aid and new degrees of strength and animation from you. But, alas, now nobody regards the design. *I walk alone. It seems as if I had discovered a new country where no other adventurer chooses to follow.* But if you were here, I am sure I should not travel alone."

Here is an item which has a pleasant sound, and would be agreeable even in the ears of Sunday school teachers to-day:

"I have invited all my Sunday school children to dine with me on New Year's Day [1795], on beef and plum pudding. I wish you could step in and see what clean

* Luke, chap. xvii., verse 20.   † *Ibid*, verse 21.

and joyous countenances we shall exhibit, and you would not be displeased to hear how well they sing their Maker's praise."

Mr. Raikes, on his own showing, was not "a myrtle flowering in the desert," but a careful cultivator of the new life, which seemed to have sprung into being in a Sahara where all before was desolate.

NOTE.—These letters from Mr. Raikes to Mr. Lewelyn have been preserved by Mr. J. B. Froysell, into whose possession they passed on his marriage with a member of the Rev. gentleman's family. To Mr. Froysell's care the Sunday school world owes a great deal.

CHAPTER VII.

OPPOSING FORCES.

"No good thing was ever started without its being opposed; but when a thing is good and is wanted, opposition is the best thing that can happen to it."—MS.

ONE of the earliest of Mr. Raikes's public supporters was the Earl of Ducie, and he formed one of the members of a School Board for the management of five schools, to which there were admitted 77 boys and 88 girls; and in December, 1784, the Committee met for the purpose of framing rules of management. Altogether sixteen rules were passed for the conduct of these schools in Gloucester, and so business-like are they that one would suppose they had been framed beforehand by someone already expert in management. The language contained in some of the rules is precisely that which we have grown accustomed to read in Mr. Raikes's newspaper and letters, and there is internal evidence that these first rules were framed by him and, perhaps, the Rev. Thomas Stock.

These rules are most important now, as showing that the Committee treated themselves as the acting board of trustees to a charity which was to be supported on the Voluntary principle. Apparently it never occurred to these gentlemen, or any kindred body during Mr. Raikes's lifetime, that the education of the young was the business of the State. The business of the State was then thought to be punitive, and not preventive. Mr. Raikes had for many years been preaching to deaf ears that prevention might render punishment unnecessary, and certainly would reduce its frequency. He did not, however, look to the State for aid.

Nearly everything in this country, outside of punishment and repression, has had its origin in Voluntary effort, and in the last century in the county of Gloucester charitable bequests seemed to be the soul of everything. There were charities of all descriptions, and the feeding, clothing, and educating of children were not forgotten. Even to-day the old parish churches are decorated with letters of gold on black panels, spelling the various gifts of pious donors. The saying, "As sure as God's in Gloucester," had a special significance for the poor at all seasons of the year, and especially in the winter. This spirit of charity in perpetuity was, perhaps, rooted in pre-Reformation practices, and the Church remained the almoner of the nation whatever changes took place in ritual and doctrine. So it came about that Robert Raikes, growing up in the habit and practice of treating everything unselfishly undertaken and given for the public good as charities, and their managers as trustees, fell into the prevailing custom with regard to Sunday schools.

Very soon after the formation of the Sunday School Board, with the Earl of Ducie as a member and Lady

Ducie actively benevolent, we find Mr. Raikes judiciously publishing paragraphs in the *Journal* in favour of weekday schools and schools of industry. So soon did this take place after the formation of the Sunday School Board, that the presumption is the acting committee gave extended popular education their support. Nothing was wanted but funds, and, from 1784-5 onwards, the columns of the newspaper were made the vehicle for chronicling donations, the formation of fresh charities, the creation of new trusts and trustees, the opening of new schools—Sunday, day, or industrial—throughout the kingdom. Here are specimens taken pretty much at random :

"The parish of St. James and St. Paul, in the city of Bristol, exhibited on Monday last 450 children rescued from idleness, filthiness, and vice, and trained up in habits of industry and good order. This is an experiment to show how far prevention of crimes is preferable to punishment."

"A sermon was preached at Manchester, in the Methodist chapel, by the Rev. Dr. Coke, for the benefit of Sunday schools for the children of all denominations, where £100 3s. 10d. was collected." "At Tetbury the collection amounted to £73 4s. 3d., and it was thought that, if some of the principal inhabitants had not been gone from home, it would have been more." "The inhabitants of Great Malvern [April, 1800] gave the S.S. children a dinner of roast beef and potatoes, plum pudding and cyder." "Donations of £300 East India stock have been given to the parish of Painswick in support of Sunday schools, and a like sum in like stock in support of day and industrial schools." A donation of £1,000 is then recorded for the use of Sunday schools in a small parish.

These are specimens of items inserted every week, and enable us to understand how and in what manner a voluntary movement, spreading to all the corners of the kingdom, was able to meet all demands without once soliciting the State for aid. It was at the commencement, and it still is, one of the triumphs of the Sunday school that children were never excluded because there was no room or no funds; another and not less triumph is, that in an old Aristocratic State the Sunday school performed the purest piece of democratic labour ever achieved since the days of the Apostles—the people taught the people free and freely.

After the novelty had passed there appears to have grown up prejudices against the education of the children of the poor. The political agitations of the times made many anxious to believe that the masses of the people could only be "kept in their places" and content so long as they were ignorant. The upheaval in France struck terror into the souls of easy-going, untravelled people in the country, to whom the word "revolution" meant the guillotine, and any and every change disturbing the social balances was looked on with distrust.

The minds of the poor sought to be benefited were prejudiced and inflamed against those who wished to benefit them. When Mrs. Hannah More, a personal friend of the Raikeses, attempted to form a Sunday school in the Cheddar district parents would not allow their children to attend, because it was said she wished to convey the children beyond sea, and sell them for slaves in the West Indies! It took her two years to make appreciable progress. According to the *Imperial Magazine*, the common people, having no idea of the first principles of Christianity, said : " Whoever heard of people taking pains to bestow benefits on the poor without having some selfish object?" They also said: "Religion will neither fill our bellies nor clothe our backs, and as to reading, it only serves to make poor folks proud and idle."

That the plan received the support of the wealthy and educated is certain; but there were times when Raikes himself felt isolated and alone.

Writing to Mr. Lewelyn in May, 1790, he says: " I did not conceive that I held any degree of esteem among my neighbours, and am, therefore, the more astonished at your having heard anything praiseworthy of one that *here seems to be walking alone.** I can prevail on no one to second me in my little efforts to civilise the long-despised and neglected children of indigence."

That Mr. Raikes had seasons of depression is evidenced by this open confession, which, however, is tinged with extravagance. This may be pardoned, because all

---

* After a man has done his very best, adverse, though kindly, criticism entails this feeling of loneliness. When Dean Stanley and other friends severely judged John Richard Green's *History of the English People*, he said with simple pathos that their judgment left him "lonely."

men, working unselfishly, feel keenly when those around them fail in sympathy, and do not appear to wish to understand the spiritual movement of the motive which inspires them. If those around them work only on the lower plane, and do not understand that beyond the present there is an ideal which must be aimed at, then the feeling of isolation and weariness comes over them and inflicts positive pain. Men are often so isolated among their co-workers that the burden of effort seems too heavy for them, and they are saved from despair sometimes by natural combativeness, and sometimes by an appeal to a higher power for strength and endurance.

How long adverse forces were gathering strength we cannot say, but it must have been some time before "Mr. Urban" threw open the *Gentleman's Magazine* to an old and valued contributor for him to make a slashing onslaught on Sunday schools and their founder. This was in 1797, a period when we have been in the habit of looking upon the system as secure from all opposition and malice; and it seems almost certain that the editor of the *Magazine* must have known that there existed a great deal of dislike to Sunday education before admitting an article which ran counter to all his previously pronounced sympathies. We may take it for granted that John Nichols, knowing of an adverse opinion amongst educated men, felt compelled to admit the article, so that he should not suffer in his reputation for fairness.

The article was written, and probably by a clergyman, under his usual signature of "Eusebius." It is very long, and the writer voiced the growing apprehension that the education of the poor would unfit them for menial* service, raise discontent, and foment rebellion. The shadow of the great French Revolution rested on his page. The article concludes with the following words:

"We may, therefore, conclude that the Sunday school is so far from being the wise, useful, or prudential institution (it is said to be) that it is in reality productive of no valuable advantage, but, *on the contrary, is subversive of that order, that industry, that peace and tranquility which constituted the happiness of society; and that, so far from deserving encouragement and applause, it merits our contempt, and ought to be exploded as the vain chimerical institution of a visionary projector.*"

There is no evidence that Mr. Raikes himself took any notice publicly of the attack, but he was not wanting in defenders, month after month. It is, however, curious to notice that even those who supported him at this crisis confessed that at one time they feared the experiment. They were well-wishers to education, but feared secretly that the bold experiment of teaching the masses only on one day in the week would have far-reaching and dangerous consequences. Mr. Edwin Goodwin (vol. lxvii.) said frankly:

"At the first institution of these schools I was doubtful indeed whether these poor children, who have thus an opportunity of being instructed on Sundays only, could

* *See Appendix C, Sunday Scholars' Companion.*

make much improvement. But, thank God! I have lived to find my mistake." *

There are no means of ascertaining what the results of this impeachment of Sunday school education were; but we do find, only three years later, that the Bishop of Rochester was popularly credited with having expressed himself as an opponent of these schools in a speech in the House of Lords. So well was this known, and so generally was it believed, that the Right Rev. Prelate, at his Second General Visitation in the year 1800, said in his Charge :

" A report has been circulated, by a misrepresentation, I suppose, in the public prints, that in a debate in the House of Peers, in which I had a considerable share, at the close of the last Session of Parliament, I spoke with decided disapprobation of all these institutions.

" The report is false. I spoke of them on that occasion as I have always spoken, and always shall speak, as institutions that may be very beneficial or very pernicious, according as they are well or ill-conducted, and according as they are placed in proper or improper hands. I said that schools of Jacobinical rebellion and Jacobinical politics—that is to say, schools of atheism and disloyalty—

* Eusebius replies [December 14th, 1797], and says: " There is an idea of humanity and benevolence annexed to the institution of Sunday schools which captivates the ignorant and superficial observer, and makes many look with a malignant aspect on a writer who questions their utility." He insists " that *industry in the lowest classes of society is better than scholarship*, and that to give them the latter without the former is to put swords into their hands which may be instruments to their own destruction." In closing the correspondence, " Mr. Urban" lets his readers into the fact that " Eusebius" is " an old and respectable correspondent."

abound in this country; schools in the shape and disguise of charity schools and Sunday schools, in which the minds of the children of the very lowest order are enlightened—that is to say, taught to despise religion and the laws and all subordination. This I know to be fact; but the proper antidote for the poison of the Jacobite schools will be schools of the same class under the management of the parochial clergy.

"Sunday schools, therefore, under your own inspection, I would advise you to encourage. Leave nothing to the inspection of the master or mistress. Suffer no books to be introduced but such as have had your previous approbation. And in the choice of the Expositions of the Church Catechism, which are almost the only books requisite in such schools besides Psalters, Prayer-books, Testaments, and Bibles, you would do well to fix on those which you find in the list of the Society for Promoting Christian Knowledge, upon which you will be sure to find none that are in any way exceptionable."

This precise and guarded language shows the existence (at all events) of a terror in the minds of men living when France was under the shadow of the guillotine, and England clamouring for more popular franchises.

What Mr. Raikes had been trying to do may be given in his own words to Mr. Lewelyn:

"In my visit to my Sunday school last Sunday I remarked some of my sheep had gone astray. On my enquiry, one of the boys told me that they were at play with a set of wicked boys in a neighbouring field.

"'Alas!' said I, 'the wicked one was afraid we should lead all the poor boys to Heaven. He has, therefore, set up a Sunday school against us to lead some to his place of torment.

"'Let those now who take pleasure in wickedness go to their master; but I know that all who wish to call God their *friend* will come and take part with *me*. But do you now mark the end of these boys who have joined our adversary; and their fate, I am convinced, will confirm you in your duty.'

"By this mode *I endeavour to avail myself of the folly of the bad to strengthen the good.*" *

The struggle, even if keenly felt by those who were put upon the defensive for attempting to do good, was not for long. The time had arrived when human ingenuity had prepared the way for a future which could not be satisfied with the old restrictions, and the bonds once burst could never be re-united. At the time that opposition was keenest no less than 250,000 children were receiving the rudiments of education, and learning to bring themselves under that disciplinary self-control necessary for the stability of social order and to progress.

There is another passage in the MS. letters in which Mr. Raikes shows himself conscious of occasional feelings of depression, and his determination to make the best of

---

* For this he was censured and reviled and misrepresented, an allowed to "walk alone."

it. He says: "Perhaps the depression of what is mortal may be necessary to elevate the immortal part of our nature," and then again he shows where he was in the habit of turning for consolation. "I am never," he writes, "in so proper a frame of mind as whilst I am reading or repeating passages from that heavenly composition [the Psalms of David]. They are my chief comfort and consolation when any distress approaches; they furnish the language of thanksgiving when the heart rejoices."

Singular as it may now appear, strongly-worded opposition to Sunday schools came from Scotland. In 1798 the Rev. Thomas Burns preached in the parish church of Renfrew two sermons directed against the introduction of Sunday schools in Scotland. These sermons were considered to be of sufficient importance to be printed and published. Some of the passages will be now read with curiosity and interest. The preacher said :

"I can see no necessity for the institution, and I am afraid men do not consider the effects that are likely to follow. In England necessity may be pleaded, as we are told there are few parents in common life who are qualified to instruct their children in the principles of true religion. . . . But whatever may be said on the point of necessity with respect to England, there can be no such argument with regard to Scotland. From the wise institution of parochial schools, every parish in Scotland is provided with the means of instruction. Children are taught, at least, to read and write, and instructed in the principles of our holy religion as contained in our confessions of faith and catechisms longer and shorter.

"Sunday schools, then, are reflections on every parish where they are appointed; nay, more, they are reflections upon every parent in that parish. It is declaring to the world that there is a parish where the parents are either grossly ignorant or shamefully negligent. Negligent they may be, but ignorant they are not, as I might easily show from several parishes which are under my own observation. . . .

"The mode of appointing these Sunday schools is strange. Here I shall say nothing but what falls under my own observation. A number of young men, perhaps well-meaning, meet together and consult where a Sunday school shall be erected. One says that such a place would do; another says such another place is very much in want of a Sunday school. They go and talk with some people in these places, who approve without thinking. They apply to some society, which sends out a deputation, and formally erects a Sunday school; and then old and young are put in motion upon the even of a Sabbath, when they ought to be quiet in their own homes and employed in the duties of family religion."

The preacher then goes on to consider Sunday schools as forming lay preachers:

"It is well known to some of you that there is a number of young men, some of them day labourers, now preparing for what is called lay preachers; and I understand they are to be fully qualified for this in twelve or eighteen months, and then they are to be sent as missionaries over Scotland to instruct the people in the principles of religion. Perhaps this institution of Sunday schools was originally intended to prepare for them congregations by the time their teachers shall announce them qualified to preach.

"Be that as it will, I repeat it again, *my great objection to Sunday schools is that I am afraid they will in the end destroy all family religion*, and whatever has tendency to do this I consider it is my duty to guard you against. I might also show that *these schools are hurtful to public religion*, for it consists with my knowledge that children stay at home from church to prepare their questions for the even; and their families are divided when they ought to be together."

On one point we may now all agree with the preacher. It was a reflection, with which we may now grow scarlet with shame, that at the end of the eighteenth century Sunday schools were necessary in England and Wales to teach children their A B C, and to teach their tongues to say "GOD" with a knowledge of what the word meant. It was this feeling of shame which inspired Raikes to speak and act, and every decade which passes only increases our wonder, until we find ourselves becoming more and more incredulous that such things could have been, and that men and women, Church and State, slept soundly!

CHAPTER VIII.

WHERE RAIKES WAS TAUGHT.

"A successful teacher must himself be taught."—MS.

THE institution of Sunday schools was for so many years presented to the world as an "inspiration"—a sudden idea evolved by the contact of two benevolent minds—that it is even now difficult to efface the image of the good men meeting in the streets, bemoaning the wickedness of youth, and then each going his own way and setting-up Sunday schools forthwith. The picture is pretty, and may be true. It is so simple that it deserves to live; but we shall not show much sagacity if we do not divine that there was antecedent preparation, without which it is very doubtful if the experiment would have been tried when it was. Certainly there is no reason for supposing that Mr. Raikes would have tried it. His mind caught at principles slowly, but held them tenaciously; and, but for a conviction that mastered him, there is nothing to induce us to believe that the opulent citizen with a touch of "swagger" about him, and a vain man in his dress and bearing, would have passed his time in the chimney-sweeps' quarter, and marched to church with filthy, ragged, fighting, cursing children longing to be free.

Littleworth was his favourite recruiting ground—there was no lower quarter in the city. The jail was there—another of his haunts. He, however, found some good there. He found Mrs. Critchley leaving the "Trumpet Inn," and induced her to take charge of the little ruffians in the more respectable corner facing the Grey Fryars and Southgate Street. Later he found his apprentices there; and so well was his weakness for Sooty Alley known, that the educated "Eusebius," in the *Gentleman's Magazine*, playfully taunted him with his love for sweeps and suggested the opening of a Sunday school for them.

A trifle galling to a vain man this—a man who entertained the Duke of Gloucester, and the French *savants* who visited the city and inquired of him about these Sunday schools, and who had respectfully declined the invitation of the great Catherine of Russia to come to St. Petersburg and stay there! "Eusebius" did not know of all this at the time, or he might have been more respectful to the man, if not to the institution.

When there was so much outwardly to gall and mortify a man a little vain with regard to appearances, it is worth seeing what was the sustaining motive and from whence derived. When we inquire closely, we find that for twenty-five years before gathering the little outcasts around him in the sweeps' quarter he had been a very consistent student of social problems. He had found his object lessons in the county and borough jails, and, after doing all in his power to alleviate suffering, he seems to have had it slowly inborne upon him that it was an inversion of the pyramid, first, to make criminals, and then to punish the manufactured article.

For years he attempted to deal with adult criminals, and failed : he paid the debts of small debtors, and they returned to jail ; he interceded for prisoners and got their sentences commuted, only again to find them naked and chained to others in their dungeons. To deal with the criminal adult was to invite defeat; to deal with the prison authorities, and, through them, the Government, was heart-breaking to ordinary men. The only possible solution, as it appeared to him, was *to prevent criminals being made*.*

For years he preached this in his *Journal*. Week by week he preached and illustrated and enforced this old idea, which, however, had the appearance of being new. The natural slowness of the man's intellect is shown in this, that it was not until 1780 that it occurred to him that the way to prevent the manufacture of criminals was to "train up a child in the way he should go."

* If Mr. Raikes had possessed Sir Thomas More's *Utopia*, he would have found the results of his work and experiences anticipated by about three centuries. In *Utopia* every child is educated, and afterwards technically instructed in industrial schools. What one marvels at is this : if Mr Raikes was in advance of his time, how far behind Sir Thomas More and his friends must his time have been ? If I had found the following passage in one of Mr. Raikes's letters, I might have taken it as the original expression of his views : "If you allow your people to be badly taught, their morals to be corrupted from childhood, and then when they are men punish them for the very crimes to which they have been trained in childhood—what is this but to make thieves, and then to punish them ? " Although Raphe Robinson's translation was published in 1551, it was probably unknown, except to scholars, in Mr. Raikes's days. Mr. Arber's reprint (1869) has placed many a student under great obligations.

When he once saw it in this light he tried his experiment, and practically in secret for three years, which shows that he was not a hasty generaliser.

Where he was taught and what he learnt we shall find principally in a careful study of the old files of the *Gloucester Journal*.

He had the great good fortune to possess a father of sterling character, who was Robert the printer, son of Robert, minister of Beeford, in Holderness, Yorkshire. Of this Robert the printer we know little; but we do know that fear was not a mastering weakness with him. At a critical period of the history of the newspaper press he twice incurred the wrath of the House of Commons for committing "breaches of privilege"* in reporting votes or minutes of proceedings. The breach was technical, but the punishment might be formidable—fine and imprisonment in Newgate during pleasure. The Clock Tower apartments were not then ready. He was also a clean-minded man, and excluded epigrams, *vers de société*, and little balderdash, spiced to liking, common in metropolitan and provincial newspapers of his day. He was also a man who pitied men, and went out of his way and encroached on the little space to spare in his small sheet in order to chronicle distress. He died at the age of 68, having been three times married,† leaving Robert, his eldest son, then 21 years, sole proprietor of the newspaper. This

---

* *See* Appendix D.

† Nothing is remembered of the first two wives. *See* Chapter XVII.

was in September, 1757, and in August the following year the business premises were removed from the Black Fryars to Southgate Street.

From this time onwards the pages of the *Journal* present pictures of the social life of the Cathedral City, which, as years roll on, become more and more precious to the historian and antiquarian. From the commencement of his editorship, Mr. Raikes made the paper a means of communication between the prisoners and debtors, whom he found naked, starving, and rotting in the jails. He begged for them, and printed the prisoners' acknowledgments. From 1757 down to 1787 (when there were improvements to record) the note was the same, only varying in intensity. We need not trouble the reader with the dates of the following paragraphs:

"The debtors return their sincere thanks to the High Sheriff of the County for his kind donation of one guinea, and also to Abraham Isaac Elton, Esq. From him they likewise received one guinea yesterday, which was faithfully divided among real objects of charity. Some of these unhappy sufferers had little other support than the benefactions they received."

The prisoners return their thanks for benefactions, and Raikes adds: "If it had not been for a private fund, *many of the prisoners must have perished for bread!*"

"From private benefactions placed in his hands last winter for alleviating extreme distress in the county gaol the printer has been enabled to give an allowance of *two pennyworth of bread per day* to debtors who, not able to pay for a bed, are obliged to lay upon straw, and without such assistance must have perished for want. This charitable fund is almost exhausted."

"There are now in our Castle [the county gaol] fourteen or fifteen persons confined for small debts of £10 or £11. These poor men are in such distress that they are near perishing for want of sustenance. About a fortnight ago *one unfortunate man, they say, was starved to death there*. Who in possession of the good things of this world can refuse a small share to alleviate such a state of wretchedness?" *

It is only to be mentioned that this announcement, that a small debtor was starved, is made without the slightest attempt to excite notice. There is no "headline" to the paragraph—not even a note of interjection. It might have been the commonest event in the world, and no one would have known of it but for Raikes.

The state of the gaol was certainly bad, but not worse than the rest of our gaols about a century ago, and these, again, were sometimes held up as models for the imitation of some European countries. This is how matters appeared to Raikes:

* "An old gentleman, nearly 80, told me that he has heard his grandfather, a farmer, say that when he was a young man his wife always gave him, on market days, a basketful of eatables—black bread and cheese and broken bits—for the poor debtors confined at the Northgate, then standing and used as a debtors' prison. On market days the poor starving debtors cried from the top of the gate, from the roof or windows: 'For God's sake, have pity on the poor debtors!' These poor miserable wretches dropped a basket down on the end of a cord, and benefactions were put in it by the charitable. The gifts were acknowledged by pathetic and heart-rending cries of gratitude."—Mr. TAYLOR.

"Our gaol at this time [March, 1785, when he had been working nearly twenty years to improve matters] exhibits a melancholy scene of wretchedness and profligacy beyond the example of any former period.

"One hundred and twenty unhappy creatures are there confined together, increasing, if possible, their own natural depravity. Shirts have been distributed to several who were naked, which were no sooner washed and hung out to dry than they have been stolen.

"The prisoners are locked up at night in a large apartment called the Main, *with a chain run through each man's link.* During the night they steal from each other— shoes, buckles, bread, or anything which it is possible to conceal. In the box of an old Welsh woman, confined for stealing, no less than seven or eight stolen shirts were discovered on Monday last, which she had bought at a low price.

"As there is no separation for the sexes in the daytime, one of the women, sentenced to a long imprisonment, is now ready to lie in, and would be destitute of every necessary for such a situation had not private beneficence placed a fund for the relief of occasional distress in the hands of an individual.

"In short, the inhabitants of the prison give a more affecting picture of the miseries entailed on mankind by the corruption of human nature than it is in the power of the imagination to paint."

The "humane Mr. Howard," as Raikes invariably calls him, had visited this hell in miniature nearly two years before and inspected it, and *spoke so well of it* that he reported that he knew of only one or two prisons in the kingdom that were to be compared with it! Sir George Onesiphorus Paul, the truly humane Governor, who had the satisfaction of carrying out some of the reforms for which he and Raikes and Howard worked incessantly, however, reported "that, in consequence of there not being sufficient accommodation for prisoners, the Judges of Assize often remitted the sentences of criminals, and turned them loose on the public."

Five years after the Sunday school in Sooty Alley was opened, "between twenty and thirty vagrants were publicly flogged and sent to their parishes."

So that prisoners should not escape even if they broke loose, mastiffs were kept to pursue them. The dogs seldom lost scent, the prison taint was so strong on the prisoners. The cost of maintaining these dogs appears in the old county accounts preserved in the Shire Hall.

Mr. Raikes did not lose sight of criminals when they left the gaol, but followed them on board H.M. transports. He had correspondents on board some of these ships. Here is a specimen paragraph:

"One thousand prisoners sent to Botany Bay, of both sexes; and it is said in a letter from one on board the vessel in which they were sent that such is the sickness that it is expected that four-fifths will die before they land,"—eight hundred out of a thousand! To have scuttled the ship in the Channel would have been more humane.

The enterprise of the newspaper manager is shown by the publication of a "special" article in the form of a letter from one of the women convicts who sailed from England in the *Lady Juliana*, and dated "Sydney Cove, Port Jackson, July 24th, 1790." It describes a state of things which he sought to have remedied, and now that it has long passed, never to return whilst England remains civilised, the letter possesses much interest for the historical student. The letter reads:

"We arrived here safe after a long voyage, in very good health. We landed here 223 women and 12 children. Only three women died and one child. Five or six were born on board the ship. This place was in a fair starving condition before we arrived, and our allowance [has been] only two pounds of flour and two pounds of pork for each man [sic] per week, and we had hardly any clothes. But since the *Scarborough*, *Neptune* and *Surprize* arrived, we have had a blanket and a rug given to us.

"If you had but seen the shocking state of the poor creatures that came out of these three ships it would make your heart bleed. They were almost dead. Very few could stand, and they were obliged to sling them as you would goods and hoist them out of the ship, they were so feeble, and they died ten or twelve daily when they first landed; but some of them are getting better. There died on their way on board the *Neptune* 183 men and 12 women; and in the *Scarborough*, 67 men; and the *Surprize*, 85. They were not so long as we were in coming here, but on account of their [the convicts'] bad behaviour they were confined and had bad victuals and stinking water.

"I don't think I shall ever get away from this place; for some of the men's times were out, and they went and spoke to the Governor and told him they would not work. He told them he could not send them home without orders from London, and if they would not work they should have nothing to eat. So they almost all went to work again, except ten [who] were saucy, and the Governor ordered them a good flogging, which brought them to compliance."

Mr. Raikes's interest in Society's victims and outcasts ended only with their lives, and after death or execution he sought to impress upon the public certain ideas which, for him, were gathering the force of axioms. Having by its neglect bred criminals, Society relieved itself of the responsibility by hanging them. Thieves were hanged, and, according to the *Journal*, after every Assize public executions were plentiful. Very often the number of men and women to be hanged was simply given, as, for instance: "At the Assizes, which lasted nearly a fortnight, two Judges engaged, eight criminals received the sentence of death for stealing." Again: "Heavy Assize. Twenty-one condemned to death."

Sometimes the fact would be followed with a sigh, as: "How deplorable that Society cannot be secured without so great a sacrifice!"

Hangings were so common that "graphic descriptions" were dispensed with. What was reported was, however, pathetic. Some men were hanged one morning, and on the scaffold were recommended to pray. One of the poor fellows said:

"Pray! I was never taught to do so. I don't know what it means; and if you hang me now I shall go to hell, cloathes and all." *

Another said: "Make the Sabbath a day of holiness to the Lord: then it will be a blessing to you. Take warning before it is too late."

Another said: "Thieving is a poor business. I never gained much by it at the best, and now I pay my life for it."

This, then, was the school in which Mr. Raikes studied, and these some of his object lessons. Going through the files of the paper year after year, we see how painfully he followed these human wrecks with eyes of pity, and yet how difficult he found it to do more than heap regret upon regret. When he met these people he could do no more than get up compassionate funds and dole out loaves of bread, or find suitable linen for women in the agonies of maternity. His first conclusion was that *idleness* (and all which it involved) was the root of all this social evil. When sentences were commuted and had expired he set himself to obtain work for the discharged prisoners.†

The *Journal* bears ample evidence that this was the

* There was a sly jest in this reference to clothes levelled at the gaoler, whose perquisites they were.

† One man (Edward Eager or Eagar) whose sentence was commuted became a reformed character and started a Sunday school at Sydney This is probably the man Mrs. Ladbroke refers to in Chapter XV.

uppermost idea in his mind for years. So far as adults were concerned, the idea never forsook him that industrious habits would alone meet their case. He put it in a sentence in the *Journal* of the 22nd August, 1785, when Sunday schools were spreading rapidly everywhere: "When the common people know that *work they must*, and that it remains with themselves to choose whether they will work in a prison or with the enjoyment of liberty, it is to be hoped they will prefer the latter." Even then he was not very sanguine.

Although he deplored ignorance and bracketed it with filth and idleness, the idea does not appear to have come early to his mind that the minds of children must be cultivated *before* habits of idleness were formed. It did, however, come to him, and it came slowly. First of all he got some children to meet him at or after early morning service in the Cathedral. He gave them presents of coppers and combs, and this went on for some time before Mr. Raikes had the courage of his apparent convictions that the child must be trained before the adult can be reached. There has been much conflict of testimony about this practice having been commenced prior to the opening of Sunday schools; but when Mr. Raikes speaks of it, it is as though the habit was a long established one. Some testimony on this point was collected in the Sunday school Jubilee year; and there is no sufficient reason for doubting that this was one of his numerous experiments. He constantly tried some new plan, and the mental improvement of prisoners was one of his schemes for carrying out prison reform. The meeting of untaught children in the Cathedral yard or in the Church was, in his case, only the variation of an old plan. He had attempted, on the testimony of his friend, the Rev. Samuel Glasse, D.D., to make the prison a place of instruction by engaging prisoners who could read, to read to those who could not; but this was only a makeshift experiment. According to the story told by Mr. Lancaster, the word "try" was inborne suddenly upon him one day with all the force of an inspiration. Whether this is literally true or no, it is certain that he had done his best to work out for himself a solution to a then momentous problem. He engaged four people to teach the children, whom he sent to them from time to time, of whom three were—Meredith, Critchley, and King; and he assured himself that the fruits would be lasting before venturing to take the public into his confidence.

It will now be seen that Mr. Raikes was a student in moral pathology and a practical worker; that he worked out his problems carefully and painfully—and, it may not be presumptuous even now to add, prayerfully. Whatever may be said of all the worthy men and women during the centuries who made Sunday education a pastime or study, it has not yet been claimed for any one of them that his convictions rested on experiences so variously, painfully, and laboriously acquired as Robert Raikes's. This is his great distinction and separates him from all disputing with him the title of "Founder."

NOTE.—Mr. Higgs, engaged at the *Cheltenham Examiner* Office in 1862, said: " Mr. Raikes visited the prisons—chiefly the city one—and was very kind to the prisoners. As to the small debtors, he frequently paid their debts so that they might be discharged. I cannot say that the money came out of his own pocket. My grandfather knew him well and worked for him, and from what he has told me, I believe Mr. Raikes was large-hearted enough to give money out of his own pocket."

The following anecdote is contained in a letter to the Author from Mr. John Crowse, Redmarley Mill: "Mrs. Jones, now [1862] landlady of the 'Crown Inn,' Redmarley, told me that a woman named Harding stole and pawned some of Mr. Raikes's shirts. When he accused her, she seemed sorry for what she had done. He very seriously admonished her, forgave her, paid for the things and said no more about it." This anecdote shows that Mr. Raikes was sincere in his professions.

CHAPTER IX.

MR. RAIKES THE SABBATH-BREAKER.

"If you desire to judge a man without prejudice, you must consider when and where he lived, and all the surrounding circumstances of his life."—Sir GEORGE JESSEL.

BY an "accident" of his profession, the Founder of Sunday schools was a systemtic Sabbath-breaker! This was charged against him in no kindly spirit during his lifetime, and remembered against him with more or less of bitterness in the city of Gloucester, according to the quality and quantity of venom distilled in the periodical contests over "the first Founder of Sunday schools." It is usually as hard to discover the first true Founder as the "first true Inventor," to borrow a phrase now familiar in Patent law. The "first true" anything seems to be always going further and further back, as we learn more of what our fathers did; and Mr. Flinders Petrie would not be at all surprised if he disentombed ancestors of our Stephensons and Edisons from the buried civilisations of the Nile Valley. We are now quite satisfied to treat as the first true Founder, or Inventor, the man who made the thing known and secured its adoption for the public benefit.

The citizens of Gloucester, feeling much interest in a

question which they regarded sometimes as "local," were not always accustomed to take broad and generous views in the Sixties, and it was quite a common thing to hear in conversation Robert Raikes labelled "hypocrite," "canting humbug," "vainglorious self-seeker," and other names more or less offensive. When investigated, it was found that this odium arose mainly from two things—the manner of the man, and the printing of the *Gloucester Journal* on Sundays.

A certain "swagger," as Mr. Paul Hawkins Fisher describes it, was natural to him, and the first comer could see it—the observant but sprightly Miss Burney, the Diarist, saw it at once. Raikes was "too flourishing, too forward, too voluble" for that young lady's taste; still she tolerated him because of his wit, benevolence, and good nature, thereby showing her good sense and capacity for seeing two sides of a man in one glance.

In addition to appearing so, Mr. Raikes was, and, apparently, had been a flourishing man all his lifetime. He inherited the valuable quality to flourish as some plants inherit the quality to bloom. His ancestors were flourishing, pertinacious, and combative men in Yorkshire before they came South, as will be seen by-and-by when we reach the family history. His own father had rooted kindly in the Gloucester soil and flourished; and when Miss Burney saw "I have flourished" written upon Robert Raikes in the year of Grace 1787, she only saw what was there and not any simulation. Still, a man may not even show himself as he is without offending someone, and it was registered against Raikes that he had flourished when and where other men, perhaps, had failed. So the benevolent-looking man, with a large heart and practical brain, with a slight "swagger" in his gait, a "buckish" air about him, and with a good balance at his bankers, was sometimes discounted because of these things.

But printing the newspaper on Sundays was quite another thing, and, during his lifetime, it was charged against him, so that he discontinued the practice for a time, but resumed it, finding it impossible to publish the *Journal* in country districts, and in parts of Wales, when most wanted, without setting up in type his "latest news," and then working off his edition on a little hand-press, the only machine then available.

In order rightly to understand Mr. Raikes's position, and to form a just opinion of his conduct, it is necessary to give a few facts about the old *Gloucester Journal*, and to show the position in which its printer stood towards the public. Everything relating to the newspaper world was so entirely different in 1722, when the *Journal* was established, that the history is not without an interest entirely independent of the Raikes's connection with it.

Amongst provincial newspapers in England, the *Journal* stands about nineteen in point of precedence, though only some half a dozen have survived. The *Encyclopædia Britannica*, which does not include the *Cirencester Post* (1719) and the *Gloucester Journal* (1722), dates the English provincial press from 1690, when the Worcester *Postman* (now *Berrow's Worcester Journal*) was started. The first number of the *Journal* was published April 9th, 1722. The paper was a very small, and, to modern eyes, a curious-looking sheet—thick, coarse, dirty-white-looking paper, with an elaborately got-up headline. The top of the front page was quite a work of art. On the left hand was a ship (representing Commerce) and a child bearing heads of corn (Agriculture). In the middle stood Old Time dictating to a scribe—or it may have been an angel dictating to St. John, and so symbolising the Church, for a good deal was left to the imagination. Between these figures stood " Prudentia." On the right was the Coat of Arms of the City and a figure with wings, meaning, perhaps, the spiritual protection over the Cathedral City. The contents of a number printed in 1723 were:

> THE LONDON BILL OF MORTALITY.
> BOOKS PUBLISHED SINCE OUR LAST.
> FOREIGN AND HOME NEWS.
> POETRY AND ADVERTISEMENTS.

No "leader" of course, and very little matter apparently of any interest. This was not only a first-class, but the only paper for several English counties and Wales. In the language of the day, it was a "very spirited undertaking," and a fuller reference will be made to it in another chapter dealing exclusively with the family history.

The paper was improved and enlarged from time to time, but when Robert Raikes succeeded his father in 1757 it was still what we now look on as a curiosity;

but such as it was, it was the only source for early intelligence for a large portion of the West of England and Wales, and was even published at two places in London. When improved road coaches shortened the journey between Gloucester and London—doing the journey under twenty hours in summer—then the paper was permanently improved.

The young and spirited editor was able to obtain, *per* Flying coach, a London Letter, the latest foreign news, agricultural prices, and a copy of the London *Gazette*, and from these news-letters and official paper he was able to get about one thousand words of what, on the Monday morning, formed the very soul of the paper, and of the greatest value from Gloucester to Hereford and through a large portion of Wales. Many and important interests depended in those days upon the due publication of the *Journal*. But the paper could not be produced without the matter being edited, set, read and revised, and then printed on the Sunday. By doing this, and working through the night with a hand-press, the paper could be sent away from the city by the earliest stage-vans and coaches on the Monday morning.

With improved modes of transit, the newspaper almost leaped into prosperity and influence. Its appearance had long been improved. A less fantastic heading had been adopted, and the issue of Nov. 3, 1783, containing the editor's modest announcement about Sunday schools, is precisely the same size as the *Times* of October 3rd, 1798, containing "Nelson's Victory of the Nile"; namely,

19½ ins. by 12½ ins.; but whilst the *Journal* contains nine columns of advertisements, the *Times* contains but seven and a-half, and those of an inferior class. Measured by this standard—a weekly against a daily—practical journalists can make a shrewd guess as to the value of the property, and its influence as a newspaper. The price was 3d., with a halfpenny Government stamp impressed; then raised to 3½d., when the stamp duty was raised to one penny; and before Mr. Raikes retired the price per copy was 6d. The "make-up" of the paper was: Page 1, two columns advertisements and two columns foreign news and paragraphs. Page 2, advertisements and odd paragraphs. Page 3, letters on various topics, News of the Nation, local news, markets, London Letter, social paragraphs, obituary notices, &c. Page 4, advertisements and imprint. So important was this paper that the volumes were bound up and passed on as heirlooms, and not infrequently found fifty years after Mr. Raikes died in old farmhouses stowed away with the Family Bibles.

What time the Flying coach, leaving London on the Saturday with the precious news-letters and copy of the *Gazette*, would reach Gloucester was always a matter of uncertainty—so much depended on the weather and the chapter of accidents; but when the parcels did reach the editor's hands, his work commenced. Then the "copy" was set up; and when all was ready, the two inner "formes"—pages 2 and 3—were locked up and put upon a hand-press. One half of the paper—pages 1 and

4—were already printed, probably on the Saturday; and to facilitate matters a notice appeared apprising the public that "all advertisements brought after five o'clock on Saturday evening will not appear,"—no space being left for anything but the precious London news, letters, and clippings from the *Gazette*.

We now see Mr. Raikes, the "up-to-date" journalist, catering for a widespread public, representing important interests and depending upon him for the latest market prices. We have also to remember that even in the commencement of the present century Sunday trading in Gloucester was a recognised traffic. The shops in the city and the principal towns were regularly opened on Sunday mornings for the convenience of people living in the outlying villages.* Sunday labour in connection with the editing and printing of the *Journal* would never have formed the ground of complaint against Mr. Raikes, but

---

* Timothy Exall, in his pamphlet on the *Rise and Progress of Wesleyan Methodism in Dursley*, 1854, says at the end of the last century "buying and selling were commonly practised on the Sabbath." This is how the Sunday was spent at Dursley in Raikes's day: "Men, women, and children rambled the woods and fields; or dog-fighting, cock-fighting, badger-baiting, ball or marble playing,—these amusements with drunkenness was the common way of spending" the Sunday. This is not introduced by way of apology, but only for the information of the thoughtful reader.

Licenses were regularly granted *temp*. Elizabeth to poor men fallen into decay to practise sports on Sundays. The following is a curious copy of a license at one time in the possession of Sir John Evelyn, Bart.:

"Middlesex. To all Mayors, Sheriffs, Constables, and other Hed officers, within the Countie of Middlesex.

"After our hartie commendations. Whereas we are informed that one Seconton Powlter dwellinge within the parishe of St. Clement's Daines, beinge a poore man, havinge fower small children, and fallen into decay, ys lycensed to have and use some playes and games at uppon nine

for the position which he occupied in respect to Sunday schools at a time when public opinion, stirred into activity, insisted on a purer code of morals.

In 1863 there were still living in Gloucester old men who, as lads, worked for Mr. Raikes in the *Journal* office, and were able to tell what they did and what was done, and we give their statements without comment.

WILLIAM WHITEHEAD, College Court, aged 89, said: "I was engaged as a lad for three years at the office of Mr. Raikes, and I should have been apprenticed to him, but there was a law among printers which compelled them not to have more than a certain number of apprentices at one time, and I should have been obliged to wait two years longer. The printing office in my time was in Bolt Lane.

"We used to set up type on Sundays—the compositors were at work during the day, and we used to go severall Sondaies, for his better relief, comforte, and sustentacion, within the countie of Middlesex, to commence and begynne at and from xxii[nd] daie of Maye next comynge, after the date hereof and not to remayne in one place not above three severall Sondaies: And we consideringe that great resort of people is lyke to come thereunto, we will and require you, as well for good order as also for the preservation of the Queen's Majesty's peace, that you take with you foure or fyve of the discrete and substantiall men within your office or libertie where the games shall be put in practice, then and there to forsee and do your endeavour to your best in that behalf duringe the continuance of the games or playes: which games are hereafter severally mentioned, that is to say the Shotinge with the Standarde, the Shotinge with the Brode Arrowe, the Shotinge at the Twelve Shore Prick, the Shotinge at the Tarthe, the Leppinge for Men, the Runninge for Men, the Wrastlinge, the Throwinge of the Barre, with all such other games as have at any time heretofore or now be lycensed used or played.

"Geaven the xxvi[th] Daie of Aprill in the eleventh year of the Queen's Majesty's Raigne."

to press at seven o'clock in the evening, and get away from the office at four o'clock on Monday morning. On Mondays we had holiday."

Q. "What did people think about Sunday work?"

A. "The opinion of the public was not then as now. I don't remember anyone saying anything about our printing the paper. Everybody was too glad to get it on the Monday."

Q. "Did you ever hear Mr. Raikes say anything about his breaking the Sabbath?"

A. "I never heard him say anything on the subject. I went with him in 1786."

Q. "Did you ever see Mr. Raikes set up type?"

A. "No; but he knew his business. He had a desk in the composing room, and used to sit there and correct the proofs and give out copy. He used to come there on Sundays and do what work there was for him to do. I never heard whether he was brought up to the business."

Q. "Was he a go-ahead or sleepy sort of a man?"

A. "Oh, go-ahead for those times. His was the best office in the city to work for. The wages paid the comps. were one guinea a week. His was the first printing business in the county—I mean in reputation. We did good bookwork. Mr. Raikes always adopted the latest improvements. I do not know what the circulation of the *Journal* was."

JAMES WHITEHEAD, King's Holm, 76 years of age, said: "I was apprenticed to Mr. Raikes, and was with him till he sold the paper to Mr. Walker [1802].

"I never went to school or church on Sundays because I had to commence work early,—light fires, make paste, run errands for the men, and, when all was ready, call the pressman from chapel. He was a Wesleyan, and we used to go to press about seven or eight o'clock. Sunday was my busy day, and I stayed up until six o'clock Monday morning—folding papers and doing anything."

Q. "Did you hear people complain that Mr. Raikes broke the Sabbath?"

A. "No; people did not look upon it as Sabbath-breaking to print a newspaper. Shops in those days were regularly opened on Sundays for the convenience of country people. Everybody was satisfied then, the printers with their work and the public with their news."

Q. "Was yours a temperance office?"

A. "My goodness! no. I was the boy, you know, and when gentlemen came to the office I used to 'wipe their shoes.' We used to give a crown a quart for egg-flip made with mint, eggs, sugar, and beer. It was a 'Chapel'* affair, and I had my share for fetching it."

Mr. SIMPSON, aged 65: "I was apprenticed to Mr. Walker at the *Journal* office. The reason why the paper was printed on Sundays was because the *Gazette* was

* A trade term. Every printing office has its "Chapel" and "Father."

published in London on Saturdays, and as it contained the bankrupts, &c., it would have been ruin to publish it on any other day than Monday. In my time, we went to press at seven, eight, or nine o'clock, according to the time the coach arrived—and that would depend on the weather and accidents; it might come in early on Sunday morning, or not before eleven or twelve o'clock in the day."

Q. "Have you heard people say that Robert Raikes, the Founder of Sunday schools, was a Sabbath-breaker?"

A. "Yes. People may say what they like; but Robert Raikes seemed quite angelic as he walked through the streets of Gloucester—there was no one like him. Everybody seemed anxious to have the *Journal* on the Monday because there was no news in that day to be had, and no literature hardly. The Dissenters used to complain much about the paper being printed on Sundays. It is a Saturday paper now. Things are all different now."

The paper was printed first on a "screw press" and then on a hand-press, after the old Stanhope pattern, and the types were inked with balls covered with skin,— not composition rollers as now. The reader who is accustomed to-day to hear of hundreds of thousands of papers being printed from "endless rolls" in a short time, will learn with surprise that with a hand-press it would take ten hours to print five hundred "insides" of the

Journal. Pressmen were a distinct class to compositors. The "Printer's Devil" was the man who worked up the ink on the stone with the balls and inked the types; and after a time, what with ink and perspiration, he looked very terrible, hence the name.

It never occurred to Mr. Raikes that the setting up of type and printing his *Journal* was an offence against good morals; but when he attempted to take advantage of an improved postal service and get off some of the papers on Sunday nights, he laid himself open to adverse criticism, and on the 9th May, 1791, the *Journal* contained the following singular notice :

"As the printer's exertions to favour the despatch of his paper to Hay and Brecon by the advantages of Sunday's post are found to expose his conduct to much misconstruction, he intends to discontinue the circulation by that mode, and flatters himself his connection in these quarters will accept his best endeavours to supply them with the *Gloucester Journal* in the most expeditious manner he can of another kind."

In the present day Mr. Raikes will not be judged severely, and probably a bill of complete indemnity will be given him. But the charge of Sabbath breaking has been brought against him again and again, and made an excuse for much adverse criticism and aspersion. When the facts are known just judgment is certain to be pronounced.

NOTE.—Mr. Charles Cooke, surgeon, Cheltenham, writing on this subject, says: "That his [Raikes's] paper was printed, and therefore corrected, on that day [Sunday] I can bear testimony, having often as a boy been sent for one on the same night. But when I add that this was at a time when my Aunt Sophia [afterwards Mrs. Bradburn] used to be bitterly scoffed at for the regularity of her attendance at the Cathedral daily service, and invited out to parties, as she has often told me, in order to be made jest of, it cannot be wondered at that religion should not have had much to do with business customs, and that in the part which he took in the foundation of Sabbath schools, *he should be considered as in advance of himself* as well as of the times in which he lived."

CHAPTER X.

FIFTY YEARS IN THE VINEYARD.

> "Pleased to do good,
> He gave, and sought no more, nor questioned much,
> Nor reasoned who deserved, for well he knew
> The face of Need."
>   POLLOCK.

ROBERT RAIKES spent the best fifty years of his life in forming and carrying out plans of social reform; and he had the great satisfaction of seeing his plans adopted and accomplishing their purpose.

The names of Howard, Paul, and Raikes are inseparably associated with the work of prison reform which commenced in Gloucester and gave its name to the "Separate System." Sir G. O. Paul perfected and carried the system into practice; and in 1807 a Commission from America visited Gloucester, and on their return inaugurated the "Solitary System," which, in its turn, was modified and introduced into Great Britain. Identity is often lost under various disguises, and the general reader, knowing Raikes simply in connection with Sunday schools, may be interested in finding that the energy which he expended on prisons and prisoners is still vital.

In October, 1791, he was able to write in his *Journal*: "The prison is in every way calculated to the ease, health, and benefit of the prisoner, who has every comfort he can wish to render confinement agreeable and life desirable."

The " prisoners " here refer to " debtors," who before were herded by day and chained at night with criminals. This view was taken by the twenty-one debtors who signed a petition to Sir G. O. Paul praying that their wives and children might have admission to their apartments.

In July, 1792, Mr. Raikes, writing to his friend, Mr. Lewelyn, at Leominster, says:

" I have some satisfaction in acquainting you that the state of the county is so much improved by the late Regulations, and the attention to the improvement of morals among the common people, *that we have not for the whole county one culprit to hold up his hand at the Bar at the next Assizes. A circumstance that the history of this county could never before record.*

" The number about ten years ago was from 50 to 100 that we usually tried. *That was the period when Providence was pleased to make me the instrument of introducing Sunday schools and regulations in prisons.*—Non Nobis Domine, sed Nomini tuo da gloriam! "

The conviction is pressed upon us that Mr. Raikes felt keenly the want of sympathy amongst the citizens, towards whom he was entitled to look for generous appreciation and support. The extravagant praise often bestowed upon him, and the adoption of his system so universally as to become more than national, would have been sufficient to overfill the souls of the vainest men of his generation; but at home, where he had worked without fainting, he was "Bobby Wild Goose," and the Sunday schools in the city did not thrive by comparison with those in the rest of the world. The Queen (Charlotte) was pleased to see him at Windsor and to encourage him.* Writing to the Rev. Bowen Thickens, Ross (quoted by Nichols, *Literary Anecdotes*), June 27th, 1788, he says :

"I rejoice to hear that Sunday schools are producing the same happy effects with you that are springing up in all parts of the kingdom, when the high ranks of people will condescend to overlook the management.

"At Windsor, the ladies of fashion pass their Sundays in teaching the poorest children. The Queen sent for me the other day to give Her Majesty an account of the effects observable on the manners of the poor, and Her Majesty most graciously said that she envied those who had the power of doing good by thus personally promoting the welfare of society in giving instruction and morality to the general mass of the common people, a pleasure from which by her position she was debarred. Were this known to the ladies of the British nation, it would serve to animate them with zeal and follow in the example which the Queen is so desirous to set before them. You may mention it to the ladies of Ross, who

* *See* "Royal Anecdote," Appendix E.

will not then, perhaps, be above noticing the children of their poor neighbours, if they are present."

Putting his own wishes into practice, he induced two of his own daughters to attend the school of St. Mary de Crypt, and personally promote "the welfare of society in giving instruction and morality to the general mass of the common people."

King George III. paid a visit to the Sunday schools at Brentford and uttered the pious wish, in Mrs. Trimmer's hearing, "That every poor child in my kingdom should be taught to read the Bible." The Duke of Gloucester—as before mentioned—visited at Mr. Raikes's house whilst quartered in the city with his regiment. He was the President of an Eclectic Society and affected an acquaintance with popular science. He was also so good-natured a man that Thomas Raikes, the Diarist, says he was known as "Silly Billy" by the young bloods about town. Being a good-natured man and given to intellectual pursuits, it may fairly be presumed that in Mr. Robert Raikes's company the Sunday school project was, at least, discussed; and probably the noble Duke was an early subscriber to the institution. Members of the French Academy came over from Paris in 1787 and thoroughly investigated the new plans for raising up a new race. Dr. Adam Smith wrote: "No plan has promised to effect a change of manners with equal ease since the days of the Apostles." Opposition had burnt itself out, and yet Mr. Raikes, writing to his friend Lewelyn, said:

"It is, however, some recompense for the *scorn and contempt* of my neighbours that I am frequently honoured with visits from strangers the most dignified and respectable, one of whom told me the other day that he would rather have been the instrument of so much good to the world than to be the possessor of a million of gold."

The Empress Catherine of Russia, for whose enlightened policy in the matter of education Raikes frequently had a good word to say in his *Journal*, did invite him—as she had invited Voltaire before him—to come to Russia. His brother's connection with St. Petersburg makes this circumstance not at all surprising, only no one apparently would have known of the great compliment paid to the citizen of Gloucester had it not been for the following lines slipped into a gossipy letter to Mr. Lewelyn* :

"You would smile were you to see how many applications I have received from men in different parts of the kingdom desiring me to recommend them to the Empress of Russia in my room. Alas! we have too much need of aid in the work of instructing the ignorant and enlightening the darkness that overhangs this nation, to spare one individual who has zeal and capacity to be useful at home."

This is all the notice which was taken of a compliment which a public man might be excused if he blazoned all over Europe. The society magazines of the day had no inkling of this very interesting fact. That his name

* Mrs. Ladbroke was not aware of the fact.

did fill the minds of men is beyond dispute. The erudite and pious Etheridge notes that Dr. Adam Clarke by his long-continued appeals on behalf of Sunday schools greatly aided those important institutions; and Dr. Jabez Bunting, afterwards President of the Wesleyan Conference, preached, May 15th, 1805, "at the Rev. Mr. Sharpe's Meeting House, 4 New Court, Carey Street, London," so powerful a sermon in support of Sunday schools that the *Gentleman's Magazine* recommended its publication, which recommendation was adopted.

The Sunday School Union was in existence then, though Mr. Raikes does not appear to have been connected with it. He was, however, an honorary member of the Sunday School Society, as appears from this minute:

"At a general meeting of the members of the Sunday School Society, held June 11th, 1787, it was resolved unanimously: That in consideration of the zeal and merits of Robert Raikes, Esq., of Gloucester, *who may be considered as the original Founder* as well as *a liberal supporter* of Sunday schools, he be admitted an honorary member of this Society."

It has never been sufficiently noticed that from the time of his becoming its responsible Editor, the *Gloucester Journal* was the staunch advocate of Temperance. The crusade commenced as early as 1757, and here again we find Raikes a long way in advance of the popular sentiments of his time. In this year there was scarcity of corn, and the price was consequently very high. The columns of the *Journal* were thrown open to correspondence on the liquor traffic and the impolicy—not to say sin—of converting breadstuff into spirit, which demoralised instead of feeding the people. Some of the ideas are crudely expressed, but the whole argument used by Mr. Hoyle—*Our National Resources and How They are Wasted*—is to be found in them. The payment of taxes on grain for distilling is set forth as a " melancholy truth " and the following bold question is put : " Whether those poor wretches who have lately risen in different parts of this kingdom impelled by extreme hunger to commit outrages on their neighbours, and have thereby in the eye of the law forfeited their lives, are not in the more lenient eye of humanity real objects of compassion ? "

There follows a long article taking up the ground of modern Temperance advocates, that it is the duty of Parliament so to restrict the manufacture and sale of intoxicating liquors as to prevent the waste of food, the corruption of morals and the bodily impoverishment of the poor. Distillers as a class are denounced as " avaricious men whose unrelenting hearts and thirst after gain (without the interposition of Parliament) would starve the poor, and destroy with intoxicating liquors one-half of the common people who, under proper regulation, would be made very civil members of society and add strength to the State."

The article is signed " Britannicus," but it reads very much like Mr. Raikes's own composition, and there are two chords touched in the whole treatment of the question which he never ceased to play on, namely: (1) That it is a crime to degrade and starve the masses; and (2) That the masses when elevated are sources of wealth and strength to the State. From internal evidence it seems probable that a *nom de plume* is adopted so as not to offend the great maltsters and distillers in the country.

The nail is driven home with much force in the same issue in a letter (also anonymous) on the scarcity of corn. Here is an extract:

"A family in great distress made application to the parish for assistance. Some of the officers went and saw a pot boiling on the fire, at which sight they seemed to disbelieve the presence of poverty. But this [disbelief] was soon dispelled by throwing out *the carcase of a dead dog*, which was the *second* that they had been compelled by extreme necessity to procure in order to prevent their starving.

"The very relation of this matter," says the correspondent, "makes 'my heart bleed with sympathetic sorrow'; nor can I look upon it in any other light than as a judgment of the Almighty on this false sinful nation for the abuse of His merciful and glorious bounty to us."

So that there can be no mistake as to the editorial sympathies, an innocent but official-looking paragraph is inserted reminding the local authorities of not the least important of their duties, namely, the visiting of alehouses by constables and Tything men of the city on

Sundays. If tipplers are found therein during prohibited hours, they are to be brought before a Justice of the Peace and fined. The penalty to the tippler is 3s. 4d. and to the ale seller 10s.

It is the fact that a single issue of the *Journal* in February, 1757, is as completely a temperance number as the habits and modes of thought of that day would tolerate, and was certainly more in advance of public opinion than any temperance magazine of to-day can be in advance of public sentiment. It was not a passing fad: he was a consistent and persistent enemy to alehouses and Sunday drinking in them. Thirty years afterwards—after all his prison experiences and after Sunday schools were prosperous—he describes them as "nests of crime," and adds that "the magistrates have given orders to the constables to look well after them."

At the end of fifty years of work we do not find that Mr. Raikes changed his views much on social questions, or ever repented of the part which he had taken in respect of them. That he really believed that criminals were made so in consequence of the neglect and carelessness of society to teach them better, is proved by the fact that he would not *prosecute the woman who stole and pawned his shirts.** He looked on all such with compassion—and this compassionate feeling, founded on experience, was never absent in his public and private career.

Whilst he was a progressive man, the tone and

* *See* Note end of Chapter VIII.

habit of his mind was conservative in this: having once thought out a problem, he seldom changed his attitude towards it. In respect to Sunday schools we only find him saying that they were insufficient to meet the necessities of the day, and that he went heart and soul with the establishment of day and industrial schools. He records in the *Journal* for July, 1801, that the Dean of Lincoln preached in the Abbey Church, Bath, to 700 children attending Sunday schools and schools of industry.

What the world most thanks him for is this: *he founded and organised Sunday schools in an unsectarian spirit and on the principle of voluntaryism*. The voluntary principle has never been departed from. The Sunday School Society was, from the first, a voluntary Society, and this tradition is carried on by the Sunday School Union established in 1803. The widest Catholic feeling was shown from the commencement. The Church of England and Nonconformist schools often shared the proceeds of the same collection. This was a great advantage to the movement from the very first, because its aims were not obscured by sectarian prejudices or bitterness. Children were cared for *because they were human*, and not because they were called by any particular name. It was not uncommon to meet in the *Journal* acknowledgments of subscriptions for the benefit of *all* the Sunday schools in a certain district. If there were jealousies, Mr. Raikes wisely ignored them on paper.

The Sunday School Society was founded in 1785,

and in ten years did a great deal of work, though it only professed to give aid to other societies and struggling schools out of funds arising from legacies and donations. That these were generous, the report at the end of the ten years will show. The report was presented at the annual general meeting, held at "St. Paul's Head Tavern," Cateaton Street, London, on the 18th July, 1795, Thomas Boddington, Esq., in the chair. During ten years the Society had distributed 91,915 spelling books, 24,232 Testaments, and 5,360 Bibles for use in 1012 Sunday schools containing about 65,000 scholars. The committee were able to report the gift of a legacy of £200 Bank Stock. This Society, although working on the lines of a charity, was much in advance of most charities, which were tied down to particular purposes to be performed in a particular way. This Society had more freedom and exercised it judiciously.

So little were the Sunday schools of the United Kingdom dependent on any central body or dependent on the magic of a name, that the "passing away" of Raikes never affected them in the least. The principle of self-help had never before been so admirably adapted to the educational necessities of a great people, and we know that the principle is as elastic now as then; and, speaking for the Anglo-Saxon race throughout the world, there is no reason for the suggestion that the time may come when Sunday schools will fail to adapt themselves to any and all future social and religious conditions.

At the end of half a century of work in a vineyard

which seemed bare of promise, Robert Raikes saw that his "little grain of mustard seed" was full of growth and promised one day to cover the earth. Before he died about 400,000 children were on the books of well-organised Sunday schools, and this knowledge was his exceeding great reward whilst in the land of the living.

CHAPTER XI.

SOME PIONEERS.

"It is the first men who do who are great."—MS.

NO book pretending to take into account the conditions under which Mr. Raikes lived, and the moral atmosphere around him, will be complete without referring to some men and women in Gloucestershire who certainly did work on pretty much the same lines as himself on the question of education. If for no other purpose, then to show that thinking men, acting independently and in different centres, arrived at the same conclusions, and that society was ripe for the change so soon as the organiser should appear. When we know all that can be known, the pretensions to originality of design so long set up for Mr. Raikes, and so hotly combated, are somewhat reduced, but without detracting from his merit and the position which must be accorded him in history. Moreover, the county of Gloucester stands in relation to the rest of the country as the Galilee of the movement, so full was it of first disciples.

THE REV. JOHN MARKS MOFFATT.

A quiet, studious, unobtrusive man was John Marks Moffatt, Independent Minister of Nailsworth, Gloucester-

Dea[r]
great a[...]
I regre[t]
when y[ou]
glad. [...]
little t[...]
to you [...]
in a M[...]
I ha[ve]
that I [...]
on anot[her]
has me [...]
It [...]
that I [...]
Visit fro[m]
tion. —
be expre[ssed]
good is [...]
Mustar[d]
upon t[he]
Spirit.

Promoters, w[...]
and princi[pally]
I have
where they
I than[k]
tracts. — [...]
we shall
towards a[...]
ing the t[...]
which ren[...]
of Blessing
I hop[e]
my sincere

Gloucester
Nov: 24.1[...]

Dear Sir

Another of my Friends having a great Desire to inspect Mr Howard's Book, I requested Mrs Wade to tell you that when you had done with it, I should be glad if you could return it for a little time. — If it will be of any Use to you it will be again at your Service in a Month's time.

I have inclosed the only Part of your Paper that I can find; there were a few lines more on another Piece of Paper, but my Man I fear has mislaid it. —

It has been a great Mortification to me that I have never yet had leisure to pay a Visit from which I should derive so much Satisfaction. — It gives me a Pleasure that is not to be expressed to hear from all Quarters how much good is springing up from this little Grain of Mustard Seed — The City of Bristol is entering upon the Plan of Sunday Schools with a degree of Spirit that reflects great Honour upon the

Promoters, who chiefly consist of a few of the Clergy and principal Merchants —

I have also had Letters from Exeter where they are going to introduce it

I thank you, my good Sir, for the tracts. — I hope by using the Means we shall in time gain some Ground towards attaining the End, of preventing the Growth of those Enormities which render Mankind a Curse instead of Blessing to each other. —

I hope Mrs Moffat is well. — With my sincere good Wishes to you both.

I am, Dear Sir, your most,
obliged and obedient Servant
R Raikes

Glocester
Nov. 24. 1784.

ho chiefly consist of a few of the Clergy
ral Merchants —
also had Letters from Exeter
are going to introduce it
h: you, my good Sir, for the
I hope by using the Means
in time gain some Ground
taining the End, of prevent
rowth of those Enormities
der Mankind a Curse instead
to each other. —

e Mrs Moffat is well. — With
good Wishes to you both.
I am, Dear Sir, your most
obliged and obedient Servant
R Raikes

84.

shire and afterwards of Malmesbury, Wilts, where he died and was buried. In 1774, when labouring at Nailsworth, and as yet unmarried, he continued the practice of teaching the children of his congregation on Sundays. How long before 1774 he commenced it it is impossible now to say with certainty, for although a literary man and the author, amongst other things, of *The Duty and Interest of every Private Person and the Kingdom at Large;* the *Protestant Prayer Book;* and the *History of the Town and Abbey of Malmesbury,* he left no account of his attempt at civilising the young generation. Even after Mr. Raikes's "scheme," as it was termed, became talked about, and some honour was attached to the name of the man who suggested it to the world, Mr. Moffatt kept silence. But for the fortunate circumstance of his only daughter preserving a letter to her father from the Rev. Thomas Gibbons, dated August 26th, 1774, there would have been nothing authentic to show that the claims put forward for Mr. Moffatt as having ante-dated Mr. Raikes were not as shadowy as scores of others.

Mr. Raikes also wrote to Mr. Moffatt in 1784, and that letter, too, is in existence. It is a good specimen of Mr. Raikes's composition and handwriting, and we give a *facsimile* of it in this volume.*

Mr. Gibbons wrote to his "dear friend" in August, 1774, and then confesses with much self-reproach that he has

* The earliest specimen of Mr. Raikes's handwriting which the Editor possesses is his signature to the church register on the day of his marriage in 1767. The letter now reproduced is the earliest specimen of a letter by him ever exhibited. A tracing from the church register is also given on p. 267.

been behindhand with his epistolary correspondence for the two years previous, and that his dear friend's last letter should have been answered months before. So we may take it that it was in 1773 that Mr. Moffatt wrote to him about his plan for instructing children, and it may be assumed that it had been in practice some little time before he wrote. We may, therefore, fix 1772 as the probable date when he began his plan, or eight years before Mr. Raikes commenced operations in the city of Gloucester.

The material parts of Mr. Gibbons's letter* are as follow :

"The scheme you have suggested of instructing the children, &c., is excellent, and I shall be ready to assist you in it—if I cannot any otherwise, yet by procuring you books from our Book Society. Indeed, I had a nomination t'other day, and I divided it half to you and half to another minister in the country. [He wrote from Bishop's Stortford, Herts.] The books I suppose you have, before this letter arrives, received : they consist only of Bibles and Testaments.

"Let me know whether you have proceeded upon this plan, whether you are likely to meet with success in it, and what aids you could immediately wish. Though my purse is but scanty, there are sparings from it for other purposes, and much cannot be expected from that quarter, yet I may be able, after I have had an account from you, to procure assistance from the liberality of others, either by books or money.

* The original is in the Editor's possession.

"Assure yourself that as it is a very laudable scheme, so I must heartily wish it success, and I am ready to forward it as far as lies in my power. Go on and prosper, my young friend, in the work of the Lord, and may He enlarge and influence your heart for doing good, and fulfil all your desire. Oh! 'tis a blessed thing to be a servant of the Lord, to be the instrument of blessing to others, and especially in their most important, their everlasting interests. And, considering how short and uncertain Life is, how ready should we be to gather up the golden sands of time that nothing may be lost."

Standing alone this letter would not clearly convey the idea that Mr. Moffatt's plan had anything to do with the Sunday instruction of children; but in 1863 Miss Moffatt was living near Stroud, and in an interview she informed the Author that her father's was a Sunday school for the instruction of children, and that it flourished under his care until he removed to Malmesbury, where he died. Her mother told her that Mr. Raikes wrote to her father and received from him information about the Nailsworth Sunday School; and she used to say: "Your father was a most humble-minded man, and did not care to have any honour."

There is not the slightest reason for doubting a single word uttered by Miss Moffatt, who at that date (1863) had herself been a Sunday school teacher for forty years. She had recently been presented with a handsomely bound copy of *Bagster's Comprehensive Bible* by the "teachers and friends of the Old Chapel Sunday School,

Stroud, for her unwearied attentions as superintendent during the period of thirty years."

The material portions of the letter which Mr. Raikes sent to her father in 1784 are as follow, and a *facsimile* of the whole is annexed.

"It has been a great mortification to me that I have never yet had leisure to pay a visit from which I should derive so much satisfaction. It gives me a pleasure that is not to be expressed to hear from all quarters how much good is springing up from this little grain of mustard seed.

"The city of Bristol is entering on a plan of Sunday schools with a degree of spirit that reflects great honour upon the promoters, who chiefly consist of a few of the clergy and principal merchants.

"I have also had letters from Exeter, where they are going to introduce it.

"I thank you, my good sir, for the tracts. I hope that by using the means we shall in time gain some ground towards attaining the end of preventing the growth of those enormities which render mankind a curse instead of a blessing to each other."

MRS. BRADBURN *née* SOPHIA COOKE.

Both of the Wesleys were personally acquainted with Mr. Raikes, and John Wesley gave his support, wholehearted and immediate, to Sunday schools. The plan was in harmony with the democratic instincts of the early Wesleyan societies. The lay element was paramount—

free to labour, free to teach, free to bring little children to the arms of Jesus. There are many cases in the country in which Sunday schools were adopted so early —and no proper record kept—that it has been claimed that some of them were prior to 1780. It has often been claimed for Mrs. Bradburn—the wife of the talented and eloquent preacher, sometimes called the Demosthenes of Methodism, who did so much to bring Wesleyanism into repute—that she met Mr. Raikes in Gloucester, and in conversation with him *first* suggested to his mind the idea of Sunday instruction. The stories told and published are defective and do not hang together well. The following biographical facts relating to Sophia Cooke (Mrs. Bradburn) are from the mouth of her nephew, Mr. Charles Cooke, surgeon, Cambray Terrace, Cheltenham. He said:

"Sophia Cooke was the daughter of John Cooke, an eminent surgeon, and a native of the city of Gloucester. John Cooke had, I believe, six children. His eldest son was the Rev. George Cooke, Fellow and Tutor of Oriel College, Oxford, and afterwards for forty years the Rector of Dortworth.

"Sophia, like the rest of her relations, was strongly attached in her early days to the Established Church, and her friends were what was called 'High and dry Church people;' but very early in life she happened to be in the neighbourhood of Stroud, and heard the Rev. Samuel Bradburn preach. He was a Wesleyan. She was deeply impressed with the religious truths uttered by him, and subsequently sought and obtained pardon for her sins. She was thrown into London by the Providence of God, and Mr. Bradburn was appointed to preach in Southwark Chapel, Borough, to a congregation which numbered generally 3,000 people.

"She was married to him. He was contemporary with John Wesley, and was a very eminent minister in that day.

"Mrs. Bradburn was greatly persecuted in her time for marrying a Wesleyan preacher, by her friends and relations. She suffered great privations of many kinds, and from being a fine and beautiful woman, she became a poor shattered creature, but we cannot learn that she ever regretted the course she had taken.

"My Aunt Sophia, before her marriage and whilst she was living in Gloucester, used to collect children in the nave of her parish church and ask them religious questions, and this practice of hers, I have always understood, was the first step towards the establishment of Sunday schools in Gloucester.

"I never heard my aunt say that she was the first founder of Sunday schools, and never heard her challenge anyone for saying that she was *not*, or that other people were.

"I wrote to the Rev. Samuel Lysons in 1861, informing him exactly the position which my aunt occupied, and he wrote to me saying that had he known the facts earlier he would have given her 'her proper position' in his sketch of Raikes in the book entitled *What has Gloucestershire Achieved?*"

The following items were extracted from an old MS. in the possession of Mr. Cooke:

"Mrs. Bradburn was brought to the enjoyment of the pardoning mercy and renewing grace of God in the eighteenth year of her age.

"It is stated from good authority that she *first* suggested to Mr. Raikes, with whom she was personally acquainted, the plan of Sunday school instruction.

"Commiserating the case of a large number of ragged children whom he saw in the streets, he said to Miss Cooke, 'What shall we do for these poor neglected children?' and she answered, 'Let us teach them to read and take them to church.'

"The suggestion was adopted, and Mr. Raikes and Miss Cooke conducted the first company of Sunday scholars, exposed to public laughter as they passed along the streets with their unpromising charges.

"From early life Mrs. Bradburn* enjoyed the personal friendship of John Wesley, and lived two years in his house in the City Road, London. She used to remark that his morning salutation, uttered with great cheerfulness, was: 'Safely live to-day.'"

SAMUEL WEB DE HILL.

When the Author visited Painswick, near Stroud, in 1862, sweet remembrances lingered in the minds of the then aged of Mr. Samuel Web, son of John Web de Hill,

* Mr. Cooke possessed a portrait of Mrs. Bradburn in Indian ink, and he gave the Author a copy, which has unfortunately been lost.—ED.

a wealthy cloth manufacturer. Samuel was baptised in the parish church of Painswick, October 14th, 1737. The certificated copy reads: "Baptizings. 1737. Oct. 14. Sam¹¹· son of John Web de Hill." In 1862 he was always called Samuel Webb. The Rev. Samuel Lysons, in a note to the Author, says the origin of the family is Dutch, and that the name "Web" was given to one of the family settled in Gloucester as a sort of nickname by the Merry Monarch—Charles II.

Samuel Webb was born to wealth and to misfortune, and both these estates endeared him to those who knew him. He was open-handed with his wealth and pitied the poor, and in his evil days he was "always the gentleman." The aged were ever pleased to talk about him—his great wealth, his great benevolence, his handsome countenance, his genial manners, his elegant dress. A tradition grew around him which the aged would not willingly let die; and it had this for its foundation: He employed a cloth weaver named William Twining to hold a Sunday school in the kitchen of his house in Rutchill Bottom, Sheepscombe. He took a personal interest in the children, walking over from the Hill to Sheepscombe, talking to and examining them. To all the children he gave something. The good had twopence and the bad one penny. All had something. He carried a large green umbrella, the first which had ever been seen,[*] and those who saw it never afterwards

---

[*] Mr. Jonas Hanway is said to have been the first person to publicly carry an umbrella in England. He will always be remembered in connection with Sunday schools.

forgot it, or the gold buttons on his blue coat, or the beautiful lace about his waistcoat and cuffs.

He was acquainted with Mr. Robert Raikes, and many old people remembered seeing Mr. Raikes with Mr. Webb when he visited Twining's school at Sheepscombe. From this circumstance, and from the fact that the Gloucester schools became pre-eminent, the scholars as they grew up obtained the fixed conviction that Mr. Raikes came over to Painswick and "borrowed his idea" from Mr. Webb. A careful investigation, however, resulted in nothing more definite than this—a Sunday school was established by Mr. Webb's agency at or about the time that Mr. Raikes made known the result of his experiment in Gloucester, and that Mr. Raikes visited the school with Mr. Fox from London, but that was not until 1784, after which a local committee was formed and Painswick became one of the show places in the early history of the Sunday school movement.

John Twining, gardener, son of William Twining, gave the Author all the information and assistance in his power. His uncle, John, conducted the girls' school in Sheepscombe—also with Mr. Webb's patronage—and in the course of his narrative he said: "These wicked children were soon reclaimed from the worst of their ways, and we used to assemble them every year in Painswick churchyard and arrange them around so as that any person might come and examine them. After I grew up I was a teacher for several years, and I once took as many as 110 scholars from Sheepscombe to Painswick, through the corn-fields, and not one of them broke the ranks. They marched in twos. . . . Robert Raikes gave my father a Bible; this Bible contained, I believe, a complete history of my father's Sunday school. I cannot possibly find where it is." *

In 1861 the Rev. Edward Lightwood, Wesleyan, wrote to the *Wesleyan Magazine* stating that in 1772 a pious woman, a member of the Wesleyan Methodist Society, started a Sunday school in Painswick. Then followed the usual story about Mr. Raikes seeing her and "borrowing" the idea, &c. Mr. Pullen, master of the National School (1862), informed the Author that he had made a house-to-house examination, but could never find any trace of any old Sunday schools in the parish of Painswick, except those kept by the Twinings and attributed to Mr. Webb's benevolence. He was very doubtful about the dates of origin—1784, in his opinion, would be the earliest.

WILLIAM KING, OF DURSLEY.

Very strong claims have been put forward and supported with warmth on behalf of William King, a woollen card maker, of Dursley, and an acquaintance of Mr. Raikes. He was a Dissenter, an admirer of Howard's, and a follower of Whitefield's. It was claimed for him that he ante-dated Mr. Raikes's first school in Gloucester. The following are the letters which the Author received

* This Bible was sold by auction, and all efforts to trace it have been fruitless.

from Mr. King's nearest surviving relations :—Mr. EDWARD WEIGHT, Norfolk Terrace, Gloucester, wrote :

"Upwards of fifty years since my late brother John wished to take the matter up, but my father and mother disapproving of it, lest their intention might be misconstrued and considered mere vanity, he refrained from doing so. . . . I well remember, when young, hearing Mr. Adrian Newth* (a man noted for his piety) repeatedly saying it was my grandfather (Mr. King) who first promoted Sunday schools. . . . I much regret the subject was not taken up when my brother wished."

William King, of Dursley.

Mr. Weight obtained from his aunt, Mrs. M. Oldland, one of William King's daughters, a letter which is perhaps

---

* This Adrian was the father of the Rev. Elisha Newth, one of the early converts of the Rev. Rowland Hill, and was " for nearly thirty years in the pastoral oversight " of Surrey Chapel. That eminent Greek scholar, and one of the New Testament revisers, the late Dr. Samuel Newth, was his grandson.

the best and most reliable testimony now obtainable. It is as follows:

"*March* 5*th*, 1863.

"My dear and honoured father, Mr. William King, of Dursley, being at Painswick on business, finding there were two men in Gloucester Prison for execution on the Monday, came to Gloucester on Saturday evening in order to visit them, intending, if permitted, to remain with them the preceding night. But the keeper did not think it safe, as they were so bad characters.

"On Sunday morning he called on Mr. Raikes. Both walked together towards the Island, and seeing several lads at different sports *my father observed to Mr. Raikes* what a pity it was the Sabbath should be so desecrated, when Mr. Raikes replied, 'Mr. King, how can it be altered?'

"'Sir,' said my father, 'if Sabbath schools were begun so as to give the poor education it would be [the] means of great good. I have endeavoured to open one myself with the help of a faithful journeyman of mine, but from multitude of business through the week I could not attend as I wished.'

"Mr. Raikes replied, 'It will not do for Dissenters; it must be from the Church.' My father belonged to the Tabernacle—[and was] a follower of George Whitefield.

"Mr. Raikes told a Mr. Stock, I believe a clergyman, who employed a person to instruct a few poor children, *and in three weeks after Mr. Raikes put it in his Journal.*

"Some years back the question was sent to your dear mother, my sister, and she answered nearly or quite the same as above. It was then put in print, in a book called *The Origin of Sunday Schools*, and I have to rejoice that that small cloud, no bigger than a man's hand, has spread over the land, and many thousands reap the benefit.

"From your affectionate Aunt,

" M. OLDLAND."

This claim, made no doubt in all good faith, does not bear close investigation. If Mr. King did not see Mr. Raikes until *three weeks* before the announcement in the *Journal* of November 3rd, 1783, then that was about three years after Mr. Raikes had collected children in Soot Alley, Gloucester, six years after Samuel Lee, on the authority of a painted board, opened a Sunday school at Pagan Hill, and eleven years after Mr. Moffatt certainly taught children on Sundays at Nailsworth. Many genuine errors with regard to the dates of "original" schools in isolated districts have, no doubt, arisen through Mr. Raikes's printed announcement being taken as the first inception of the idea of Sunday schools. This we now know to be wrong; and if it were not, the claims set up would in no way affect the true historical position of Mr. Raikes.

Outside of Gloucester there have been many genuine attempts to inaugurate local social reforms, and at Little Lever, Lancashire, Raikes was clearly anticipated. The points of resemblance in the methods are interesting.

ADAM CROMPTON, LITTLE LEVER.

Perhaps the best thought-out and most systematic plan of Sunday education, apart from catechising in places of worship, is that of Mr. Adam Crompton's, of Little Lever, paper manufacturer. He worked entirely on the same lines as Raikes—establishing a school and supporting it at his own expense—only he put his plan in operation some years before Mr. Raikes put his. The one vital difference between the two experiments was, that one was local, isolated, individual; and the other, universal. The one died, the other lived. Both were organically the same, but one, and one only, had breathed into it the breath of life.

Through a little carelessness the thoughtful efforts of Mr. Crompton have been attributed to James Heyes, a poor bobbin-winder, of Little Lever, known locally as "Jemmy o' th' Hey." Mr. Peter Turner, of Wednesbury, gave currency to the "Jemmy o' th' Hey" tradition, and gave it picturesqueness by stating that he used to summon the Sunday scholars together by means of an old brass mortar and pestle, which is not improbable. But Jemmy was a paid teacher in the employ of Mr. Adam Crompton.

The *European Magazine* for 1793 (in Robert Raikes's lifetime) contains a thoughtful and judicious article by Dr. Thomas Barnes, of New College, Manchester, on Mr. Adam Crompton, who died October 30th, 1793, at the age of 72. Dr. Barnes claimed for his personal friend the honour of being *the first person in England who formed* the plan of a Sunday school and supported it at his own charge. Dr. Barnes is not certain about the date, although he is about the fact that James Heyes was paid a regular salary by him for teaching poor children at his own house on that day. The date fixed for the commencement of James Heyes' school is 1774-5, and so Mr. Crompton precedes Mr. Raikes by five or six years, and in his turn was preceded by the Rev. John Marks Moffatt, of Nailsworth, by about two years, who likewise (as we have seen) organised a school and supported it at his own charge. What makes the parallel between Mr. Raikes and Mr. Crompton more interesting is, that both were laymen. In one sense it was not their duty to look after the spiritual welfare of the little outcasts, and Society laid no claims upon them to do so. There the parallel justly ceases—Raikes gave the nascent institution his unceasing personal attention, advertised it, stood the chaff and ridicule and abuse connected with it, and when praise came he took that and absorbed that also. In Mr. Crompton's case no one knew of it but "Jemmy o' th' Hey," who received his wages when due.

Dr. Barnes says: "This was done in so secret a manner that his [Crompton's] own family was at the time ignorant of it, and cannot now [1793] therefore fix the exact year when it was begun. But I can state, that for several years before the institution of Sunday schools by that good man, Mr. Raikes, of Gloucester, Mr. A. Crompton maintained a school of this description at Little Lever, under the care of James Heyes, to whom he paid a regular salary for teaching poor children at his own house on that day. I lived for many years a near neighbour to this poor man, and admired what I then thought to be his disinterested kindness in devoting every Sunday, when by infirmity disabled from attending public worship, to so charitable an office. It was not till long after that I discovered the plan and the support of it to be the work of Mr. Crompton, who had concealed this, as he wished to do his other charities, even from his nearest friends and relations, among whom I had the pleasure of being numbered." Dr. Barnes for himself then follows out a train of thought just towards Mr. Raikes's claims to be the central figure in the Sunday school system by saying: "This circumstance will not be considered as any diminution to the praise, nor will it lessen the satisfaction, of the worthy man before mentioned, since Mr. Raikes did not borrow the hint from hence or any other quarter. He, in the generosity of his own soul, like Mr. Crompton, conceived and executed the plan; and he has had the noble pleasure of seeing it adopted, extended, and patronised in such a manner as to gratify the warmest feelings of his heart."

Many men and women besides these have, doubtlessly, in their own way endeavoured to improve the intellectual and spiritual condition of the ignorant poor about them. They have done good—all of them—and the fact has been forgotten or recorded on tombstones; but from no effort of either of them did there spring a system or institution which lasted longer than they lived to support it.

They were, however, pioneers, and as such deserve remembrance.

CATECHISING IN CHURCHES.

The wholesome and ancient practice of catechising children publicly in churches has from time to time given rise to much misapprehension as to the antiquity of Sunday schools. In pre-Reformation times, and after, it was the custom to transact most of the business of life in or near the church. The church was "shot," like a coloured thread in silken stuff, through all the concerns of life. Feasts and fairs were held in unconsecrated portions of churchyards, and rents and tolls were received by the Abbots and Priors and Lords Ecclesiastical from all persons using Church lands for secular purposes. The church itself was the great meeting place in bitter trouble and in great joy; and for buying or selling, people met either in the church porch or just outside of it—a practice not yet altogether obsolete in rural counties.

In pre-Reformation days the Church and teaching were associated in the minds of the laity, and there were Catechisms so old that their age is said to be doubtful. In Reformation days the great value of catechising was recognised, recommended, and then insisted on under heavy penalties. As a general observance, the catechising of children so fell into disuse that when practised it seemed a new thing, and pious donors gave legacies for its perpetuation. The value which the Church placed upon the practice—which grew into a kind of domestic inquisition in Scotland, but which lost its hold in England —may be seen by reference to the Constitutions and Canons Ecclesiastical.*

By the 59th of the 101st "Constitutions and Canons Ecclesiastical," agreed upon with the King's Majesty's license in the Synod begun at London 1603, it was made binding on "ministers to catechise every Sunday": to wit, "Every parson, vicar, or curate, upon every Sunday and holyday, before evening prayer, shall, for half an hour or more, examine and instruct the youth and ignorant persons of his parish in the Ten Commandments, the Articles of the Belief, and in the Lord's Prayer; and shall diligently hear, instruct, and teach them the Catechism set forth in the Book of Common Prayer. And all fathers, mothers, masters, and mistresses shall cause their children, servants, and apprentices which have not learnt the Catechism, to come to the church at the time appointed, obediently to hear, and to be ordered by the minister, until they have learned the same.

"And if any minister neglect his duty herein let him be sharply reproved upon the first complaint, and true notice thereof given to the Bishop or ordinary of the place. If, after submitting himself, he shall willingly offend therein again, let him be suspended; if so the third time [he offend] . . . then excommunicated, and so remain until he will be reformed."

The Church could not pronounce itself more strongly; but its sympathy may not have gone with the pronounce-

* For the opinion of the late Bishop of London, see Chapter XVI.

ment, or "the times were out of joint," and there was no power to enforce its authority. The Canon was disobeyed and forgotten. Had it been acted on, the energies of Mr. Raikes might have been more profitably employed in other directions, and Sunday schools, as we now know them, probably would never have had an existence. Catechetical instruction is very ancient, and the *Encyclopædia Britannica* (ninth edition) says it "was doubtless common among the ancient Jews, and the modern Jews possess several Catechisms. The earliest with which we are acquainted are, the *Thirteen Articles of Belief*, by the famous Maimonides, which belongs to the twelfth century, and Rabbi Levi's *Book of Education*, which belongs to the thirteenth." The most important and authoritative of the Catechisms of the Roman Catholic Church is that of the Council of Trent, which was published in 1566, prepared under the superintendence of Cardinal Borromeo, Archbishop of Milan, who certainly did his best to enforce catechetical instruction. He enacted a Synodical decree obliging all curates to assemble the children of each parish for catechism on Sundays and other festivals. He organised a teaching staff of both sexes to teach the children on Sundays, and at his death (1584) he left 740 schools, 273 superintendent officers, 1,726 minor officers, and 40,098 scholars. The plan never spread beyond the Cardinal's personal influence, and, after his death, the schools declined.

Apart from this ancient and most salutary practice of catechising known to our own Church, there was the example of the Cardinal Archbishop of Milan for the imitation of those who should not have been ignorant of the duty so clearly set forth in the "Constitutions and Canons Ecclesiastical."

The clergy and Nonconformist divines who started what have, in their names, been called "Sunday schools" never claimed for themselves any new discovery. They viewed the matter in quite a different light to Raikes. They were Catechists, and so looked on themselves, and made no special note or parade about the matter. In this way they differed greatly from Mr. Raikes, who estimated himself as the originator of something. To use his own words: "*That was the period when Providence was pleased to make me the instrument of introducing Sunday schools.*"

The Rev. Joseph Alleine, one of the most sympathetic of souls, and by some reckoned as the last of the Puritan divines, catechised children in St. Mary Magdalen's Church, Taunton, about 1655, and afterwards at Bath.

The Rev. Theophilus Lindsey, of Catterick, Yorkshire, and his wife, in 1763 catechised and expounded the Scriptures to the children in the parish on Sundays. He also had adult classes in his study on alternate Sundays.

In 1769 Miss Hannah Ball used to hear children their Catechism, and hear them read the Scriptures, in her house and in the nave of the parish church at High Wycombe, Bucks.

It has been claimed for these and for many others that they were true and original founders of Sunday schools.

They were really Catechists, and when their efforts ceased things fell back into their original grooves.

What was understood by catechising is pretty well shown by the legacy of Mrs. Rebecca Powell, of Cirencester, who, dying in 1722, gave £10 a year to the minister for catechising the children and for expounding the Catechism, and £2 a year to provide the candles necessary for that service. The catechising was to extend from the Feast of St. Luke (October 18th) to the Feast of St. Matthias (February 24th). This bequest was meant by the pious donor to be for "the better propagation of Christian knowledge, and the *breeding up* of the children of the town in the principles and doctrines of the Established Church of England." This practice was common in Cirencester in the reign of Queen Anne.

In 1732, among the "Orders" agreed upon by the trustees of the charity schools at Stroud were the following: "All the children in the town [schools] shall be brought to church every Sunday before Divine service begins, and the children of each school out of town shall be brought to church every Sunday in the afternoon during the summer season, in order to have their proficiency entered into by some of the society after Divine service. All children shall be instructed in the Church Catechism, and learning the Morning and Evening Prayer and the Grace before and after meat; and every child in their turn shall repeat the Morning and Evening Prayer and the Grace to be used before they sit down and rise from table."

Some years ago inquiry was very active into the claims of "first founders," and a disposition was shown to accept an assemblage of children on a Sunday anywhere—provided only that they were taught something—as a "Sunday school." The catechising of children by Cardinal Borromeo was often quoted to show how absurd it was to look for "first founders" in England in the eighteenth century. But the parallels between the examples only run short distances.

Everyone who has attempted to make poverty less painful and bitter is deserving of honour, and it is for this reason that Mrs. Catharine Boevey, of Flaxley Abbey, Gloucester, is deserving of mention. She was a wealthy and charitable lady, and set up a charity school in her village. She liked to see the children beholden to her bounty and know they were well cared for, and so she had six of them each Sunday, turn and turn about, to dinner with her; and, after they were satisfied, she herself heard them say their Catechism. This fact is duly chronicled on her monument in Flaxley Abbey, erected after her death in 1726. Ballard notes the fact, and Bigland gives the inscription in full. Mr. Raikes might have read both, or gone to Flaxley Abbey for inspiration and returned again, without being one step nearer to the institution of a system possessing the power of universal adaptation to social needs.

CHAPTER XII.

THE PLACE OF MR. STOCK.

"A truly modest divine."—Gentleman's Magazine.

THE position which the Rev. Thomas Stock, so frequently mentioned in this volume, must take is one of three: to be placed *before* Mr. Raikes; to be bracketed *with* Mr. Raikes, or to fall in line with, but at the head of, all the good and kind-hearted men and women, in the Church and out of it, who pitied misery when they saw it and tried to enlighten ignorance.

The Rev. Thomas Stock.

To place him *before* Mr. Raikes with regard to the Sunday school movement is impossible. In 1780 the Rev. Thomas Stock, M.A., first Curate and then Rector of St. John the Baptist, Vicar of Glasbury, County Brecon, and sometime Headmaster of the Gloucester Cathedral School, was, comparatively speaking, a new man in the city. He had had a living at Ashbury, in Berkshire, where he started what is sometimes called a "charity" and sometimes a "Sunday" school, because he was in the habit of catechising children in the parish church. This was in 1776, and one condition for admission to the weekly reading school then started was a regular attendance at Divine service on Sundays.* He is said to have opened a similar weekly reading school in the parishes of Leigh and Hempstead, in Gloucester, and to have catechised children in the parish churches also,— which is highly probable, though must not be accepted implicitly in the absence of direct evidence. If he did act in this manner, the only strange element about it is that it was so unusual a thing for a clergyman to do, at that time, as to make it a matter worthy of comment.

He came to Gloucester, wherein he had relatives, in 1777-8, and the social conditions were very different to what they were at Ashbury. There is no record in the minutes of any of the local institutions of his taking any active part, or indeed any part at all, in the city, to stem the living stream of vice and misery which surged around him; but in 1863, the old people who once had known him spoke of him in the sincere language of respectful praise. They said he was "an humble man," and, notwithstanding his plurality of livings and headmastership,

* This is from a note made by the late William Griffiths, a well-known scholar at Gloucester, and a personal friend of Mr. Stock's. This striking of a bargain with children shows how entirely different they were to the children in Gloucester. If Raikes had bargained so, he could not have succeeded.

he was always spoken of as a "poor man"—certainly poor when compared with Mr. Raikes. He was not a Prison Chaplain, either paid or honorary, and there is no paragraph in existence stating it as a fact that he did visit the prisons. The experience of life which he brought to Gloucester was acquired in rural pastoral districts, where he cultivated a certain literary finish and style highly appreciated when he preached at the Cathedral.* Lysons states that when Mr. Stock preached in aid of the Musical Festival, in 1796, the collection amounted to £385 15s. 6d. So little is known of the rev. gentleman, that this fact even is valuable when we are endeavouring to learn something of him beyond his professional appointments.

It is said that he was connected by marriage with the Raikes family, which is not improbable, though the claim made (referred to at the end of this chapter) is very obscure. The Stock family was very respectable, and, socially, on a level with the Raikeses in the city. Certain it is that they were on good terms in 1780. Mr. Stock was then 30 years of age, and Mr. Raikes had for about twenty-five years been studying social questions, life in prisons and the streets, and slowly evolving plans for the permanent improvement of the masses.

The experiences of the two men were at this time

* " The Rev. Thomas Stock wrote and published a Greek Grammar. He also published some sermons which he preached in the Gloucester Cathedral. I have seen one on the Restoration of King Charles. It was written in bold, resonant and classical English." (H. Y. J. TAYLOR.) This sermon was published at the request of the Dean and Chapter, with illustrations by Dean Tucker, in 1782. (*Gentleman's Magazine*.)

widely different. Mr. Stock had run a creditable University career, and was for some time Fellow of Pembroke College, Oxford. His knowledge of life obtained in his country curacies would, in the course of things, not be large. By his side, Mr. Raikes was already a veteran. He had never been to the University, and probably had never spent more than a few days at any one time outside of the city. His had always been the practical side of life, and he had been under the guidance of a father with leanings towards social economy as a science, and philanthropy as a virtue.

In 1780 the sum of experience of the two men was unequal. Mr. Stock could say at that date that he had tried a reading school for children, and found good arise from catechising them. No more than this could be expected from a young man almost fresh from his University, already distinguished for his scholarship, his literary attainments, and, for three years, already the Headmaster of the Cathedral College School. Mr. Raikes's knowledge at that time was vastly more—he had learned to know crime and misery and want in the alleys and courts and gaols where they were generated and full-fledged. When these two came to compare notes, it was the elder who was in the position to teach.

For more than a century now an irritation, ill-suppressed at all times, and at times breeding much ill-feeling, has existed on the vexed question of the claims of Thomas Stock and Robert Raikes to precedence. This is all it amounts to. Fortunately the area of disturbance has never spread much; but within the area it may be fairly said that Raikes the Thinker has been largely lost sight of, and what is superficial in him has been compared most disadvantageously with Stock the Christian and Scholar.

The life's work of the man shows that he cannot be treated in this manner without doing violence to our sense of right, and breaking down a true standard of criticism. He had been training himself, unconsciously perhaps, all his life for the work in which he at last succeeded. According to all the statements, Mr. Raikes and Mr. Stock met by accident one day and determined to *do* something. Each engaged women to look after children on Sundays, and it is said they went together and engaged Mr., or Mrs., James King. This is the legend, and it may rest there.

Almost from the commencement, however, Mr. Raikes went beyond his co-worker; he paid two of the women two shillings per week extra to teach children out of work hours on *weekdays*. Moreover, he kept his own experiment apart and distinct from Mr. Stock's; and though it appears certain that they visited all the schools together at times, Mr. Stock confined his labours to his own, and was but little known until Mr. Raikes had obtained a monopoly of recognition and praise. The means for publication were his and his only. Mr. Stock might have used the Press outside of Gloucester to make known the new scheme and educate public opinion, but he remained passive. The only plan known or copied was Mr. Raikes's—and but for his intelligent industry, Sunday schools might never have existed as far as the public knew.

It results then that Mr. Stock cannot stand *before* Mr. Raikes; and it also results that he cannot be bracketed *with* him. It would have been a gracious thing to have bracketed them in the "honours" list, but that is impossible. However admirable Mr. Stock's schools may have been, however well conducted and free from the cursing, badger-fighting, laughter-loving ragged robins whom Raikes managed to get hold of and lick into shape, *his schools were never known*. He was not the man on whom the citizens turned the laugh and flung the nickname of "Bobby Wild Goose." Equally, too, when honours came—and they came soon—it was Raikes and not Stock who got them. The public did not bracket the men then, and it is too late to do so now.

The privilege of Mr. Stock in this connection is, that he was associated with Mr. Raikes. He certainly is one of the "two clergymen" whom Mr. Raikes mentions more than once with gratitude as working with him. The other is his own brother, Richard, whose name stood for a blessing in the city. The catechetical exercises of Mr. Stock, at Ashbury, do not count for much when considering the scope and interest of this particular movement after its publicity in November, 1783. It is always open to the observation that Sunday instruction was his *duty*, for the doing of which no special honour accrues to any man. In Raikes's case, what he did had *merit.* Here again a sharp line must be drawn between the two workers, and due account taken in making just criticism.

The children whom Mr. Stock had under his control were, it seems, more amenable to discipline than Mr. Raikes's "ragged regiment." He brought with him the authority and personal dignity of his sacred office, and greater experience in the handling of children *when in school* than Mr. Raikes. He was also more disciplined himself in his conduct towards them. His methods were not so violent. His patience and firmness were not so liable to be broken down by disorderly conduct. Neither Miss Priscilla Kirby *—a scholar and afterwards the sole mistress, who spoke the truth of him as though she were at "the table of the Lord's Feast"—nor anyone else gave an instance of sudden explosions of temper—birching the boys, taking them home to be punished, or blistering their fingers for lying. There were no stories told in 1863 of boys being dragged, or driven, to his schools with heavy weights and logs of wood attached to their legs to prevent their running away.

He was a disciplinarian, but of another and gentler kind. Miss Kirby says she learnt much from him; and the "rules" which he drew up for the conduct of his schools are said to have formed the foundation of those adopted later by the Sunday School committees. "Rules" in the Soot Alley School, and in Mrs. Critchley's early days in the Grey Fryars, would have been simply grotesque,

* Chapter II.—" Human Documents."

and have had but little meaning without the sweet but manly patience of the Rector of St. John's to illustrate and enforce them. Later, these distinctions between the two sets of scholars disappeared, but at first there were marked differences between the character of the scholars and the management and discipline of the schools.

When all is said that can be said, one is conscious of the feeling that it would have been a more natural process in the evolution of this most Christian idea, for the Sunday school system to have proceeded from a mind and temper chastened and modelled like Mr. Stock's than like Mr. Raikes's. In this case, however, the finer tool must give place—not for the first time in history—and Mr. Raikes must remain where mankind, by an instinctive sense of right, have placed him.

Mr. Stock was a much younger man than his friend, was without his special training, and without his business push and tact in making known the success of a plan for evolving the "new race" which had been the subject of painfully slow but persistent study. Had there been no Raikes the reputation of Mr. Stock must have been purely local. As it is, he will live in the hearts of men, and in the history of the Sunday school movement rank next to Robert Raikes.

NOTE.—Mr. Thomas Ensor, writing to the *Wesleyan Methodist Magazine* for August, 1870, said that the sister of Mr. Thomas Stock was the mother of the celebrated Robert Raikes. This could not be so, Robert Raikes's mother's maiden name being Mary Drew. But as a Miss Stock may have been some relation by marriage to Robert Raikes the elder, the Author wrote to Mr. Ensor, and was by him referred to Mr. J. Gould Avery, of London, from whom he had obtained his information. Mr. Avery at once replied: "I fear I cannot assist you much. My grandmother died at an advanced age, when I was a little boy, and I only learned what I know by conversation with my sister, who died two years ago, and by other family gossip. My grandmother's name was Stock, daughter, as I understand, of the Rev. Thomas Stock, of Gloucester. She always spoke of Mr. Robert Raikes as 'My Cousin Raikes,' and was evidently very familiar with him; but whether Mr. Raikes's mother or Mr. Stock's wife had changed her maiden name I cannot say. . . . Of course, all this is family gossip and nothing more. I have nothing in my possession worthy to be called historical or biographical in reference to the matter." The Rector of St. John's was fifteen years younger than Mr. Raikes, and although there may have been a family connection, it certainly was not so close as Mr. Avery here suggests.

The *Gloucester Journal*, January 2nd, 1804, contains the following obituary notice, the writing of which is attributed to Mr. Raikes: "On Tuesday last died, in the 54th year of his age, the Rev. Thomas Stock, A.M., Rector of St. John the Baptist, Perpetual Curate of St. Aldate, in this city, and Vicar of Glasbury, in the County of Brecon. Possessed with sincere and ardent piety, with fervent and active charity, devout and impressive in the services of his ministry, eloquent and animated in the preaching of those awful truths of which diligent investigation had convinced his correct and learned mind—attentive, affecting and solving, in his visitation of those who were sinking under the weight of sickness or the terror of death—scrupulously just in all his dealings—inoffensive, kind and cheerful in domestick and social life, he will long live esteemed and lamented in the memories of his parishioners, his acquaintances, family and his friends."

The *Gentleman's Magazine* supplied the omission about Sunday schools by calling him "the first suggester of Sunday schools."

The rev. gentleman sometimes preached anniversary sermons. Here are two records:—"September 25th, 1796. The Rev. Thomas Stock, Rector of St. John's, Gloucester, preached the anniversary sermons for the benefit of the Sunday School at Painswick." Again: "September 23rd, 1798. The Rev. Thomas Stock again preached for the Painswick Sunday School." The memory of the rev. gentleman is perpetuated in St. John the Baptist Church and in the Cathedral, Gloucester. His remains, however, lie in St. Aldate's Church, but the memorial tablet originally placed there has unaccountably disappeared!

CHAPTER XIII.

SUNDAY SCHOOLS IN GREAT BRITAIN.

" The nurseries of the Church."—Dr. GUTHRIE.

WALES.

THE name of "Charles of Bala" casts a spell over the Welsh soul as enthralling as, though differing from, the inspiring notes of the "March of the Men of Harlech." It is a march of another sort—a march of the soul in subdued tones.

With reference to the Sunday school movement, "Charles of Bala" to Wales is the "Raikes of Gloucester' to England. Working on independent lines, he arrived at very similar results. The following letter is from the pen of his grandson, the Rev. David Charles, formerly the Principal of Trevecca College, dated December 24th, 1863, and written after a long and interesting interview with the Author:

"In reference to the Welsh Sunday schools and the part my revered and honoured grandfather had in their formation, &c., I would beg to submit the following observations:

"It was the Rev. Griffith Jones, of Llanddowron, in

the county of Carmarthen, who gave the first impulse to the work of educating the people by means of catechising his parishioners every Sunday at the public service in the parish church. This was about the beginning of the last century.

"Before this time there were no schools in Wales, and the mass of the population were lying in the grossest darkness.

"The success that attended his public catechisings led him to the establishment of Circulating Charity Day Schools, which proved very beneficial in the several localities to which they were removed from time to time, and which were the first glimmerings of the dawn of day.

"It was in the neighbourhood of Llanddowron that my grandfather was born, and in Llanddowron it was that he received his school instruction, as well as some of his first religious impressions. There lived at Llanddowron at that time an old man of the name of Rhys Hugh, who had lived with Mr. Griffith Jones, and who was the means of infusing Mr. Jones's spirit into Mr. Charles while he was yet a boy; and it appears that this spark of inspiration, first excited by old Rhys Hugh in the mind of his youthful friend, was never extinguished, but broke out into a conflagration which was to embrace Wales and the world.

"Mr. Charles in after years, when he went to reside at Bala, in North Wales, established similar circulating charity schools to those of Mr. Griffith Jones; and it was in the working out of these charity schools that Mr. Charles first saw the grand principle of the Welsh Sabbath schools.

"The day schools, which survived for about twenty years, were especial means towards preparing teachers for the work of the Sabbath school. For this purpose Mr. Charles himself undertook the instruction of those whom he intended to become Sabbath school teachers, and he composed two catechisms in the Welsh language for the benefit both of the teachers and scholars of the Sunday schools.

"These schools Mr. Charles first set up about the year 1785—about three years, I believe, after Mr. Raikes. Still, we believe we are authorised to say that the *principle* of the Welsh Sabbath school was practically wrought out by Mr. Charles; *and to attribute to him the independent thought of establishing these schools* does not involve the idea that Sabbath schools had not previously existed in other places, but on another and a more inefficient principle.

"A reference to a prior institution as evidence that we are not to attribute the originating of the Welsh Sabbath schools to Mr. Charles alone, proves that they who do so do not fully comprehend the nature of the schools which Mr. Charles established.

"The distinguishing principle of the Welsh Sunday schools which Mr. Charles incorporated in his institution for the religious instruction of his countrymen was, that the object of the Sabbath school was the instruction not only of children but of adults also, and that it was intended not merely to teach spelling and reading, but to bring all classes together to examine the Word of God and to exchange thoughts upon its all-important truths.

"The Welsh Sunday school thus became an institution in which the great doctrines of the Christian religion were learnt, and understood, and practically enforced by men who had themselves experienced their power.

"The Church of Christ was taught that it was the duty of every one of its members to care for and instruct the world in the saving precepts of the Gospel; and the Sunday school was put forth as the arena in which the zeal, the love, the knowledge, and the spiritual power of the Church were to be brought to bear upon the masses of their fellow-men. *Thus our Sunday schools were intended to become real missionary institutions for the Church to exert its influence upon all classes of the people.*

"This is the distinguishing feature of our Welsh Sunday schools, which is a great advancement upon the ground taken by those which had been previously established in England, and this, we say, was the distinct and original idea of the Rev. Mr. Charles.

"He was probably the first also who established regular public meetings in connection with the Sabbath schools—meetings to which the public at large assembled to witness and listen to the regular catechising of several schools which had come together from different localities. On those occasions large multitudes flocked together, and very powerful impressions were generally left on the minds of the audience, as well as upon the Sunday scholars and teachers, and, through them, upon their families.

"These meetings afforded opportunities to the people in general to see what kind of instruction was given to their children, and also what the efforts were on the part of the teachers to instruct them in the great truths of religion. *Thus the prejudices of the people against religion were gradually worn down;* their attention was drawn to the Sunday school, and at length they were attracted to place themselves under its fostering care.

"In this way the Sunday school wore more the aspect of a church in active operation than a school—prayer and praise being blended with earnest exhortations to all. Instruction was given in every branch of scriptural knowledge, and, at the same time, the teacher exhibited not so much the character of a master as that of a friend and a Christian, who was willing to lecture for the good of others.

"The Welsh Sunday schools, are then, to this day well-springs of religious instruction to men of every age, and contain generally more adult members, both male and female, than children. They are specially the nurseries of our Churches, both as regards members and ministers.

"Trusting the above brief sketch may meet your object, and with Christian regards,

"I am, dear Sir,
"Yours very faithfully,
"DAVID CHARLES."

It will be seen that one great advantage which the Sunday school system in Wales had over the kindred system in England was an organisation subject man control. In England there was no "patent," so to speak, for civilising the children of the masses, but it was left to individuals to frame what rules they liked, teach what they pleased, when they pleased, and where they pleased. People anxious for the survival of strongly-marked social distinctions in rural districts often looked askance at these Sunday meetings, and regarded them as secret societies for the propagation of Jacobite principles. In some districts, however, these schools won confidence by the openness with which they were conducted.

Mrs. Hannah More (who possibly may have heard of the Welsh system) introduced into her schools at Cheddar the teaching of adults with children.

A delightful little sketch of a day with the ladies (who took their dinners with them) who taught in the schools appears in the *Gentleman's Magazine*, vol. lxviii The following extract shows that Mr. Charles, of Bala, was not alone in thinking that the communion of adults with children was of advantage:

"After our return to the school in the evening, such farm servants and others as were prevented from attending before by the necessary avocations of the day—milking cows, &c.—were not ashamed to make their appearance at the school *and give answers along with the children;* nor could I learn that the knowledge thus acquired made them in the least above their duty in that state of life in which it had pleased God to call them. The children being then dismissed, were succeeded by two hundred grown persons, who in a very devout manner, sang a hymn, which was followed by prayer and a printed sermon read by one of the ladies. That being over, we finished with prayer and another hymn, and whilst the congregation were singing—

'Lord, dismiss us with Thy blessing,'

we entered our carriage and proceeded home, well pleased with the occupation of the day."

That this was not an isolated method is shown by the foot-note, which says that the same practice was going on in various other villages, where the master or mistress reads over the sermon when the ladies cannot attend. The "ladies," we learn, were then living at Cowslip Green, five miles from Cheddar, hence the necessity for them to take their dinners with them. Mrs. Hannah More was at this time engaged in writing "spirited rhymes and prose tales in the *Cheap Repository* series, to counteract the doctrines of Tom Paine and the influence of the French Revolution." That her sketches were in one sense "living" we know, and we know now, in part, where and how she studied her "living documents." Two millions of these sketches were circulated in one year—in those days an unprecedented number.

Still, the admission of adults with children and teaching them together, as a system, was not generally followed in England. For Mr. Charles's idea of mixed classes we must probably go back to the earliest Jewish schools in Palestine, which were open to all classes and all ages, the presence and sayings of young children being always welcome and highly prized.* We must not, however, go to the Old Testament, or even to later Jewish practices, for the model of our Sunday schools. The late Dr. N. Adler (Chief Rabbi in London) says :† " I may state that Sabbath schools for children [Jewish] are of comparatively recent origin. The Sabbath assemblies in ancient times were devoted more to the instruction of the adult than to that of the young."

SCOTLAND.

In Scotland, as in England, there are now known to have been many instances of Sunday teaching of children early in the eighteenth century. If, however, the education and care of children by ministers and parents had been as intelligently active in England and Wales as in Scotland, there is no good reason for supposing that Robert Raikes, or Charles of Bala, would have founded and organised systems which became national. When Sunday schools after the English pattern were introduced into Scotland, there was already in existence the habit and practice of family teaching, and the very salutary practice of Scotch ministers closely to examine the

* "The Kingdom of God is in the souls of children," was thought to be the true meaning of the Psalmist's words, "Out of the mouths of babes and sucklings;" and Jesus gave currency to familiar language when saying, "Out of the mouths of babes and sucklings Thou hast perfected praise."

† Letter to the Author, October 6th [1863].

members of their congregations in spiritual matters. What would now be considered impertinent and inquisitorial was then the custom; and the minister would be wanting in his duty, and be subjected to severe penalties, if he did not make periodical searching examinations into the hearts and consciences of his flock. For example, a young man's marriage might be delayed until the minister was satisfied that he was a fit and proper person to become the head of a family. The introduction of Sunday schools from over the Border met with much opposition by both ministers and laity. The holding of Sabbath evening schools made some headway, and a society was formed in Edinburgh in March, 1797, called "The Sabbath Evening School Society," having for its object the establishing of others in Scotland.

"At Aberdeen," says the *Gentleman's Magazine*, vol. lxxiii., "no children under eight years old, or who cannot read,* are admitted. They meet at six o'clock on Sunday evening, repeat the texts, and give an account of the sermons they have heard. After prayer a portion of Scripture is repeated, and the teachers endeavour to draw forth the ideas of the children on it, and they are examined on eight or ten questions from the Assembly's Catechism. After a short and affectionate address, singing a few verses, mentioning the texts to be learnt against the next meeting, and a short prayer, they are

* This alone shows the great difference between the state of things in Aberdeen and Gloucester. It was *because* the children could *not* read that Raikes collected them.

dismissed. . . . An extraordinary reformation has been wrought among the youth of Dundee."

It is only necessary to compare this state of civilisation in Aberdeen with that of Gloucester, when " Winkin' Jim" brought his live badger into school and let it loose, and cursing and swearing during Divine service in church had to be somehow provided against and checked.

Dr. Chalmers's claims to making Sunday schools popular in Scotland are fully recognised, and the number of scholars is now 713,360, and the teachers 63,939. These teachers (men and women) are considered to be the flower of the Churches. With such teachers, the seedlings must flourish.

IRELAND.

The Rev. Dr. Urwick, Dublin, contributes the following account of the history of Sunday schools in the Sister Island:

" So far as I have been able to ascertain, the earliest gleam of 'Sunday school' work in Ireland appeared in the parish of Bright, in the county of Down. It matured into a professed and fully-arranged Sunday school in 1786, but it had been less formally in operation perhaps ten years before. Two Sunday schools were opened in Dublin, led on apparently by the movement in England in the same year; namely, 1786."

The history of this germ of Sunday school work is given by the rev. doctor in the interesting paper which he read at the General Sunday School Convention, held in London in September, 1862. He said:

"About the year 1770, the Rev. Dr. Kennedy, curate of Bright parish, in the county of Down, was painfully struck with the total disregard of the Lord's Day among the young people and children in some villages through which he had to pass in going to and from his duty at the church. His congregation was very small. A gentleman of the name of Henry, with his family, joined it, and with him Dr. Kennedy consulted by what means it could be improved.

"Having engaged a well-conducted and competent man in the capacity of parish clerk, *they got boys and girls together to practise psalmody.* This made a little stir. In 1774 to singing was added exercise in reading the Psalms and lessons for the day, which, being rumoured abroad, excited further attention. Ere two more years had elapsed, the numbers had considerably increased. Those who came were desired to bring what Bibles and Testaments they could, in order to their being better instructed and examined in what they read. Then the children of other denominations were invited to share the advantages of the meeting. And thus by the year 1778 *the gathering, which had begun as a singing class* a few years previously, had *matured into a school held regularly every Sunday* for an hour and a half before the morning service.

"The good work went on and prospered until the latter part of the year 1785, when Dr. Kennedy heard of the proceedings in England for the establishment of

Sunday schools. His own was in reality a Sunday school already. But he and the gentleman he advised with agreed that its plan should be made more comprehensive and systematic, according to the English method. . . . The Bright Sunday School was opened on the first Sunday in May, 1786, with Robert Henry, Esq., as its superintendent; members of his family, and other respectable individuals, as teachers; and honest Thomas Turr, the parish clerk, ready to help in it as he might be able or occasion require."

THE CHANNEL ISLANDS.

Mr. Joshua le Bailly, St. Heliers, was instrumental in obtaining some particulars respecting the early history of Sunday schools in Jersey, and of the somewhat remarkable woman who organised them in 1804. Mrs. Susan Perrot was a young lady mixing in the best island society, and the miniature taken of her when about twenty years of age shows that when young she was possessed of great personal attractions.

Mrs. Susan Perrot.

Energetic by nature, she commenced field preaching in the island, and was very soon made the object of much persecution. She had two grandsons, both of whom she induced to join the ministry, and whilst her eldest grandson was studying at Gosport she commenced a Sunday school. A letter which she wrote to her grandson (F. Perrot) has fortunately been preserved, and establishes the fact. Translated, the material paragraph reads:

"I have commenced the Sunday school, and have now from forty to fifty scholars from six to twelve years of age. I have ordered more catechisms to be printed, having given the school all I had. I hope they may be the means of doing much good, and that the blessing of God may be upon the work."

The "Parish Sunday School" in St. Peter's le Port, Guernsey, was established about the same time, as appears from a very clear statement made to Mr. Peter Machon by his aged aunt, and transmitted October 8th, 1862, to the Author:

"I believe," she said, "that the Parish Sunday School, as it was called, was established by the Messrs. Le Cocq and Dobree, at least sixty years ago [1802]. The girls' school was kept by a Mrs. Nichols at her own house, and the boys' by my father (my own grandfather assisted by my own father) at his own house.

"About fifty-six or fifty-seven years ago Mrs. Nichols resigned, and I then took charge of the girls, the school being removed to my father's—he occupying the top room of the house and myself the room underneath. The hours in the morning were from nine to twelve; the children met again in the afternoon at one, and were taken to church by my father and myself and dismissed at the conclusion of the sermon.

"In the school the children read in the Testament and learned the Catechism. I cannot exactly say when the school was discontinued; but I was married in 1808, and gave up my charge and was paid my salary of £6 per annum. There were about one hundred and thirty boys and eighty girls in the schools. From what influence the school was established I cannot say."*

The Church Sunday school was established in 1820. The following minute is preserved: "17th April, 1820. At a highly respectable meeting of the friends of the Sunday school, the Very Rev. the Dean in the chair, it was resolved that a French Sunday school should be established for the parish of St. Peter's Port (town), the committee being empowered, if expedient, to appoint English teachers."

The Channel Islands are ecclesiastically in the diocese of Winchester, and it is to the lasting credit of the Sunday school connected with the parish church, that Bishop Wilberforce left it on record that it was "the best in his diocese." Victor Hugo, soon after he came to reside at Hauteville House, visited the schools, and afterwards established what he called "the festival of poor little children," forty of whom, without distinction of race or creed, he was in the habit of having to dinner with him once a week. On one occasion he said: "I know of

* The question asked was, whether this school was the offspring of the Gloucester movement.

nothing more sad than to see little children suffering: the livery of rags touches my heart."

If they had nothing else in common, the "livery of rags," the appearance of want, and the degradation of children's souls, when they should exude the perfume of heaven, would form a bond of union between men so dissimilar as Victor Hugo and Robert Raikes.

CHAPTER XIV.

MR. RAIKES AT HOME.

"Let me see the man at his own fireside."—JOHNSON.

"I always want to know as much how a great person thought and spoke as what he did."—Countess POMFRET.

MR. RAIKES was a domestic man—the home instinct was strong within him. When he spoke of his family it was with an affectionate caress. "I have now six excellent daughters and two lovely sons," said he, when writing of them in the plenitude of his own days. And he loved them equally, and put them all upon the same level when he made his will—the two sons to share and share alike, and the six girls to share and share alike. "My dear wife, Anne Raikes" was appointed sole executrix, with life interest in all his real and personal estate, should she survive him—which she did; but should she predecease him, then his two sons were to be joint executors; all of which shows the love and confidence in his heart, and the atmosphere of affection in his home. A very dry document like a will may be made to speak and breathe sentiment and affection, when family love exists.*

---

* Mr. Raikes's will is a short document and was made only two years before his death. He possessed no real estate. By a codicil added twelve months afterwards [1810], he gave to his wife for life "all my benefit and advantage from the Stock of the Stationers' Company." After her decease

The house in which he resided in Bell Lane was shut out from the noise of the streets. The streets of the city were not paved and drained as they are now, but were full of filth and garbage, and the "kennel" was always running, to the great annoyance of gentlemen of the dandy sort wearing white stockings and knee-breeches. Mr. Raikes has been described as "buckish," and we learn that he disliked dirt. A vain man in his dress is generally a clean man in his habits—Raikes was certainly clean, for he had a crossing made between his house in Bell Lane and his place of business. On dark nights he carried a lantern to light him between the two houses, so that the prosperous, well-dressed, citizen left as little as possible to chance and dirt.

His household appointments were those of a gentleman of the period. He kept a good table and a manservant. His two lovely sons and six excellent daughters were not expected to grow manly and bloom beautifully without, at least, some paternal encouragement. When distinguished strangers came to the city it was their habit to visit my Lord Bishop at the Palace, the Mayor, and Mr. Raikes, so that the two sons and six daughters saw a good deal of "the best company."

People who reside in a house are, when judges of character, the best witnesses of the dispositions of the

it was to form part of "my general personal estate, and be applied accordingly." At one time the testator possessed some small parcels of freehold land in the county, but these were probably sold and the money reinvested in the Stationers' Company's Stock, hence the codicil. The will explains why, after the death of Mrs. Raikes, the whole of his estate was sold. The will, with codicil, was proved in London, 28th June, 1811.

master and mistress. Even when their own judgment is not to be relied on, they can often state facts of much service to interested strangers. We possess, fortunately, the statements of servants, which enable us to judge with some accuracy of Mr. Raikes at home.

JAMES WHITEHEAD, the office boy, already quoted on another point, said: "I was about the house a good deal. Mr. Raikes was a good, liberal master and kept his servants a good while. He paid good wages, and no family in Gloucester had more company than the Raikeses. I used sometimes to help the footman clean the plate in the butler's pantry. There was no regular butler, but extra servants were employed on occasion. Mrs. Raikes was never happy unless her house was full of company. She was very 'pettish' but very good, and had her own way; but she kept the maids a long time, and she was very charitable. We all knew she was a lady—an admiral's sister.*

"I knew most about Mr. Raikes. Mrs. Raikes took no part in the Sunday schools, but I never heard her object to the poor children coming on to the lawn, when they lived in Bell Lane, and into Mr. Raikes's room; and she would send pieces of cake in for them.

"I believe he liked to have children about him, and he'd get them to sing on the lawn. I never saw John Wesley or Charles Wesley at the house during the

* *See* Chapter XVII., "The Raikes Family."

Musical Festivals. If they stayed there, it would be before my time.

"He had a nice way about him with children. I was in the office one day, before the fire, making paste. Mr. Raikes came in and said to me: 'James, are you a good boy?' I said, 'Yes, sir.' He then put half a guinea in my hand, and said that that was for a Christmas box for being a good boy."

WILLIAM WHITEHEAD (who has also been quoted) said: "All I know of Mr. Raikes is, that he was a kind-hearted sort of man, and that he was very strict in all his business matters and in all that he did. When I was with him I was fond of reading, and he said to me: 'Any books you want you shall have, but don't take any without asking me.'

"Mr. Raikes was a constant attendant at morning prayers [at the Cathedral]. I was one of his Sunday scholars, and he took me into his office.*

"Mr. Raikes was a nice good-looking man. I do believe he was a pious man. He kept a footman and a capital establishment. It was one of the first establishments in the city. After the battle of Trafalgar, it was "open" house for several days. I suppose seventy or eighty persons were entertained every day. I mean ladies and gentlemen and persons of respectability—their acquaintances and connections. Captain Thompson, of

---

* In his letter to Mrs. Harris, of Chelsea, 1787, Mr. Raikes says he has taken one of the Littleworth boys into his employ. *See* Appendix A.

the *Leander*, married one of the daughters. He did a fine and gallant thing, and broke the line of the enemy.

"When Mr. Raikes died, the general feeling was that Gloucester had lost a good man."

Mr. Simpson, who was engaged at the Normal College, Cheltenham, in 1863, said: "I often saw Mr. Raikes with Mr. Wood, the banker—old Jimmy Wood, the miser, you know. I used to see them going to early morning service at the Cathedral. Mr. Wood had a short, quick step and was very active. His shop was in the main street; he had a sort of haberdashery shop and bank—one counter for each. On one side he'd sell you a farthing's worth of pins, and on the other shovel out gold to any amount.

"I went to Mr. Stock's and not to Mr. Raikes's school. I have had many a penny from Mr. Raikes, but nothing from Mr. Wood—he never *gave* away anything, not he! I never heard anyone speak badly of Mr. Raikes —only say he was 'a crank.'"

In 1862 there was residing with Mr. John Crowse (a retired miller), Redmarley, an old man named William Redding, who was in Mr. Raikes's employ as indoor servant from the year 1807. This was after the transfer of the *Journal* and printing business, and when he was residing altogether in Bell Lane. Mr. Redding, on being applied to, expressed himself willing to answer any questions in his power, and a schedule was sent to him, to which he replied in the following terms :

Q. " What were Mr. Raikes's habits in his house ? Did he rise early; have family prayers morning and evening ? And did his servants attend those prayers in his house ? "

A. " Regular in his habits — not an early riser, or late. Never had family prayers except Sundays, and then his servants always attended them."

Q. " Did his servants go to church, and how often ? "

A. " His servants attended church every Sunday."

Q. " Did he often speak to his servants respecting their souls' welfare ? "

A. " He never held any conversation on religious subjects with any of his servants."

Q. " Did he ever speak to them respecting Sunday schools, and what was the nature of what he said ? "

A. " I never remember hearing him speak to anyone respecting his schools."

Q. " Did he ever speak of any other gentleman or lady in connection with these schools — if so, what were their names ? "

A. " I never recollect hearing him mention any other person's name."

Q. " Did he keep much company, and was it religious or otherwise ? "

A. " He did not keep much company in my time."

Q. " Was his house ruled in the spirit of Christianity ? "

A. "He always kept a very quiet house."

Q. "Was he in the habit of drinking alcoholic liquors? Did he drink them to excess, or only in moderation?"

A. "I never remember him drinking any spirits, only his wine after dinner. *Never* to excess."

Q. "How did he spend his time on Sundays?"

A. "He generally spent his time at home—excepting going to church."

Q. "Was he a very sociable man, or gloomy and reserved?"

A. "He was a very sociable and pleasant-spoken man."

Q. "What sort of health did he enjoy?"

A. "Generally very good."

Q. "What sort of husband and father was he—kind or otherwise?"

A. "A very kind husband and father."

Q. "How many servants did he keep?"

A. "Three maid-servants and myself."

Q. "Was he a benevolent man?"

A. "He was."

Q. "What kind of mistress had you?"

A. "A very good, pious woman."

Q. "Did his family live affectionately together?"

A. "Very much so."

Q. "Did you ever hear that Mr. Raikes was accused of Sabbath-breaking?"

A. "I never heard anything of the sort."

We have seen that Mr. Raikes spoke of his own children as though satisfied with them — as fathers should be—and how he trusted his "dear wife Anne" when he made his will; and now we are able to quote one passage in a private letter, showing how tender and distressed he was when she was ill. He had deferred sending in an account for book work, and says:

"I have been greatly distressed by the indisposition of my wife, whom I have been obliged to attend into the country for the benefit of her health. This misfortune, I dare say, will be admitted by your benevolent and sympathetic heart as an apology for the apparent neglect." *

All this gives one the notion of domesticity and comfort; a pleasant house at which to visit, and dine, and drink claret, and be agreeable to the six excellent daughters, whom Miss Burney found passable enough, being only country bred. That the home was in truth what it seemed is evidenced by the fact that all the girls married well, and that their marriages appeared in *Dodsley's Annual* and the *Gentleman's Magazine* and all the fashionable Gazettes of the time.

The eldest daughter (Anne) married Admiral Sir Thomas Boulden Thompson, Bart., when he was Captain Sir Thomas, Knight, but marked out for promotion for his gallant conduct when Commander of the *Leander*. He lost one arm, like Nelson, whom he sailed under, and was praised in Nelson's despatches. It was in his

* Raikes to Lewelyn, July 12th, 1790.

honour that Mr. Raikes kept "open" house after the victory at Trafalgar, and the young officer did not belie his early promise.*

The second (Mary) married Henry Garrett, Esq., R.N., afterwards Admiral Garrett.

The third (Albinia) married John Birch, Esq., of Charlotte Street, Bloomsbury Square, Lieut.-Colonel of the Royal Westminster Volunteers.

The fourth (Eleanor) married Daniel Garrett, Esq., of Gower Street, Bedford Square.

The fifth (Charlotte) married William Stanley Clarke, Esq., Commander of the *True Briton*, East Indiaman; and the sixth and youngest (Caroline) was married to Captain Weller, 23rd Regiment of Light Dragoons, afterwards General Weller-Ladbroke.

There was a beautiful regularity about the marriages of these young ladies—they went off year by year with the regularity of clockwork. The marriages commenced in 1796 and ended, when there were no more daughters to marry, in 1803. And this, if nothing else, can be fairly said about the fact: the home of Robert Raikes was the home which young English gentlemen of position were pleased to enter, and to marry from.

Whatever his fads or fancies about neglected criminals in fever-stricken prisons, or the education of ragged outcasts in schools, or slumming in the sweeps' quarter, he did not bring a gloomy ascetic air into his home, or avenge upon his family the snubs and slights which he

* *See* Appendix F.

got from his fellow-citizens, of whom he complained for letting him walk too much alone. He was not an extreme man, but a man of gay and joyous temperament, and too simple minded to hide satisfaction when he felt it. Miss Burney made a note of this transparency of character. The shrewd little Diarist promised to name the institution of Sunday schools to Queen Charlotte; and then Mr. Raikes was so overjoyed that "the joy with which he heard this was nothing short of rapture!"

Mr. Raikes, being a social man, was a member of the Gloucestershire Society. At the annual meeting, held in London in 1803, Robert Raikes and Dr. Jenner were elected Vice-Presidents, the Duke of Norfolk being President, of the Society. Raikes and Jenner were then world-wide celebrities. At the annual dinner the old Gloucestershire song of "George Ridler's Oven" was sung in the vernacular. The Society, founded in 1657, was originally political and intended to hasten the restoration of the Stuart dynasty. "George Ridler's Oven" was a political song; but so unintelligible had it become in 1803, that the Society in its annual report printed a version of it with elucidatory notes. When Raikes and Jenner were Vice-Presidents the Society was charitable, and, amongst other things, found the necessary premiums for the apprenticeship of Gloucestershire youths.

In religion Mr. Raikes was an Evangelical and had strong leanings towards mysticism. In the course of his correspondence with the Rev. Mr. Lewelyn, of

Leominster, his religious views are given with singular candour. Mr. Lewelyn was strongly touched with pious mysticism, and Mr. Raikes considered him to be the possessor of an "illuminated soul." Amongst other books, Mr. Lewelyn wrote ΜΟΡΦΗ ΘΕΟΥ; or, *The Form of God;* an *Exposition of the Revelation;* and *Christianity; or, Science of Christ.* Mr. Raikes printed these books, and opened his mind freely when forwarding "proofs." The following passages give an insight into the workings of his mind in secret, and enable us to understand, as nothing else could, the precise meaning of the words used by his youngest daughter concerning him: "His favourite study was always on serious subjects. With great truth, I may add, he was a very holy man."*

May 16th, 1790.—" I rejoice that I have some kindred spirits who are anxious to promote the glory of Him who is invisible, and who wish to enlarge the Kingdom of His Son."

December 9th, 1791.—" I wish to ask you what you understand by the Seven Spirits, like the Seven Lamps, burning before the Throne. Do they mean any particular attributes of the Deity?"

February 27th, 1792.—" You could not have gratified me more highly than in the freedom with which you say you write to me on the subject of the love of God. Were all men by such communications to provoke each other

* *See* Chapter XV., " Mrs. Ladbroke's Letters."

to good works, manifesting their love to the Giver of all Good by imitating His beneficence in their conduct to their fellow-creatures, what a happy world should we live in—how well adapted to prepare us for that city whose Builder is God!"

March 12th, 1792.—"I wish my spiritual part was subtilised and refined like yours. Heaven grant we may one day meet and pass a happy eternity together in that blessed society, where the praise of God is the only enjoyment."

March 24th, 1792.—"When you can write, indulge me with a few of those heavenly ideas that are preparing your faithful spirit for its glorified state: that state in which you will be admitted to see even as you are seen. Oh, that I may be preserved, like you, faithful unto the coming of the Lord Jesus, and that we may meet in the realms of everlasting bliss, there to celebrate the praises of Him who sitteth on the throne, and the Lamb that was slain!"

June 2nd, 1792.—" I have lately discovered new improvement and delight in a kind of examination after I have read the Gospel. The heart enquires of the head what he [sic] understands by such doctrine, what application he [sic] proposes to make in the future government of the thoughts, the words and manners. How earnestly ought prayer to be made for power to imitate the Heavenly Pattern."

July 3*rd*, 1792.—" Perhaps we may not meet on this side the grave, but I pray that we may pass eternity together, and join in the delights of adoration, thanksgiving and praise to Him that sitteth upon the Throne, and of the Lamb and Holy Spirit, for ever and ever."

January 15*th*, 1793.—"It is the failure of the knowledge of your most excellent principle, *humility*, that keeps mankind tied and bound to the chains of everlasting darkness. It is looking up to Jesus, the Author and Finisher of our Faith, through the medium of *humility*, and a due sense of our own vileness and unworthiness, that appears to me the only means of following Him whither He has gone before. It is in this sentiment that we so cordially agree. This agreement binds us together in unity of spirit and the bonds of peace. Upon this rock let us build a temple to Friendship, which time shall not destroy."

November 8*th*, 1793.—"Our relish for David's Psalms is exactly similar. I am never in so proper a frame of mind as when I am reading or repeating passages from that heavenly composition. They are my chief comfort and consolation when any distress approaches; they furnish the language of thanksgiving when the heart rejoices."

December 31*st*, 1794.—"Your writings have strengthened and refreshed my drooping heart. I see my own unworthiness more clearly, and with this plea I go more boldly to the Throne of Mercy, keeping in my eye the leper, the publican in the Temple, the lame, the blind—all who came to Jesus brought by conviction of their own misery, having faith and confidence in His power to restore. Without this hope of relief, the pressure of my sins would be a burden too heavy for me to bear.

"However, *this is language which I speak only to you and to my own heart.* The world would laugh. They conceive that notorious crimes are all that we have to guard against. But you and I have not so learned Christ!"

These extracts form of themselves a complete answer to the suggestions, thrown out in the earlier portions of this book, that Mr. Raikes acted as he did simply because his sympathetic and emotional nature was uppermost in the presence of physical suffering. Mr. Paul Hawkins Fisher, man of the world and scholar, and Mr. John Powell, Q.C., and M.P. for the City of Gloucester, accustomed to trace human motive to its secret springs, both came to wrong conclusions. They had not before them a correspondence which lays bare the inner workings and questionings of a soul certain of what its ultimate destiny should be, and anxious not to miss it.

The world has been in entire ignorance of the religious, as apart from the merely benevolent, side of Mr. Raikes. He has been misunderstood greatly, even by those who wished to regard him with affection, because they have credited him with "benevolent" instincts which stood apart altogether from religious consciousness. Robert Raikes in this way became a character in whom a large benevolence was founded on a much larger personal vanity. What he really was his own pen reveals; and his own testimony of himself may be taken as true, as there is not the faintest reason for supposing that he ever dreamed his private confidences would be preserved.

In politics* Mr. Raikes was a Church and Constitution man, and studied the Apocalypse and some of the prophetic books with special reference to the politics of France. At times he feared greatly that England, on account of her wickedness, had been abandoned by God, and he took every occasion to express his hatred of Tom Paine. When Paine was tried, in December, 1792, and found guilty of treason and sentenced as an outlaw, Mr. Raikes joyously attended his mock execution. "In the evening," he wrote, "the figure of Tom Paine was hung upon a gibbet, and ceremoniously burnt by the populace in a meadow adjoining this city." Had he lived now, he would have been an Imperialist, for in his lifetime he believed it was the duty of an Englishman to put England before the world, and light bonfires and keep open house and rejoice when her sons won victories. He was attached to the persons of his Sovereign and his Queen, and did not obtrude himself upon their privacy when they visited Gloucester, or when he took his family over to Cheltenham to see and admire them with the rest

* *See* Note at end of chapter.

of the crowd from a distance. The year before [1787] he had had an interview with the good Queen Charlotte at Windsor, and might have presumed a little, but he was content to be on bowing terms with the bright-eyed second keeper of the Queen's robes, and Miss La Planta, maid of honour. A comfortable man in the family circle was this prosperous citizen of good lineage, and, as he styled himself, " botanizer in human nature."

Still, he was not always left in peace. Believing, with his old friend John Wesley, that Satan was quite capable of setting up an opposition Sunday school, he found that Beelzebub was mean enough to persecute him in the person of a " pettyfogging lawyer," and draw £50 out of his pocket. Here is the story as he told it to Mr. Lewelyn on the 27th August, 1792:

"Since I wrote to you last I have been the subject of a most infamous prosecution, which has been instituted against me by one of those miscreants of the law who are seizing every occasion to oppress and worry those who are endeavouring to do good.*

"It happened whilst I was last year in London that an advertisement of a Bank bill that was lost was sent to be inserted in my paper, in which the advertiser offered five guineas reward and *no questions asked*.

"This last expression, it seems, by an old Act of Parliament, subjects the person who publishes such an

---

* Mr. Raikes forgot that "good" is quite a relative term, and that what is "good" is capable of much argument. Probably he had interfered with the Attorney's business, which was bad for the Attorney.

advertisement to a penalty of £50.* My compositor was ignorant of this law, and inserted the advertisement as it was sent. And now I am compelled by an infamous pettyfogging lawyer to pay this sum for my servant's ignorance.

"But the servants of God must expect such treatment from the slaves of Beelzebub, whose sole delight is mischief. May they never have power to hurt you, my friend." This explosion shows that Mr. Raikes could think hardly sometimes, and express himself vigorously after the event; and that the atmosphere of his small but choice library of "serious books" did not altogether subdue the "old Adam" when he felt himself aggrieved.

This was quite an exceptional event in his active life, and, reading carefully, we make this out: at home or abroad, there was much evenness of temper with Mr. Raikes; and that although there was strong tenacity of purpose with him, he took colour for the moment from that which was nearest, and was sad or gay according to his environment. But for this sympathy with what was nearest, it is doubtful if he would have ever been heard of in the world. He abounded with a living sympathy at a time when all about him were fit objects for compassion, and so the world knows him better than it knows, or ever will know, much "greater" men.

* For compounding a felony and interfering with the due course of justice. This penalty may still be enforced under 24 and 25 Vic., c. 96, s. 102. The provisions of much older Acts are re-enacted.

NOTE.—In the "good old days" newspapers were distributed in town and country by "newsmen" who proclaimed their advent by blowing horns or ringing bells. In villages the horn or bell of the newsman was an event of the week. At the end of a year after the transfer of the *Journal* to Mr. Walker, a supplement in doggerel rhyme was issued with the paper, commencing :

> " Long has the *Journal* of old *Glo'ster*
> Been of our country's Fame the boaster ;
> Long has its columns filled our eyes
> With pleasure, horror, or surprise :
> Nay, e'en our good great-grandsires knew it,
> Proud at their festive boards to shew it.
> The name which gave the paper birth
> Fostered it long, and stamped its worth.
> We've lost our good old master—RAIKES :
> Who's quitted Paper, Types, and Cares,
> T'enjoy the fruits of anxious years."

The " politics " of the paper are alluded to :

> " As to our politics, 'tis known
> We love the King—support his Throne—
> Staunch sticklers in the people's cause,
> Yet reverence the Church and Laws ! "

Then there is a word for the old newsman at this the festive season :

> " Ah, remember, sirs, my weekly pains,
> My labours hard, my humble gains !
> And whilst your board can plenty boast,
> Whilst swims in ale the nutmeg'd toast,
> Make th' *Old Glo'ster Newsman* drink—
> Nay, make once more his pockets chink :
> Then for another year he'll trot with
> Wond'rous news, or tale, or plot ;
> Adventures strange, or strange disasters,
> T' amaze, or please, his worthy masters ! "

CHAPTER XV.

MRS. LADBROKE'S LETTERS.

"My dear and honoured father was indeed a true philanthropist in the most Christian sense of the word, and his life was a constant illustration of that character."—Mrs. LADBROKE.

HAVING presented Robert Raikes as remembered by those who knew him when the memory is most retentive, as he showed himself by and through his work, and as he estimated himself in his own correspondence, we now present a picture of him as he appeared to his own daughter.

When these letters were penned, in 1862 and 1863, there was no one living capable of speaking of Mr. Raikes in the language of authority and affection as Mrs. Weller-Ladbroke could and did. She was then of great age. In 1862 she had passed her 84th birthday. The solemnities of life were crowding around her, and, in the intervals from suffering, she wrote the letters which we print in full. They are penned in the spirit of affection and reverence, and there is throughout them a scrupulous desire not to permit affection to interfere with the presentation of the truth. Mrs. Ladbroke wrote with freedom, having received the assurance that during her lifetime her letters should not be published, or her authority quoted.

Mrs. Caroline Weller-Ladbroke—the relict of General Ladbroke—was residing at Worthing when the Author was introduced to her by letter. She would willingly have received a visit, but wished to spare herself fatigue and the Author possible disappointment, and so from time to time she wrote letters to him, answering such questions as she was able, and giving any additional information which she possessed and thought worthy of record.

The information which the Author was able to obtain respecting Robert Raikes and his life's work came from many sources, overladen with much which was valueless and more that was uncertain. It was only by a process of sifting and re-sifting that material facts could be separated and preserved, because the Raikes traditions in Gloucester had even then become confused and blurred, and heated controversies had greatly distorted the original outlines. In the letters from Mrs. Ladbroke the author felt that he was breathing a purer atmosphere, and that in them he possessed a touchstone to which he could bring the facts and fancies which came into his possession.

It is the privilege of the reader of this little volume to do the same. He may take all that has gone before—the statements of witnesses, the imputations of motive, the critical suggestions of the Author—and submit them to this Ladbroke touchstone, and say what is their degree of purity. Looked at from this standpoint, no gift to the

Sunday school world which now can ever be made will be so precious as this portrait of Robert Raikes, drawn by his daughter when—as it happened—in a few brief months she herself would " cross the line." Where affection glowed so intensely the absence of idealism is strongly marked; and those who love and revere the memory of Robert Raikes will be grateful to Mrs. Ladbroke for saying of her father only what she believed to be true, and what to her was true.

The first letter was purely formal, after the receipt of a letter from the Author enclosing a note of introduction. The second and following letters are here given:

"Stanmer Lodge, Worthing,
"*October 10th,* 1862.

"SIR,—I am very sorry your letter has remained so long unanswered; but my health is so delicate that I am not always equal to the painful exertion of writing.

"My firm and unhesitating conviction is that my dear father (the late Mr. Raikes, of Gloucester) was the *original* Founder of Sunday schools. His parents died very long before I was born, and therefore I know not their early history. They left four sons and one daughter.[*]

"My father was a constant communicant at St. Mary de Crypt. He never held any office in the church, or in any public office.

"He was a most affectionate husband and father, and an excellent master. He ruled his household with great

[*] This error is contradicted in the next letter.

Christian piety, and always required his servants to go regularly to church.

"The subject of Sunday schools was nearest his heart, and he often spoke of them in confident hope of the blessings which would attend the institution.

"I believe the first Sunday school was opened November 3rd, 1783; indeed, I fear not to assert it.*

"I perfectly recollect Prince William of Gloucester visiting my father two or three times when he was quartered at Gloucester, about seventy years ago; but I do not remember hearing the subject of their conversation.

"I am not aware of my father having borrowed the idea about Sunday schools from *any* person. I firmly believe the first conception was his own.

"My father was in the frequent habit of visiting the county and city prisons, particularly the former, and much blessed were his religious instructions to the poor inmates. Indeed, he was a general philanthropist, and never so happy as when he was administering consolation and instruction to the poor.

"He had two sons, now both dead. The eldest (Robert) was Rector of Longhope, Gloucestershire; the second (William) commanded the Coldstream Guards. He had six daughters, one of whom alone survives him.

---

* It was in 1780 that Robert Raikes first opened a Sunday school in the city of Gloucester; but it was not until November 3rd, 1783, that he made the project known to the world through the medium of the *Gloucester Journal*. In a subsequent letter Mrs. Ladbroke admits that she may be mistaken in the date she here gives.

Their names were Anne, Mary, Albinia, Eleanor, Charlotte, Caroline.

"My father died of disease of the heart, and was only ill half an hour, and died in perfect peace.

"As you say Mr. Lloyd's book is out of print, I am happy to have it in my power to lend you a copy. I am sure you will take great care of it, and return it to me as soon as you conveniently can.

"I sincerely wish you success in your excellent undertaking.

"I beg to remain, Sir,
"Your obedient Servant,
"CAROLINE WELLER-LADBROKE."

"Worthing, *December 27th*, 1862.

"SIR,—There is an interesting circumstance in my dear father's life connected with Sunday schools that I have hitherto suppressed, because I am unable to supply the date, though I think it must have been between the years 1790 and 1795. I told you before that my father was in the constant habit of visiting the county gaol, and that the instruction he gave the poor inhabitants was much blessed. A man was convicted for sheep stealing, and sentence of death passed upon him. My father, being fully convinced of the man's sincere repentance and entire change of heart, made great interest with the Judge to spare his life. The petition was granted, and the man transported to Botany Bay for his life. In the course of years his conduct was so exemplary that he got a free ticket, and established a Sunday school of his own in Botany Bay.*

"I beg to correct my statement that my grandfather Raikes left four sons and one daughter. He left *five* sons (of whom my father was the eldest) and one daughter.†
I see by Mr. Lloyd's book that my father states his first Sunday school to have been established at the close of the year *1781*, and therefore I suppose the plan was fully matured in 1783. You ask me what was my father's crest. It was a Griffin's Head.

"I beg to remain, Sir, yours obliged,

"CAROLINE WELLER-LADBROKE."

"Stanmer Lodge, Worthing,

"*January* 14*th*, 1863.

"SIR,—I am very sorry that I am quite unable to give you the information you wish to obtain as to where my father was educated, but I should think it *improbable* that he was at Crypt School. There was another large school at Gloucester, 'The College School,' but I am equally uncertain as to his being placed there.

"I have never heard of his being articled to any person.

* *See* Chapter VIII.

† Mrs. Ladbroke was not aware that her grandfather had been three times married.

"I perfectly recollect he was well-informed, wrote French fluently, and was a first-rate geographer.

"I had not the pleasure of knowing Mr. Lewelyn, or that he corresponded with my father.

"I well remember that my father had the great privilege of a visit from Mr. Howard for a day or two. I think it must have been in the year 1786 or 1787, and, most probably, at the time he was visiting the gaols in Gloucestershire. I recollect he wore a large bunch of seals on his watch chain, and made impressions of them for my sisters and me; and a child's memory as to kindness is generally very truthful.

"I wish I may have been of some little use in the matters I have stated to the best of my belief. If you publish them, I must request the kindness of you to suppress mentioning ME as your authority, for at my great age (on the eve of 84) I particularly wish to avoid all notoriety, and I think I may be safely spared that discomfort by your being so good as to say that the authority is undoubted, without giving my *name*.

"And now I will conclude with the assertion that my dear and honoured father was, indeed, a true philanthropist in the most Christian sense of the word, and that his life was a constant illustration of that character.

"I beg to remain, Sir,
   " Your obedient and obliged,
      " CAROLINE WELLER-LADBROKE."

"Stanmer Lodge, Worthing,
"*February* 11*th*, 1863.

"Sir,—In answer to your letter, which I received yesterday, I lose no time in giving you the information that my mother was a Miss Trigge. She had two brothers: the eldest was General Sir Thomas Trigge, and the other was Admiral Trigge. After Mr. Trigge's death my grandmother married General Napier. I *think* Mr. Trigge lived at Mincham, in Gloucestershire; but my mother did not marry till some time after General Napier's death.

"I am extremely sorry that I cannot give you any intelligence as to where my father was educated, neither do I know to whom I can apply for the information, as all my uncles are dead.

"I never heard of my father having had any communication with the Empress of Russia; but that by no means disproves the fact.

"I beg to remain, Sir,
"Yours truly and obliged,
"Caroline Weller-Ladbroke."

"Stanmer Lodge, Worthing,
"*March* 12*th*, 1863.

"Dear Sir,—I am very sorry to have delayed answering your letter, but I have been too unwell to do so, and am now not *well* able to write.

"It was the Reverend John Wesley who my father knew. I recollect his being at Gloucester between seventy and eighty years ago. My dear father had a great respect and regard for him.

"My eldest sister married Admiral Sir Thomas Thompson; the second, Admiral Garrett; the third, Mr. Birch; the fourth, Mr. Daniel Garrett; the fifth, Captain Clarke.

"I am sorry to hear your health continues so indifferent; but I hope you will receive some benefit from the change of air.

"I beg to remain, dear Sir,
"Yours truly and obliged,
"C. WELLER-LADBROKE."

"Stanmer Lodge, Worthing,
"*September 25th*, 1863.

"DEAR SIR,—I have been extremely unwell for the last three months, and am now suffering from the natural consequence of great weakness, and am quite unequal to any exertion or excitement; therefore, I should be exceedingly sorry to be the means of your taking a journey when, perhaps, I might not be able to see you; but I will endeavour, in writing, to answer your questions as far as it is in my power.

"My beloved father was quite well in the former part of the day he died. In the evening he was suddenly seized with a severe pain in his chest, and a *great* oppression on his breath; but he was only allowed to suffer half an hour, and then expired. Dr. Cheston, an eminent physician at Gloucester, had been immediately sent for when he was first attacked, but at once said nothing could be done. I was living in Wales at the time, and, therefore, had not the high privilege of seeing my dear father ere his blessed spirit had flown.

"I quite remember that Mrs. Hannah More was a friend of his, and that they used to correspond.

"He had no *extensive* library (as it would be termed *now*), but a very good collection of books, and his favourite study was always on serious subjects. With great truth, I may add he was a very holy man.

"I have no idea where he was married, but I should suppose in London, as I *believe* my mother lived there with my grandmother, Mrs. Napier, after the General died.

"I am extremely sorry that I *cannot* give you *all* the satisfactory information you wish to obtain.

"Before I close this letter I must assure you how thoroughly I appreciate your indefatigable endeavours to make the history of my dearest father's life as truthful and profitable as possible.

"With my sincere good wishes,
  "Believe me, my dear Sir,
    "Yours much obliged,
     "CAROLINE WELLER-LADBROKE."

This was the last letter which the Author received, and the intrinsic value of the series will be most appreciated by those who have endeavoured, from time to time, to piece together a life of Robert Raikes so as to present to their own minds a man working amongst men, and not the Ideal Man of their own desire. On questions of fact —such as where her father was married, where he was educated, and whether he was ever apprenticed or articled to a master printer—it seems curious that Mrs. Ladbroke was entirely ignorant. What is more, every member of the Raikes family—direct or collateral—was, at the time, also ignorant. Where he was married we now know; but where he was educated, and whether he ever learnt the art and mystery of printing, and so qualified himself as a master printer, will probably never be certainly known. The presumption is that he was educated either at the Crypt Grammar School, or Gloucester College, and that he did learn his business. Certain it is that he understood it, and, at times, used a composing "stick,"* the same as the editor of the *Gentleman's Magazine* might have done, he having been apprenticed to that celebrated printer Bowyer. He also had the jealousy of a craftsman for the reputation of his office, and refused a valued customer point-blank to put his name to a book which he did not print.

The handwriting of these Ladbroke letters is bold and vigorous, and in no instance is there the slightest trace of confusion of thought. She lived in much seclusion with

* *See* Chapter XVII.—" Raikes Family : Gloucester Branch."

an old family servant. The Rev. Mr. Read, writing to the Author after the funeral, says:

"I much regret to say I can render you no help, for during her last illness I was not permitted to see her. . . . This I much regret, for one more truly excellent I never met with than the lamented lady, with whom I had much pleasant intercourse during many of the last years of her life."

CHAPTER XVI.

THE MOVEMENT WEIGHED.

"The Sunday schools established by Mr. Raikes, of Gloucester, at the close of the century were the beginnings of popular education."—GREEN's *History of the English People.*

"In my mind the Sunday schools have been the foundation of much of what is good amongst the millions of our people."—JOHN BRIGHT.

SUNDAY schools were commenced as an experiment in the city of Gloucester in 1780, and in 1783 some results of that experiment were made public. In 1787 the *Gentleman's Magazine* published a letter from Mr. Raikes, estimating the number of children under Sunday instruction at 250,000. This may have been an over-estimate, or else there was a falling off afterwards, for in 1800 the same magazine recorded the numbers as 156,400 —presumably for England and Wales. In the year 1818 a Parliamentary return showed the number of Sunday scholars in England and Wales to be 477,225, or rather more than 4 per cent. of the population. In 1833 a second Parliamentary return gave a total of 1,548,890, or nearly 11 per cent. of the population. In 1851 the educational census return gave the numbers as 2,407,642, or nearly 13½ per cent. of the population. In the absence of an official return, the Hon. Secretary of the Sunday School Union (Mr. Fountain J. Hartley) estimated the number of scholars in 1887 to have increased to 5,733,325, or about 20 per cent. of the population in England and Wales. In June, 1898, the total number of scholars for England and Wales as published by the Sunday School Union is 7,456,108. For the United Kingdom and Ireland the totals are: Number of schools, 53,590; teachers, 704,955; scholars, 7,875,748. Total membership, 8,580,703—about 25 per cent. of the population.

If it were possible for the Founder and Organiser of this system to have a knowledge of these figures, surely his soul would be satisfied.*

The Author endeavoured from time to time to obtain the opinions of men of "light and leading" as to the value of Sunday schools and their influence on the rising generation. A few of the replies have been mislaid, and, notably, one from the Rev. Dr. Guthrie, and another from Mrs. Beecher Stowe. There still, however, remain a large number of letters from men representing many shades of thought in the Christian Church in England, the United States, and Australia, and from them the following selection is made.

* The extension of the Sunday school system in America would, if possible, increase his joy. The figures collected for the World's third Sunday School Convention, held in London in July, 1898, showed that in the United States the number of schools was 132,697; teachers, 1,394,630; and scholars, 10,893,533. For Canada the number of schools was 8,986; teachers, 75,064; and scholars, 582,070. Not only do the numbers in the United Kingdom and the United States yearly increase, but the percentage of scholars to the population steadily increases also.

[ELIHU BURRITT—*January 7th*, 1863.]

"I thank you most cordially for your kind and interesting letter, awaiting me on my arrival from America. I thank you for your good words and wishes for my personal welfare.

"I do indeed feel a deep and lively interest in the history and influence of Sunday schools, and feel that Robert Raikes was to the youth world of humanity what Isaac Newton was to the world of matter and motion.

"To attempt to measure the influence of the great institution he founded would be *like applying a two-foot rule to infinite space, or the measure of a moment to eternity.* They have come to rank among the very first agencies of our great Anglo-Saxon race in both hemispheres.

"They have been developed to a remarkable expansion and power in America. There is probably not a church or chapel of any denomination between the oceans that has not a Sunday school connected with it.

"Sunday school anniversaries are becoming seasons of popular interest in every community. Perhaps the largest and best organised schools in America are those connected with Rev. Dr. Tyng's church in New York, and Rev. Henry Ward Beecher's church in Brooklyn. I think each numbers one thousand pupils. Dr. Tyng is an eminent episcopal clergyman, and has given his heart and soul to the work of building up these institutions to be a *working* power in the land. All the scholars under his care form themselves into Missionary Societies—Home and Foreign—and raise a large amount of money for such operations in the year. . . .

"I am sorry that I cannot tell you who founded the first Sunday school in America,* or when it was established. I remember attending one in my own native village † forty-five years ago [1818].

"Should you write to Dr. Tyng, he would be exceedingly interested in receiving one of the letters of Robert Raikes, just to show to his multitude of pupils the handwriting of a man whose name is so revered by the youth of America." . . .

[RICHARD COBDEN,‡ M.P.—*March 16th*, 1864.]

"The American schools are strictly religious in their objects and organization. They are not intended for teaching reading, as all children in that country are expected to attend the 'common schools,' which are open *gratis* on the weekdays for all the children in the country. This makes the Sunday schools a totally different institution from what was contemplated by

---

* Said to have been founded by Ludwig Hacker between the years 1740 and 1747 at Ephrata, Lancaster county, Penn., among the German Seventh-day Baptists. The schoolroom was used as a hospital after the battle of Brandy-Wines, fought in 1777. The school is said to have been discontinued about that time—four years before Robert Raikes gathered the first children together in Sooty Alley, Gloucester.

† New Britain, Connecticut.

‡ "He is above all in our eyes the representative of those sentiments and those cosmopolitan principles before which national frontiers and rivalries disappear."—M. DROUYN DE LHUYS.

Raikes and his successors, who had to teach the poor children to read.

"I am not aware of any Government returns respecting the Sunday schools of the United States."

[LETTER NO. 2.]

"I really don't know that I can add anything to my former note. The Sunday schools of the United States are exclusively for religious, and, indeed, *denominational*, training.

"*They are not relied on for teaching children to read.* Weekday secular schooling is offered *gratis* to every child in America. It is the boast in some of the New England States that you cannot walk a mile without coming to a school house where education, books, &c., are to be had free of all charge.

"Where such is the case, you must see that Sunday schools can claim no merit for affording elementary education. If a child cannot read, his parents would be open to censure for not having sent him to school; and as the weekday school is always ready to welcome him, it is *there* that he would be taught to read and not at the Sunday school.

"In Canada, a system of common schools was inaugurated during Lord Elgin's governorship very similar to that of the United States. Of course all denominational religious teaching is forbidden in the weekday schools both in America and Canada.

"In *this* country, where there has never been a system

of national education deserving the name,* the Sunday schools have often supplied, in a most important way, the deficiency by imparting a knowledge of the alphabet and a little reading to the poor children.

"In the time of Raikes this was almost the only chance for the children of the working class; but to rely on such a resource *now* would be to leave us behind every civilized Christian nation."

[Dr. H. Clay Trumbull,† Philadelphia—*December 7th*, 1898.]

"America has been practically saved to Christianity and the religion of the Bible by the Sunday school. At the opening of the nineteenth century, Bible study and Bible teaching were at a low ebb in America—at a lower ebb than at any earlier period. At the close of that century, Bible study and Bible teaching are at a higher point than ever before in the Western Hemisphere, and that chiefly through God's blessing on the agency of the modern Sunday school. But not only has the Sunday school been the means of bringing up the standard of Christianity in the regions first settled by the Pilgrims and Puritans in New England, by the Cavaliers in Virginia, and by the Huguenots in South Carolina; but in the newer portions of the United States, the Sunday school has been the chiefest agency of pioneer evangelisation.

---

* It will be remembered that this was written in 1864, one year before he died. Had he lived he would have been a generous supporter of the Education Act, 1870.

† Yale Lecturer on the Sunday school, 1888.

"In our Churches of every name, in city and country alike, the children of our choicest Christian homes are largely dependent on their Church Sunday school teaching and influence for their religious training and upbuilding. This is recognised by the best Christian parents, as well as by many of the more careless ones. Statistics, and all historic evidence, go to show that just in proportion as the Sunday school has prominence in a church community, the family life and the home training are uplifted; and that as the Sunday school is neglected, the family life declines.

"There is no agency of city missions comparable with the Sunday school in our more crowded cities, East and West. By this agency is stayed the relapsing into practical heathenism of the districts deserted by the Protestant churches, as their congregations move into more attractive quarters, carrying the church organisation with them.

"In our newer communities, on the advancing and extending borders of our country, it is the Sunday school that is the pioneer religious agency that secures an outpost of evangelistic progress, as nothing else does or could. This gathers the children of varied sorts and nationalities into a new religious centre, that prepares the way for a Church and pastor, when the parents could not have been won or reached except through their children.

"Of course, the American Sunday school is different, in many respects, from the Sunday school in England, having been adapted in its form and methods to the peculiar nature and needs of the New World communities; but it took its new start from the Robert Raikes movement, and it gives grateful credit accordingly.

"Observant foreigners have noted and commented on the dominant influence of the Sunday school in American religious life. M. Buisson, at the head of a French Commission sent here, in 1876, to study the educational methods of the United States, reported accordingly to his Government. He said that the Sunday school 'aims to fill by itself the complete mission which elsewhere is in large measure assigned to the family, the school, and the church.' Professor Émile de Laveleye, of Belgium, wrote about the same time of his careful observations: 'The Sunday school is one of the strongest foundations of the Republican institutions of the United States.' The more familiar a student of facts and principles is with America as it was and is, the firmer will be his conviction that these observers are correct in their estimate of the importance of the modern Sunday school as a basal support of American institutions and religious power."

[THE REV. JOHN H. VINCENT, D.D.,[*] TOPEKA, KANSAS, U.S.A.—*February 10th, 1899.*]

"I am delighted to read of your plan for a unique life of Robert Raikes; and, certainly, if your plan is carried out, it will be a most charming and valuable contribution

[*] Former Editor of the Methodist Episcopal Sunday School Union publications, the present Chancellor of the Chautauqua Society, and Bishop over the Methodist Episcopalian Church, New York.

to philanthropic literature, and especially to the literature of the Sunday school.

"Robert Raikes represented the activity of the laity in religious effort; his movement not only anticipated the mission-form of the modern Sunday school, but the intelligent effort of laymen to which, in these days, on both sides of the sea, the Christian churches owe so much. I shall look forward with great interest to the reading of your volume."

[REV. W. MORLEY PUNSHON—*May 9th*, 1863.]

"I suppose at this time of day there is but little difference of opinion about Sunday schools, when properly conducted and worked, so that the salvation of the scholars is kept in view as the main design.

"I believe that as an educational agency simply, Sunday schools have fulfilled their mission; but it would be rash to deny that they have been in multiplied instances effectual for lasting spiritual good.

"Their chief lack just now seems to be an appliance to meet the case of those who are, or think themselves, too big to be classed among the scholars, and who are not yet ripe for the fellowship of the Church."

[RT. HON. SIR JOHN PACKINGTON, M.P.*—*April 18th*, 1863.]

"I have had the honour of receiving your letter of the 16th inst. I am not aware that I have it in my

* The Rt. Hon. Member for Droitwich was, during his long and honourable career, very active in all matters relating to National education; and his labours—not always appreciated—did much to make the Education Acts of 1870 and since possible.

power to offer you any suggestions which would be of service to you in the interesting and laudable work you have in hand.

"The educational agencies of the present age, deficient as they still are, are a fresh advance, as compared to those we possessed half a century ago, and amongst those agencies the Sunday school system has occupied a high and important place.

"With reference to religious instruction especially, they have done much good, and, though for general educational value they are not to be compared to the day school, those who have favoured and supported them are entitled to respectful gratitude.

"In expressing these opinions, I believe I am only expressing the opinions of almost all who have studied the education question."

[THE REV. C. H. SPURGEON—*May 2nd*, 1863.]

"My first attempts at public speaking were made in a Sunday school in which I was a teacher. The exercise of addressing the school was very useful to me, and led me to engage in giving addresses to other assemblies. I was never a Sunday scholar in a Sunday school. I wish you every success in your work."

[DR. JOHN CUMMING—*May 13th*, 1863.]

"In answer to your enquiry, I may state: (1) That in the great number of instances I have found that Sunday school pupils have become afterwards Sunday school teachers. (2) That the most devoted teachers are, many of them, young persons engaged in shops, warehouses, and dressmaking establishments, ten, twelve, and fourteen hours a day during the week. (3) In many cases I have found Sunday school teaching become a passion and an enjoyment of singular intensity and endurance."

[The Rev. Hugh Price Hughes, M.A. (*President of the Conference*)—*December 1st*, 1898.]

" The benefit of the modern Sunday school is so vast and so manifest everywhere that it seems almost as superfluous to name it as to mention the benefit we derive from the sun at noonday. You are possibly aware that we Methodists maintain that there was a Methodist Sunday school before Mr. Robert Raikes started his, and I think the evidence of the fact is demonstrative. It does not, however, in the least degree detract from the immense and imperishable services of the Great Philanthropist of Gloucester, who, in the popular mind, enjoys the credit of starting the Sunday school movement.

" I believe that he is entitled to the great credit which popular opinion assigns to him, inasmuch as it was he who led to the national movement on the part of all the Churches, consequently we are deeply interested in any investigation which can throw more light upon his ever-blessed career."

In 1870, the Author addressed a circular letter to the Anglican Bishops in Great Britain and the Colonies.

The following replies were received, and they are supplemented by letters recently received by the Editor:

[DR. TAIT, *Archbishop of Canterbury—August 29th,* 1870.]

"I write a line on behalf of the Archbishop of Canterbury to say, in reply to your letter, that it would be almost impossible to exaggerate the importance of Sunday schools. They have rendered great service to religion and education; and if the secular system should gain ground in England, this importance would become even greater than it has hitherto been.

"Believe me to be, very faithfully yours,
C. W. SANDFORD,
Commissary to the Archbishop of Canterbury."

[DR. JACKSON, *Bishop of London—September 6th,* 1870.]

"I am sorry that I am unable to give you any information to assist you in your biography of Robert Raikes; but even with want of leisure I will briefly enter on the wide subject of the influence of Sunday schools on the formation of religious character.

"It is obvious to remark that this influence has varied somewhat in kind, while it has increased in extent, during the period over which it has been exerted.

"When Sunday schools were first established they provided a large proportion of their scholars with the *only* education they received: as reading and spelling, as well as Bible truths, were learnt in them for the first and only time. Day schools were rare, and by many, even by good men, were suspected and discouraged; and the duty of catechising was much neglected, although required by the law and canons of the Church of England.* Sunday schools were then invaluable as being to multitudes the only instrument, however imperfect, for opening their minds and awakening their intellectual faculties, as well as for giving them some acquaintance with revealed truth and the duties it involves, and the motives it supplies. And this office such schools still discharge in too many cases, especially in populous parishes where the children are either not sent to the day school, or attend too irregularly and leave too early to derive any benefit from them.

"But in proportion as day schools have become more general and day scholars more numerous, the secular position of the instruction given in the Sunday school at any rate has, happily, become less important, and even the religious teaching is only supplemental to the more systematic instruction which most of the scholars are receiving in the week. And the question has been asked by many whether Sunday schools have not, under these circumstances, become an evil—even if it be a necessary evil,—and whether it would not be better and more consonant to the true idea of the Christian family if the children, being carefully instructed during the week in the Bible and the truths contained in it, were on Sunday taught only by their parents, and with them went to the House of God?

* *See.* "Catechising in Churches," Chapter XI.

"Unhappily, this question does not call for an answer. As a matter of fact, parents for the most part cannot, or do not, teach their children at home on Sunday, nor take them with them to the House of God; and the question is not between the Sunday school and the influence of the Christian home, but between the Sunday school and neglect and idleness—the fields or the streets.

"Nor is the religious teaching of the Sunday school without its special advantage now, when the scholars are also carefully instructed in a good and scriptural day school, especially if the Sunday school be properly organised and the teachers duly equipped. In the day school the classes are usually too large: the teaching general, although systematic; individual application difficult; and the doctrines and precepts of the Gospel are in danger of being accepted rather as lessons to be learnt than as truths to be felt and acted on. But in the Sunday school (supposing the scholars to be well grounded in the day school), where the classes ought always to be small, the teachers should always have God's love in their hearts. The individual application of the truths taught in love should be the main object in view, and is more effective as the teaching not only of mind to mind, but of heart to heart. And this leads me to the expression of a doubt whether the happiest influence of Sunday schools has not been as great, if not greater, on adults as on children, on the teacher as on the taught.

"Our religion is worth nothing until it has made us

take trouble for God's sake, and active charity in some form or other is necessary for the soul's health. But the greater part of our more educated population are occupied unceasingly in the week by their work, professions, or home duties. Sunday only is their own. And the Sunday school gives them the opportunity of dedicating some part of their only leisure to a good work for God's sake. It is an unspeakable blessing to them.

"And it is a thought of great comfort when anxious and dispirited on account of the vice and immorality, the irreligious infidelity, which seem to surge up all around us, to remember that there are tens of thousands of men and women of all ranks—from some of the highest in the land, the most learned, the most accomplished, to those who owe all their knowledge and love of their God and Saviour to what they themselves learnt in Sunday school—who are teaching every Sunday in the schools of our land, giving often to God what rest they might fairly feel they needed themselves, learning, not seldom, what they teach, and always knitting more closely the bond of Christian fellowship, and bringing together classes which, even in a Christian land, want so sadly severs.

"This view of the character of Sunday schools, as supplying work for those who wish to work for God, has been more generally recognised, perhaps, by those who are without the Church of England, than by those within it; and they have had their reward by their attaching more closely to their own community many who find with them what the church neglected to give. But the principle, while good in itself, may be, and is, carried too far; and I have regretted to find among those who are allowed to teach others, persons who are discreditably ignorant themselves. This is unjust to the scholars, and not always beneficial to the teachers, whom it may confirm in their conceit instead of convincing them of their deficiencies.

"But this evil may be in a great degree prevented, and another important benefit be deduced from Sunday schools, if the clergyman, or other superintendent, will take the pains carefully to teach the teachers themselves; and by forming a class of all those who are not sufficiently educated to be qualified to act for themselves, and by talking with them previously what they in turn are to talk with their children in the Sunday school—to prevent the risk of mistake, teaching and at the same time conveying a lesson to the teachers which, thus given and thus repeated, will not easily be forgotten by them.

"But I have written more at length than I had intended, and begging you to pardon my prolixity,

"I am, Sir, your obedient Servant,

"J. LONDON."

[DR. TEMPLE, *Bishop of Exeter—July 8th*, 1870.]

"I am desired by the Bishop to acknowledge the receipt of your letter of 29th June, and to say that his Lordship thinks it almost certain that Sunday schools will greatly increase in importance as all education is better appreciated.

"Yours very faithfully,
"E. G. SANDFORD,
"*Chaplain.*"

[LORD ARTHUR DR. HERVEY, *Bishop of Bath and Wells—August 13th*, 1870.]

"You ask for my opinion about Sunday schools. I think that more than ever they are becoming a most important part of the Church's work in carrying out our Lord's command to feed His lambs. In the present state of the educational question through the country, and with the restrictions which, even under the act lately passed,* are placed upon religious teaching in our parochial schools, it becomes of vital consequence, for the maintenance of an intelligent faith among our people, to make use of the Sunday school.

"I also think that the opportunity afforded to voluntary teachers to lend their aid on the Sunday is of great value, with a view to the promotion of Christian sympathy among the members of our congregations; and that without some such opportunity, love is likely to wax cold.

"I remain, your humble Servant,
"ARTHUR C. BATH AND WELLS."

[DR. JACKSON, *Bishop of Chester—August 1st*, 1870.]

"I am sorry to be thus late in acknowledging your letter, and I do not know that I have any better way of

* The Education Act of 1870 is here referred to

doing this than by sending you a passage from my Charge, 1868.

"I beg to remain, your faithful servant,

"WILLIAM CHESTER."

Then follows an extract from the printed Charge, p. 19:

"It has of late become a sort of fashion in some quarters, to speak disparagingly of Sunday schools. This is very much to be regretted. Such teaching, well conducted, has great and abiding influence on after-life; and if it ever should be abandoned by the Church, it will assuredly be taken up with increased vigour by those who, conscientiously, separate themselves from our Communion. To urge that children had better be at home with their parents is to betray strange ignorance of what home and home associations generally, and the mode of spending the Lord's Day at home in particular, too often are.

"Whether the practice of dismissing the younger scholars, at all events, at some period short of the conclusion of our full Morning Service, might not be adopted more generally than at present, with great advantage, is well worth considering. And, when circumstances admit of it, a separate Shorter Service for the children by themselves is most desirable. Some little relaxation of discipline and routine may fittingly characterise the Sunday as compared with the day school. And some of the many appliances which, happily, our age supplies, for helping in an agreeable way to impart the facts of Sacred History in young minds, will, of course, be employed."

[DR. GOODWIN, *Bishop of Carlisle—August 29th*, 1870.]

"Owing to circumstances, I have for many years had very little to do with the working of Sunday schools; and it is, consequently, a subject upon which my opinion is of little value. But it has always seemed to me that when diligently managed, they are very agreeable to the young folks, and the notion of the children being wearied by attendance at Sunday school has no support in actual experience.

"The weak part of them appears to me to be the subsequent attendance at Church without sufficient and proper accommodation for the children. I am disposed to think that this conjunction of the Sunday school with much discomfort and weariness in church, is one reason why so many young people cease going to church when they cease going to school. But this is mere speculation.

"Your truly,
"HARVEY CARLISLE."

[DR. BICKERSTETH, *Bishop of Ripon—August 19th*, 1870.]

"I am glad to find that you have been successful in finding materials for a biography of Robert Raikes, the reputed founder of Sunday schools.

"It is impossible to over-estimate the good results which have arisen out of the establishment of Sunday schools. They were at one period about the only channel for the communication of religious instruction to the children of the poorer classes, and their beneficial influence is still so great, notwithstanding the enormous advances which have been made in the cause of education, that *they could not be dispensed with without serious injury* to the best interests of the whole community.

"Believe me, very faithfully yours,

"R. RIPON."

[DR. KNOX, *Bishop of Down—September 7th*, 1870.]

"I need hardly assure you of the deep interest I feel in Sunday schools, and from time to time I have brought them before my clergy at my visitations.

"I consider Sunday schools have conferred a *lasting* benefit, not only on our Church, but on the *nation at large*. Were it not for this noble institution a large number of children (especially in the manufacturing districts) would be in total ignorance, for pulpit ministrations hardly reach them. To the Founder of Sunday schools every Christian man and woman in the country, from the Queen to the humblest of her subjects, owes a deep debt of gratitude.

"The amount of Scriptural knowledge conveyed in properly conducted Sunday schools throughout the country, under the management of various Christian bodies, cannot be over-estimated. Let us only remember 'Children are the morrow of society; it is in our power to prepare for the coming day, but when that day has risen upon the earth, its destinies have escaped beyond our control.'

"I am, yours faithfully,

"THOS. DOWN AND CONNER."

[DR. BUTCHER, *Bishop of Meath—September 5th*, 1870.]

"Having been requested to state my opinion 'as to the influence of Sunday schools upon the rising generation, and the part they may be fairly said to play in forming the religious character of the nation,' I have no hesitation in saying that I believe their influence to be most salutary where the schools have a sufficient staff of duly qualified and earnest teachers, and are under the direction of sensible and careful managers.

"Under these conditions I am sure that Sunday schools are calculated to play an important part in forming the religious character of a nation.

"SAMUEL MEATH."

[DR. BRODERICK, *Bishop of Tuam—October 13th*, 1870.]

"If the experiences of thirty-five years are of any value, I can add my hearty testimony to the blessings of Sunday schools.

"My knowledge of them has been in large scattered country districts and in well peopled town parishes, and the same happy work is the fruit in all.

"I have had the old and the young filling every room of the farmhouse upon the wild hillside, and grey hairs bending over the Scriptures and learning from lips of almost childhood. What could be the result when every word (almost) spoken in those houses came direct from the Fountain of Wisdom, and when its lessons are enforced by hearts which speak not of their own abundance?

"The Sunday school in my town experience was the platform on which all classes met, as teachers and as scholars, to learn what in God's sight, and by God's good wise provision, respects not persons, but places all upon the equality of the lost or the pardoned, and forms golden ties for lifelong social interests, while it moulds into the surest form the providential distinctions of daily life.

"You only wish for my testimony, or I would go on. . . .

"Very faithfully yours,

"C. B. TUAM."

[DR. WILLIAMS, *Bishop of Quebec—December 8th*, 1870.]

"The Sunday school, so far as my observation enables me to judge, is, when inspired and directed by a zealous and efficient man, one of the most powerful influences which a clergyman wields.

"It is very difficult to give systematic religious instruction to older people, and to mixed congregations; and for want of systematic instruction a preacher's address is too often uninteresting and unintelligible to one half of his audience, while to the other half it is wearisomely trite.

"This difficulty is, in great part, obviated where the Sunday schools have been efficient.

"The Sunday school, again, forms a most convenient channel for the conveyance of the clergyman's personal influence—directly and indirectly. Directly, by bringing him into contact with so large a number of his flock at the most impressionable age; and, indirectly, by the opportunities it gives him to *teach the teachers and so diffuse his mind through the mass.*

"The customs of the country, where rich and poor alike attend the Sunday school, add an inestimable advantage in the mixing of ranks and classes, and the practical inculcation of the truth, that in Christ we are all one.

"In the thinly settled districts, where the clergyman has to be in several places on the Sunday, and where teachers are often found with difficulty, the working of Sunday schools is no easy matter; but, as a general rule, it is open to observation, that *the most successful clergymen* are those who are most strenuous in the Sunday school—where, indeed, the seed of their success has been sown, some to appear at once, some after many days.

"I am, my dear Sir,
"Faithfully yours,
"J. W. QUEBEC."

[DR. SHORT, *Bishop of Adelaide—December* 29*th*, 1870.]

"My opinion of the value of Sunday schools, properly and systematically taught and managed on Christian principles, is, that *they are the seed-plot of the Church.*

"If followed up by regular catechising at stated times,

I think they will build up children under Divine grace in Christian as well as Church principles.

"I do not think the minister of any congregation is making full proof of his ministry unless he personally superintends, and catechises, such a school connected with his congregation.

"The duty is universally recognised in this diocese. *A good or poor Sunday school is a tolerable test of the efficiency or inefficiency of the minister.*

"I am, your obedient Servant,

"A. ADELAIDE."

[THE RIGHT REVEREND ALFRED BARRY, D.D., *formerly Primate of Australia—November 12th,* 1898.]

"My experience, both here and on the other side of the world, simply confirms what I cannot doubt that you have heard from others—that the Sunday school institution is invaluable, and the main help of the Church in carrying out systematically her catechetical teaching of the young.

"To make full use of its influence, it should be, I think, united with a regular system of periodical catechising in Church, and made to lead up to the preparation for confirmation. Nor can it, of course, be a substitute for the more complete and technical teaching of the Church day schools. For, naturally, its influence is exercised over the heart and the spirit even more than the understanding, and that influence makes itself felt, both socially and spiritually, over the whole life of each parish. That it might be extended more largely still, is obvious.

"In England generally we need that extension in two directions: first, over a longer period of age of the scholars, including the formation of adult classes; and next, as consequent on this, an enlargement of the curriculum, which, after Holy Scripture and the Prayer Book, should certainly include some elementary knowledge of Church history. But even as it is, it is impossible to exaggerate its usefulness; and I am convinced that no systematising of the catechising in Church, however desirable, can ever supersede it with advantage.

"As one chief means, moreover, of lay ministration, harmonised with the pastoral duty of the clergy, it is invaluable, and it indirectly promotes all other forms of the ministration.

"Yours sincerely,
"ALFRED BARRY." *

[DR. ELLICOTT, *Bishop of Gloucester—November 17th*, 1898.]

"I hasten to acknowledge your letter about Sunday schools. I have really nothing more to say about them than this—that if the teachers seriously prepare their teaching, and the clergyman of the parish wisely superintends, they will bear blessings to the children and to the parish.

"Very faithfully yours,
"C. J. GLOUCESTER."

* Dr. Barry is now the Rector of St. James's, Piccadilly, the church wherein Robert Raikes was married in 1767. The facsimile of the entry in the church register (see p. 267) is from a tracing by Mr. J. Redman, Clerk.

CHAPTER XVII.

THE RAIKES FAMILY.

YORKSHIRE ROOTS.

THE county of Gloucester claims Robert Raikes as a son, but the county of York claims, as it is entitled to, the honour of producing, and nurturing, and developing those sterling racial qualities which have distinguished an ancient and honourable family. There does not appear to be any known authority enabling us to say what is the origin of the race.*

The name is variously spelt, but the stock has been vigorous and productive, and there has been no failure of issue in the direct line since 1507, when Johanna Rakys, of Kelfield, in Stillingfleet, near York, widow, made her will, brief and to the point: "My body to be buried in Stillingfleet. To William, my son, a cow; to Thomas, my son, 6/8; to Thomas, son of William Rakys, a cow

---

* Dr. Max Müller, Oxford, writing to the Editor, says the name seems to be Saxon. Mr. Henry St. John Raikes thinks the family originally came from Denmark. The name does not appear in the indexes bound up with Sir Henry Ellis's *General Introduction to Domesday Book*, comprising tenants in chief and other tenants, as well as the holders of land anterior to the formation of that record. The *Patronymica Britannica* suggests a Scotch derivation from rake or raik—sheep raik (or walk), cattle raik, &c. Sir John William de la Pole, editor of Sir William Pole's description of the county of Devon, speaks of Sir Adam Rake, of Rake, who served in France, and was knighted about the forty-third year of Edward III.

and an heifer. Residue to George, my son." Husband and wife did not always think it necessary to spell their names alike; for example, Alison Raks was the widow of William Rackes, of Kelfield. She was a lady of some consideration. By her will, proved at York in 1545, she bequeathed "to Richard, my son, one stott [bull] of 2 yeres olde. To Isabell Jackson one quye [cow] of one yere olde, my best gowne, a kirtle, a petticote, a mattres and one sheit. To Robert, my son, one holdinge swynne. To Elisabeth Jackson, my daughter, my marble gowne, a cape, a hate and a kirchif, a smoke and a pair of hose. To Katheryne Raks a kirchif; to Elisabeth Raks, my son Thomas, daughter, a kirchif and one pair of silver crooks [tongs]; to Agnes Raks one kirchif and one piece of hose; to Elisabeth Raks, a kirchif; to Thomas Raks, my son, 12d., whom I make supervisor of this my will. Residue to Roger Raks, my sone, whome I make my full executor."*

The Raikes family at this period were "husbandmen," and dairy produce occupied their attention, for grazing lands were mostly occupied by them at Kelfield and Eskrigg. The name was also spelt Rakys and Rakes, but Raikes seems to have been adopted towards the end of the sixteenth century, at all events by those who forsook farming, and went to Kingston-upon-Hull to live as sailors and merchants.

In 1599 Robert Raikes was admitted a free burgess of Hull, and became a Warden of Trinity House in 1616;

---

* From the Raikes Pedigree (Lieut.-Col. G. A. Raikes, F.S.A.).

and he was the son of Richard Raikes, "master mariner," who, by his father's will, came into possession of "half of one quarter [an eighth part] of a good ship *Richard Bonaventure* then at sea, or the *Marie Thomas*, or of the *Robucke*." This Richard was a younger Brother of Trinity House. So also was William Raikes in 1632, who, by his will, gave a silver cup to the Trinity Brethren, which is still in the possession of the Corporation at Tower Hill. Several members of the family were Brethren and Wardens of the Trinity House. Thomas Raikes, the younger brother of this Richard, "master mariner," took a very active and prominent part during the Civil War. He was a merchant, sheriff in 1621, and three times mayor; namely, in 1633, 1642, and 1643, when, the gates of Hull having been shut against King Charles I.'s army, the town underwent the horrors of a siege.

The following extract from the Corporation Minutes shows something of the character of this Thomas Raikes, and the estimation in which he was held : "At the election of mayor for the year to come, the burgesses assembled, taking into consideration Mr. Mayor's (Thomas Raikes, Esq.) vigilance and carefulness of the Town's affairs the year past [1642–3], and his fidelity to the public cause, and the great danger that the town is now in, being at present strongly beleaguered by the Earl of Newcastle's forces lying nigh, and daily shooting into the town with their great ordnance, earnestly prayed Mr. Mayor either to continue mayor as he is, or that he would be elected mayor again for the year to come. He consented when

Lord Fairfax, Governor, came into the said assembly and requested him to do so."

These were anxious and perilous times, and Tickell in his *History of Hull* shows that this Thomas Raikes was a prudent man. The King had set up his standard at Nottingham, and there being a rumour that peace would ensue, Thomas Raikes (then mayor) "began to apprehend no small danger to himself and his brethren, and thought it prudent to provide in time both for his own and their safety. In order to this he summoned the Bench, and laid before them the danger they were in of being called to an account for their remarkable adherence to the Parliament, and the active part they had taken against the King during the whole course of this unhappy dispute, should they not be included in the Act of Oblivion. . . . They therefore unanimously determined to write to Henry Vane, knight, and Peregrine Pelham, their representatives in Parliament, in order to entreat them to make use of their influence 'that the town and all its inhabitants, without exception, be fully included in the said Act, and, on that condition, to endeavour, as much as in them lay, to put an end to the calamities and afflictions which had so long oppressed, and threatened still more to oppress, this unhappy and divided nation.' After a few messages and answers, however, all hopes of peace entirely vanished, and the nation saw itself involved in all the horrors of a civil war."

Tickell calls this Thomas Raikes a man of "anti-monarchical principles." He was a staunch man, and when Sir John Hotham, the Governor of Hull, and his son, Captain Hotham, entered into a plot to surrender to the King, Thomas Raikes (Allen's *History of the County of York*) held a consultation with the Parliamentary party, and resolved to defeat the project by seizing the Governor and his son. This was done, and on January 1st, 1643, Captain Hotham was executed, and on the 2nd Sir John followed his son. Thomas Raikes succeeded Sir John Hotham as Governor.

This Thomas Raikes died in 1662, and both he and his brother Robert left issue, but their descendants in the male line became extinct before 1700. The line was, however, continued through Richard, the eldest brother, the master mariner and merchant in Hull, who had two sons, Richard and Joshua, and five daughters, the second of whom, Hester, married William Wilberforce, from whom descended William Wilberforce, the philanthropist and political leader of the anti-slavery party in England.*

Richard, the eldest son, M.A. Emanuel College, Cambridge, entered the Church, and was vicar of Hessle, in Yorkshire. Dying in 1671, he left three sons and three daughters, of whom the eldest, Timothy, also entered the Church, and was, first, Vicar of Tickhill. Afterwards he succeeded his father as Vicar of Hessle. He took his degree at St. John's, Cambridge, but his wife from Gloucester, having married Sarah, the daughter of — Partridge, Esq. By his marriage he had three sons—

* He sometimes visited his relative, Robert Raikes, in Gloucester.

namely, Robert, Richard, and Timothy — and three daughters.

Robert, the eldest, settled in the city of Gloucester, and was three times married. By his third wife, Mary, daughter of the Rev. Richard Drew, of Nailsworth, he had one daughter, Mary, married to Francis Newberry, of Heatherford Park, Sussex, and five sons; namely, Robert, Richard, William, Charles, and Thomas.

We here reach the point in the family history of the greatest interest to us, and have to some extent enabled the reader to account to himself for some of those traits in the character of Robert Raikes which have been so prominently brought forward in this volume. From his ancestors in Hull he had hereditary leanings towards popular rights. He was by hereditary strain to be found on the side of the people. His father (Robert), the first settler in the city of Gloucester, was a bold and progressive man, and showed that the traditions of Thomas— Mayor of Hull—were not lost in him. His conduct in the management of his newspaper brought him into conflict with the House of Commons.* This is not the place to enlarge on the subject, but it may be fairly said that the whole body of journalists of to-day owe some gratitude to this Robert Raikes for reporting the minutes of the House in 1728 and again in 1729. The action of Parliament was tyrannical, and so was the resolution of the House passed after the second offence. The subject may be pursued in May's *Constitutional History* and Lord

* *See* Appendix D.

Mahon's *History* by those who are interested in the evolution of the English Press towards freedom.

Only two of the five sons of Robert remained in Gloucester; namely, Robert and Richard. Two, namely, William and Thomas, succeeded to the business of a distant relative, an eminent Russian merchant; and Charles settled in Cambridge, married his cousin, Eleanor Raikes, and died without issue.

The Raikes family left Hull for several generations, and it was not till 1789 that Robert, a son of William Raikes, the Russian merchant, and a nephew of Robert Raikes, of Gloucester, re-established their connection with the ancient borough by marrying the daughter of Mr. Williamson, banker and iron merchant, in Hull. He succeeded to the Welton estate; and his sister, Mary Anne, marrying Mr. Isaac Currie, the Raikes-Curries, once so well known in the commercial world, were born.

It was, however, from Thomas that the literary and political honours of the family came. Thomas Raikes, of the city of London, in his day was usually referred to as "eminent" or "great." He had wealth, but, in addition, he had probity, and his name stood in the commercial world as a synonym for honour. He was Governor of the Bank of England during the crisis of 1797, and reckoned Pitt and Wilberforce amongst his friends. He was considered to be an authority on finance, and told Pitt that there was something wrong in Dundas's accounts, as appears from the Report of the Select Committee on the Naval Report, printed in 1805. Pitt disregarded the warning, and Lord Melville's trial was a result.

Mr. Thomas Raikes had three sons and five daughters. One daughter married Lord William Fitzroy, fourth son of the Duke of Grafton; and Harriet, the youngest, married Sir Stratford Canning, then envoy to the Swiss Cantons. This Sir Stratford Canning, afterwards Viscount Stratford de Radcliffe, is the "Great Elchi" at Constantinople to whose fine abilities Kinglake has done full justice in his *Invasion of the Crimea*.

The eldest son, Thomas, is Raikes, the fashionable lounger at courts and clubs, and the diarist *par excellence* of the "best" society of his day. His *Diary* was dedicated, when published, to Napoleon III., and Charles Greville wrote the preface. He was a shrewd, observant man, but gave up business, for which he was trained after leaving Eton, and became a fashionable lounger. His *Diary* is well known and appreciated for its fund of anecdote. His *Letters from St. Petersburg and Paris since 1830* is also a well-known volume.

The second son, the Rev. Henry Raikes, M.A. St. John's, Cambridge, entered the Church, and became eminent as a leader of the Evangelical School. In 1832 he was appointed Chancellor of the Diocese of Chester. He married in 1802 the eldest daughter of Jacob Whittington, Esq., of Theobarton Hall, Norfolk, and died in 1854. Canon Hugh Stowell, knowing him intimately, says of him: "His personal endowments were distinguished, his mind of no common compass and power, his imagination rich, his taste refined, his literary attainments varied and elegant, his fortune ample, the respect paid him universal, the prospects held out to his ambition full of promise; yet he was perfectly free from arrogance or assumption. . . . He was as accessible to the poor as to the rich. It was touching to see his stately figure bent down to hearken to the tale of some ragged mendicant, or to catch the accents of some suppliant child." Yet he suffered greatly: "Not even his own family suspected the anguish he must have undergone, so signally was it veiled by his patience." Again, he was "the nursing father" of charities.

With these words in our minds, we get a fuller knowledge of the man than we otherwise should in the letter which he wrote to his brother Thomas, June 5th, 1840. He was in London, and he wrote: "London is overflowing; the Park, the streets, are all too small for the multitudes that circulate through them; but the world does not look cheerful. The shops are splendid, the houses beautiful, the town itself in many respects improved; but whether I look at things with a graver eye, or whether the selfish spirit of the day is visited on itself, and the love of pleasure is the cause of its own disappointment, the Great City does not seem a happy city."

The son of the Chancellor—also Henry Raikes—inherited many of the finest qualities of his father, by whom he was appointed Registrar of the Diocese of Chester. He was also a Cambridge man: graduated at

Corpus Christi College, obtained a Mawson Scholarship, and left the University with a "double second." He entered the Middle Temple, and was called to the Bar in 1836. He married the youngest daughter of the Ven. Archdeacon Wrangham, and became Registrar of Chester in 1837. He wrote an elaborate, but not well-known, treatise on the English Constitution. On the death of his father his fortune was larger than his needs, and his private charities were on the most liberal scale. For example, to the necessitous clergy he gave £1,100 a year. All the panegyrics which appeared in the Press on his death in 1863 fell short of what those who knew and loved him best would have.

"The memoirs," wrote one of the family,* "can give no idea of the strength of his domestic affections, the playful brightness of his humour at his own dinner table, the wonderful clearness of his memory, and the extreme and self-denying simplicity which characterised all the habits of the man, whose heart and head were ever open to the claims of poverty, or to schemes for advancing the interests of our Church and helping the ministers."

When we hear so much of "selfishness" amongst men, such tributes are refreshing to the heart.

The public, well-informed as they usually are, have not been in the habit of associating the late Right Hon. Henry Cecil Raikes, M.P., Chairman of Ways and Means, and Postmaster-General, with the Founder of Sunday

* In a letter to the Author.

schools. He was, however, the son of the Registrar of Chester, and the great-grandson of Thomas, the younger brother of Robert, "the Man of Gloucester."

Now that he is dead, it may be said that the literary traditions of his family passed into safe keeping. He was educated at Trinity College, Cambridge, and the public are now acquainted with the volumes of his letters and correspondence, edited by Henry St. John Raikes, his son, on whom literary gifts have descended.

As far as the limits of this volume will allow, we have given a sketch of the members of the Raikes family outside of Gloucester; and the reader is now in possession of certain strongly-marked individual traits which have not been weakened by descent. Whatever their weaknesses, the Raikeses were a progressive race, apparently tenacious in matters of principle, shrewd in business, and showed much forethought in their marriages. Not only has there been a survival, but an improvement in descent of an old and vigorous stock, and, underlying the shrewdness and caution wanted for advancing family interests, there seems to be always a benevolent and sympathetic spirit. It was not in *one* member only, but in all of whom we get the most knowledge; and, with this in our minds, we may return to Gloucester with some hope of understanding both Robert the father and Robert the son differently, if not better, than they have hitherto been understood.

THE GLOUCESTER BRANCH.

ROBERT RAIKES THE ELDER

was baptized at Hessle, in Yorkshire, on the 22nd April, 1690, and, bearing in mind what were the habits of the period amongst Church people with regard to early christenings, we may assume that he was born about this date. It has already been mentioned that he came into Gloucester when about thirty years of age, and it is the fact that his previous life had not been entirely colourless.

Whether he was regularly apprenticed to the business of a printer is not known, but it is probable that he was, and that he served his time at York. Thomas Gent, the eminent printer of York, wrote an autobiography, and he and Raikes, who were of one age, were so friendly in the year 1718 that Gent, not himself able to accept an offer of partnership, "or take so much standing wages as would subsist me" with Mr. Hasbert, of Norwich, recommended Raikes in his room. This is the first glimpse we have of the young man on the look out to settle himself somewhere. He must also have known his trade,* or a practical printer would not have recommended him to Mr. Hasbert, of Norwich, or have referred to him later as a "master" at Gloucester. If Raikes went to Norwich he did not stay there, for in the same year (1718) he went

---

* He turned out some excellent work. "I possess," writes Mr. H. Y. J. Taylor, "'Cantatas and Songs,' by B. Gunn, organist, Gloucester Cathedral, both music and type splendidly printed by R. Raikes, Gloucester, 1736."

to St. Ives, in Huntingdonshire, and started a newspaper —a new and rare thing in the provinces in those days.

He appears to have had a passion for starting newspapers, which, however, differed very little in size from pamphlets, and it was the custom amongst the educated to call them so to a much later date. His first venture was the *St. Ives Post Boy; or, The Loyal Packet*. It is described as "A Collection of the most Material Occurrences, Foreign and Domestick. Together with an Account of Trade." This was to be a weekly production, and its price three halfpence. R. Raikes appears in the imprint, and the place of publication is "Water Lane, near the Bridge, where Advertisements are taken in, and all sorts of Books Printed."

The *Post Boy*, however, galloped too fast, and gave way to the *St. Ives Mercury* in 1720, about which time he appears to have been on friendly terms with a young man of the same habits and pursuits, and with whom he formed a partnership. This was Mr. William Dicey, of Northampton, and Messrs. Raikes and Dicey started the *Northampton Mercury; or, The Monday's Post* (a weekly) on the 2nd May, 1720. Messrs. Raikes and Dicey next set up a printing press in the city of Gloucester, and the *Gloucester Journal* was established in 1722. It seems probable that Raikes came to Gloucester alone, leaving Dicey to look after the Northampton business; and when the partnership was dissolved, on or before 1725, Mr. Dicey retained the *Northampton Mercury*, which became a very valuable family property.

It is probable that the inducement to Raikes to settle in Gloucester was his engagement to Sarah, daughter of John Niblett, of Fairford. This was a lady with property; but she did not survive her wedded happiness long, but died and was buried at Fairford, and her husband took out letters of administration on the 19th August, 1724.* There was one daughter, Sarah, who died in 1839.

The first number of the *Gloucester Journal* appeared April 9th, 1722, and a descriptive advertisement was issued about one month previously—March 10th. Robert Raikes was by this time an adept in drawing up these notices. It ran as follows:—" At the Printing Office against the 'Swan Inn' in Gloucester will be shortly published Weekly a Newspaper entitled the *Gloucester Journal*, which will contain not only the most authentic Foreign and Domestick News, but also the price of Corn, Goods, &c., at Bear Key in London, and all the Trading Cities and Market Towns 50 miles herewith. The Paper will be suitable to all Degrees and Capacities and will be collected with all the care that money or industry is capable of procuring. N.B.—At the aforesaid Printing Office any Shopkeeper or others may have all sorts of Bills and Advertisements Printed in the best Fashion, as

* The marriage took place on the 25th February, 1722, not quite two months before the *Gloucester Journal* was started. The letters of administration were granted to " Robertum Raikes, de civit. Glouc., stationer." The lady was probably very young, for in the official entry it appears that administration of the estate of Sarah Raikes, of Gloucester, was granted to Robert Raikes, *her father*. He was then thirty-four years of age. No mention is made of the nature or value of the wife's effects. The place of interment is mentioned in Bigland's *Gloucestershire*.

also their Signs with any other Ornaments very curiously Engraved on Wood at reasonable Rates."

The business was that of newspaper proprietors and general jobbing printers, and they also did book work. It may be mentioned that the press used was of a very primitive construction, namely, a screw press. The use of the lever, as in the old "Stanhope" press, was not at that date invented. The rate of production by a screw press was very slow, and it may safely be presumed that the circulation of the *Journal* was, at first, very limited.

Robert Raikes *pere* was, as already stated, three times married. His second wife was Ann, sister of William Mond, M.D., of Walthamstow, Essex.

The second wife, married about one year after the death of the first, had at least three children, two of whom died in infancy. Mr. Raikes lived in the parish of St. Mary de Crypt, and the registers of baptisms and burials furnish the only information about his family which we possess.

The first entries are: October 18th, 1726: Robert, son of Robert and —— Raykes, of St. Mary de Crypt, was born, and died the month following, namely, November 8th. In both entries the name is spelt "Raykes." The next entry is—"1729, March 18th: Elizabeth, daughter of Mr. Robert Raikes, printer, by Ann, his wife." This Elizabeth survived and was married on the 16th May, 1751, to Thomas Jeffreys, of London. This was in her father's lifetime and no more seems to be known about her. The next entry is—"1731, September

10th: Martha, daughter of Robert Raikes, by Ann, his wife." This Martha was buried on the 26th September, 1732, and on September 10th, 1733, the sickly children were followed by their sickly mother, the entry being simply—" 1733, September 10th: Ann, wife of Robert Raikes."

The third marriage was to Mary, daughter of the Rev. Richard Drew, of Nailsworth, but the date is not known, and she became the mother of one daughter and five sons, all of whom, as we have already seen, succeeded very well in the world. The third wife was twenty-five years her husband's junior, and survived him twenty-two years, so that her numerous family had all the benefit of her tenderness and judgment at periods of life when they were most needed.

This third wife alone is mentioned on the memorial tablet in St. Mary de Crypt Church.* As stated, Sarah, the first wife, was buried at Fairford; the second, Ann,

---

* The tablet is in Latin, and, translated, reads as follows :—

SACRED TO THE MEMORY
OF
ROBERT RAIKES,
LATE PRINTER IN THIS CITY,
WHO DEPARTED THIS LIFE ON THE 7TH DAY OF SEPTEMBER,
IN THE YEAR { OF OUR SALVATION, 1757,
OF HIS AGE, 68 ;

ALSO OF
MARY,
HIS BELOVED WIFE, DAUGHTER OF THE REV. RICHARD DREW,
WHO DIED THE 30TH OCTOBER,
IN THE YEAR { OF OUR SALVATION, 1779,
OF HER AGE, 65.

and the third, Mary, lie in the family vault in the south chancel of St. Mary de Crypt Church. The two first marriages seem to have been quite forgotten when the marble monument was fixed on the church wall, *not where it is now* but above the vault.

Robert Raikes the elder lived the whole of his life in the parish of St. Mary de Crypt. All his children were baptized in St. Mary de Crypt Church, and it seems probable that he never removed from the dwelling-house next to the "Swan (or Black Swan) Inn," where he started in business.* Part of the house is still standing, and is described "as old and heavily timbered, spacious and roomy." Robert, the son, was probably born and lived in this house until after his father's death, when he removed to the Southgate Street. What makes it probable that Robert the elder never removed from this house is, that the premises extended into the Black Fryars, and it was from the Black Fryars that Robert the younger removed in 1758.

Little is known in the city of Gloucester of Robert the elder, except that he lived there. He held no municipal office; but was an enterprising man, as shown by his getting his London news from the celebrated Edward Cave, founder of the *Gentleman's Magazine*, and printing Parliamentary minutes and votes when it was a serious offence to do so. That he had artistic tastes which he was unable to satisfy is shown by his

* The "Swan Inn" originally stood at Pye Corner, near the Southgate, and in the parish of St. Mary de Crypt.—Mr. Taylor.

constant changes in the headlines and "make-up" of his newspaper. He took an interest in parish affairs, and was elected Overseer for St. Mary de Crypt in 1729. He wrote a cramped, old-fashioned, hand, and always signed his name in full—Robert Raikes,—whilst the son, who was guardian to the poor for the years 1775, 1776, and 1779, always signed his name R. Raikes. This signature he used throughout his life.

The *Gentleman's Magazine* of 1749 gives us one of the very few references in existence on which we may rely for an appreciation of the character of Robert the elder. It was the custom of the time to collect money for charitable purposes by what was known as "Briefs"—the word is now disused, except in a technical sense amongst lawyers. The *Gentleman*, in an article entitled "Charges for Briefs," showed that newspaper proprietors were, on occasion, sufficiently philanthropic not to charge for them as advertisements; and by way of illustration it is said: "R. Raikes, printer of the *Gloucester Journal*, inserted *gratis* many acknowledgments concerning Honiton fire, and by his zeal, and that of other considerate persons, such handsome collections have been made upon that and the like occasions in the said county, that though its numerous monasteries and such religious houses are no more, there is not less room for that old saying, 'God's in Gloucestershire.'"

Three things he set his face against in his *Journal*: the waste of grain foods in the distillation of spirits, the inhuman treatment of debtors and criminals, and cock fighting. With regard to the latter, the following sarcastic notice appears in his paper a year before his death:

"This is to give notice to all lovers of cruelty and promoters of misery that at the 'George Inn' on Wednesday, in Whitsun week, will be provided for their diversion that savage sport of cock fighting, which cannot but give delight to every breast thoroughly divested of humanity: and for the musick and oaths and curses [which] will not fail to resound round the pit, so that this pastime must be greatly approved of by such as have no reverence for the Deity, nor benevolence for His creatures."

Those who at this distant date would make a study of the son, will share in the regret that so little is known of the father. There is, however, just sufficient preserved to enable us to see that there was in the son an hereditary bias towards unselfish social reforms.

ROBERT RAIKES THE YOUNGER.

The "Man of Gloucester" was probably born in the old premises next to the "Swan (or Black Swan) Inn," in the month of September, 1736,[*] and he was baptized

[*] The *Dictionary of National Biography* says Raikes was born 14th September, 1735. This is a common error. In the latest Raikes pedigree, "corrected to January 25th, 1897," no date for birth is given. The entry is—"b. at Gloucester, bapt. at St. Mary de Crypt, 24 Sep., 1736." The date 14th September, 1735, is apocryphal, and the error commenced with Fosbroke's *History of Gloucester*, 1819. The mural tablets in St. Mary de Crypt Church do not record the date of birth. The old practice was to baptize children so soon after birth that the baptismal register was relied on as evidence of age, in the absence of some entry made at the time in a Family Bible or Prayer Book. The age "75" at the time of death is right or wrong according to the mode of computation, whether from the last birthday or to the birthday next ensuing.

in the church of St. Mary de Crypt, in the city of Gloucester. The official entry in the Register of Baptisms is:—"Sep. 24, 1736. Robert, son of Robert and Mary Raikes, of this parish."

A much more classical quarter has been selected for the birthplace of the man who made the name of Raikes illustrious and enduring; namely, in Palace Yard, under the shadow of the Cathedral. This old house still stands, and is looked upon by strangers with veneration. It is, however, in the neighbouring parish of St. Mary de Lode, and has been the habitation of some of the aristocratic families of the city. The Mee family, one of whose daughters was an ancestress of Lord Palmerston, at one time lived there. The Rev. Richard Raikes (Robert Raikes' brother), who married Ann Mee in 1774, is said to have resided there for a short time, and so birth may have been given to an error now quite respectable for its antiquity.

So little is known of the childhood and early manhood of Robert the younger, that he has long been the despair of the biographer. Where he was educated is still open to conjecture. Mr. Charles Raikes, C.S.I., writing in 1880 to the Author, says: "My own *idea*—for I know nothing for certain—is that Robert Raikes must have been educated at or near Gloucester. No sooner was he of age than, by the death of his father, he was at once made editor of the *Gloucester Journal*. He could not have succeeded as he did in so difficult a work unless he had been specially trained, and, possibly, under his father's eye and in his father's office."

The late Canon Samuel Lysons, Hempstead Court, writing in 1870, says: "The knowledge I possess of the Raikes family is more scanty than it ought to be, considering that I am doubly connected with it. The Rev. Richard Raikes married a second cousin, and Mr. William Matthew Raikes a first cousin of my father's. . . . I cannot tell you where Robert Raikes was married or where he was educated, but probably [he was educated] either at the College school or the Crypt school in Gloucester."

Mrs. Weller-Ladbroke was equally without knowledge as to her beloved father's place of education, his professional training, and the place of his marriage.

St. John's College, Cambridge, having been mostly affected by the Raikes family, and Richard Raikes having been educated there, the following letters on the subject will not be without interest:—

"29 Jesus Lane, Cambridge,
"*March 2nd*, 1863.

"DEAR TEASDALE,—Robert Raikes, the benefactor to the city of Gloucester, is usually stated to have studied at this University, but it is certain he never graduated. I have an impression that he was a member of St. John's College. Unfortunately, however, the volume containing the matriculations at that College for the period at which Mr. Raikes would have entered the University has been lost. The only chance, therefore, of finding Mr. Raikes' College is by searching the *Matricula* at the Registrar's office. This I will do at the earliest opportunity, and, if successful, will forward you the results of my investigation.

"I should feel obliged to your correspondent, Mr. Harris, for any information respecting this Robert Raikes, whom we propose to notice in some future volume of *Athenæ Cantabrigienses*.

"Yours truly,

"THOMPSON COOPER."

"Clare College, Cambridge,

"*February 27th*, 1863.

"SIR,—I am strongly of opinion that the statement in the *Gentleman's Magazine*, to which you refer, that Robert Raikes was a graduate of this University, is an erroneous one. I have referred to the published list of the graduates (the so-called 'Graduati Cantabrigienses'), and find only two graduates of the name of Raikes—one, Richard, of St. John's College, who took his A.B. degree in 1767 and his A.M. in 1770; the other, Henry Raikes, also of St. John's, who took his A.B. degree in 1804 and his A.M. in 1807.

"It is in the highest degree improbable that Robert Raikes should have graduated here and his name have been omitted from the 'Graduati Cantabrigienses.' The absence of his name from that list leaves me without any means of ascertaining any particulars respecting him. If he ever was a student of Cambridge without graduating, it would be likely that he was entered at St. John's

College, since the other two gentlemen of the same name were both of that College.*

"If you think there is any probability of this, it might be worth while writing to the Master or one of the tutors of St. John's College, mentioning, if you can, the year of Mr. Raikes' birth as a guide to them in consulting their Admission book. I have little doubt that they would be willing to refer to that book if there were any probability of the name being found there.

"I am, Sir, yours faithfully,

"E. ATKINSON, Vice-Chancellor."

"St. John's College, Cambridge,
"*March 18th,* 1863.

"SIR,—Finding no trace of Robert Raikes in our Register, which is, indeed, defective about the period in question, I placed your note in the hands of Mr. Mayor, who has great acquaintance with the archives of the College and the University; but he, I am sorry to say, can give me no further information than what is contained in the enclosed note.

"I am, dear Sir, yours faithfully,

"W. H. BATESON."

[*Enclosure.*]
"St. John's,
"*March 17th,* 1863.

"My dear Master,—R. Raikes, of St. John's, has Latin Alcaics in the Cambridge verses published in 1763,

* Also Timothy Raikes, his great-grandfather.

signature *S. This, however, is probably Richard R., B.A. in 1767. I seem to have no other note in the name. I enclose the letter, and remain,

     Very truly yours,
        JOHN E. B. MAYOR."

A search was made by the Rev. John Griffiths, M.A., keeper of the archives of the University of Oxford, with the result that Robert Raikes did not take a degree there. The Crypt Grammar School was founded by John Coke, an alderman of Gloucester, in 1528. John Moore, D.D., afterwards Archbishop of Canterbury, and George Whitefield were educated there; and if the young Raikes was also educated there, the old Grammar School will have no reason to be ashamed of three of its scholars.*

The trouble taken in this search is not to be regretted, because it strengthens the presumption that the young Robert was, from the first, intended to carry on the business of his father, and that his education was such as best fitted him for it. The search at Cambridge has also made us more familiar with his brother Richard, whose name in the city of Gloucester is, even to-day, as a sweet incense from good deeds.

The latest investigations render it almost certain that the young Robert learnt his trade in the ordinary way, though there cannot be found any trace of indentures. It is, however, known that he was in the habit of using

* Dr. Moore obtained his Pembroke Scholarship from the Crypt Grammar School. He was translated to the See of Canterbury in 1783, and died 1805.

a "composing stick" on occasions, and there is now in the Museum at Gloucester a compositor's metal "stick" which a former old compositor in the *Journal* office declared was, in his time, always called "Mr. Raikes' stick." This man, named Cox, entered the *Journal* office after Mr. Raikes' time, and became foreman printer, or overseer; and he made a declaration to Mr. H. Y. J. Taylor to the effect that the "stick" which he offered to the Museum was known in the office as Mr. Raikes', and that he had heard the old compositors in the office say that *they had seen Mr. Raikes use it* when they were busy. This is not conclusive of anything except of a practical knowledge, which, though it might be easily acquired without indentures of apprenticeship, is yet seldom acquired except by skilled workmen.* This is the only Raikes relic in the Museum, and it is not generally known to be there.

The business of a printer in the early part of the seventeenth century appealed much more to the imagination of the public than it does to-day. The comparatively small number of persons who could read, and the rarity of printing presses invested printing, as an art, with something mysterious and supernatural. To have seen a thing in print was, in the popular estimation, to have seen the truth. To "swear the print out of the Bible" and to deny the truth of what had been "read

* Mr. Taylor informed me that a person whom he told that Mr. Raikes was "a printer by trade" was highly offended with him, thinking that some offence to the man's memory was intended. The trade of printer is rooted in honour, and no man can disdain a printer for ancestor without betraying his own littleness.

in a paper," amongst masses of people in country districts in our own century, was a current saying implying a hardihood not to be surpassed. Lord Macaulay, quoting from Nichols's *Literary Anecdotes*, says although there had been a great increase in printing presses within a few years, yet in 1724 there were 34 counties in which there was no printer, one of these counties being Lancashire! When the elder Raikes set up his press in Gloucester, he was, perhaps, the only printer from Exeter to Hereford, the whole of Wales, and part of the Midlands. A printer had a great deal to learn outside of the art and mystery of his craft, so hemmed in and hedged about was he with laws designed to make his very existence a terror. That the young Raikes was well equipped for his work is evidenced by the fact that on his father's death he "stepped into his shoes," and almost immediately afterwards extended and improved the business and the newspaper.

His father altered the headlines and make-up of the paper three or four times between the years 1722 and 1742. He seemed dissatisfied with the appearance of the sheet, and in 1760 Robert (the son) made a final alteration, the title being in large ornamental scrip, *Glocester Journal*, between a female figure (Prudentia) and the arms of the city between two lions as supporters. The original size of the paper was $12\frac{3}{4}$ by $7\frac{3}{4}$ inches. In August, 1742, it was enlarged to 16 by $10\frac{1}{2}$ inches. After the young Robert succeeded it was enlarged to 18 by 11 inches, and in 1792 to 20 by 14 inches;

and it was not again permanently enlarged during his proprietorship. On the first number the price of the paper is not stated; but it was 3d. for many years, then 3½d. (the halfpenny being for the Government stamp), then 4d. in 1793, when the impressed Government stamp was increased to 1d. In 1797 it was 6d., and was sold at this price when transferred to Mr. D. Walker in 1802.*

At the age of 21 the young Raikes suddenly found himself the responsible head of a family — children, still growing, to be educated and placed in positions becoming their rank in life. He did not marry until he was 31 years of age, and then he married Anne, the daughter of Thomas Trigge, of Newenham, in the county of Gloucester, and the only sister of General Sir Thomas Trigge, K.C.B., and Rear-Admiral John Trigge. The marriage was by Bishop's license, and took place in St. James' Church, Piccadilly, December 23rd, 1767. The mother of the bride (Mrs. Napier on her second marriage) and Thomas Trigge, her brother, were two of the witnesses. On the opposite page is given a tracing of the entry in the church register:—

* The paper remained in the Walker family until 1871, when it was transferred to Mr. Thomas Henry Chance, who was sole proprietor until 1881, when Mr. E. Bland and Mr. Harry Godwin Chance, M.A., became his partners. In the Raikes' time the paper was non-political. It became Whig, or Liberal, with the Walkers, and has never altered its political tone. The *Journal* has for many years been published on a Saturday at one penny. An evening paper is now printed on the new premises, called the *Citizen*, and the old office clock—two centuries old—ticks calmly above a scene of activity which would astonish the old Raikeses could they but witness it. This clock is one of the very few Raikes relics in Gloucester.

No. 378 Robert Rawkes of S.t Mary de Crypt in the City of Gloucester & Ann Trigge of this Parish were married in this Church by Licence from the Bishop of London this twenty third day of December 1767 by me Carparthen Trigge

This Marriage was solemnized between us

Mariticus Ann Trigge

In Presence of Jane Hemings Ann Raynier

Tho.s Trigge

The bride was at the time residing with her mother in Great Pulteney Street, Golden Square, W. All that we know is that the bride was 23 years of age, and that the wedding appeared amongst the Society paragraphs of the day. The bride was brought home, and lived in the Southgate Street in the fine specimen of an old Gloucester house, with varnished timbered front, at which every passing stranger looks with interest. In Raikes' time they were two houses, and he occupied the one nearest to Bolt Lane, wherein the printing office was after its removal from the Blackfriars in 1758. Here the family were born, and here he laid the foundations of his claim to public gratitude for his labours and the quiet, persistent manner in which he developed his successive schemes for prison reform, and the education of children. In both these matters he regarded himself as the "instrument" of Providence.

Altogether nine children were born to him. The first, a son, Robert Powell, died in infancy; his second son, also named Robert Powell, died when 11 years of age. His family consisted of daughters—five of them—until 1783, when (happy omen!) on the very day on which he announced to the world his plan of Sunday schools, a son was born. The name of "Powell" had overshadowed the first two, and fortune was not to be tempted again, so this boy was christened Robert Napier, and he was followed the next year by another son, William Henley, both of whom survived —the one going into the Church, and the other into the Coldstream Guards, in which he attained to the rank of colonel.

The eldest son graduated B.A. Oriel College, Cambridge, and took holy orders. In 1811 he was presented by the Bishop of Norwich to the vicarage of Gayton, near Lynn, Norfolk; the following year he became Rector of Hillesden with Drayton, in the same county, and was lastly preferred to the living of Longhope, Gloucester, in 1837. He married, September, 1810, Caroline, the second daughter of the Very Rev. John Probyn, by whom he had five sons and four daughters. Two of the sons attained to the rank of general and major in the army, and three died in India. Three of the daughters married, and became respectively the wives of General Sir Henry Gee Roberts, Captain John Henry Dighton, and Admiral Sir Thomas Thompson, Bart.

The Rev. Robert Napier Raikes (their father) was a very amiable man, of domestic habits and evangelical tendencies. It is related of him that he used to write texts of Scripture on fly-slips of paper, and give them on appropriate occasions to the servants. One evening, seeing a maid-servant very tired after a day's work, he wrote and gave her the following:—" It is in vain for you to rise up early and to go late to rest from labour, eating the bread of sorrows; for to His beloved ones He will give food and sleep."*

Mr. Robert Raikes never held any municipal office in

* This came from the possession of the servant to whom it was given, living at or near Redmarley in 1862.

Gloucester, and it is not quite certain what is to be understood by his appointment on a city commission, unless it was for city improvement or in connection with the improvements in the County Prison. There exist no records of this prison prior to 1783.* He was not a magistrate, and "no trace or record of his exertions" in obtaining the great prison improvements of the place— writes Mr. H. Cartwright, an official in the prison—can now be found. So were it not for the existence of the old files of the *Gloucester Journal*, and a few fugitive notices by Howard in his book, we should possess no reliable knowledge of Robert Raikes's exertions as a prison reformer, and also be without the most useful means of knowing under what circumstances, and in what atmosphere, his own plan of Sunday schools was evolved and the purpose which he intended it to play. What these circumstances and atmosphere were may be faintly understood by reading Howard's description of the condition of Gloucester Castle, which was also the county Bridewell. There was one court for all the prisoners, and one day-room (11 ft. 9 ins. by 10 ft. 7 ins.) for men and women felons. "The free ward for debtors is 19 ft. by 11 ft., where, having no window, part of the

* Letter from Mr. J. Huddleston, deputy governor, to Mr. Harris: "We have no record books in this prison prior to 1783. I am, therefore, unable to give you the information required. I failed to discover any traces of either Mr. Robert Raikes or Howard from the above period, excepting the Grand Jury at the Gloucestershire Assizes, 29th March, 1783, recommended that proper places of confinement and discipline, similar to those recommended by the humane and intelligent Mr. Howard, should be erected in the county."

plaster wall is broke down for light and air. . . . The whole prison was much out of repair, and had not been whitewashed for many years." Many prisoners died of small-pox and gaol fever. "There is no separation of the women or of the Bridewell prisoners. The licentious intercourse of the sexes is shocking to decency and humanity. Many children have been born in the gaol. There is a small chapel, but all the endeavours of the chaplain to promote reformation among the prisoners must necessarily be defeated by the inattention of the magistrates, and their neglect of framing and enforcing good regulations. *Perhaps this is the reason the chaplain seldom attends.*" The chaplain, whose salary was £40 a year, was the Rev. A. B. Evans, curate of St. Mary de Crypt. This gentleman was afterwards headmaster of the Gloucester College School. Mr. Raikes says of him that it was not until at the end of six years' work that he "at last condescended" to take notice of the Sunday school movement.

Robert Raikes's was almost the only kindly, pitying eye which the prisoners saw. He enlisted others to join him in contributing towards the feeding and clothing of these poor creatures, so brought up and treated as scarcely to be held responsible before God or man. It was here that Mr. Raikes learnt his lesson. Mr. Howard perceived this, and said so: "This gentleman [Mr. Raikes] is also the founder of a benevolent and useful institution for the children of the poor of this city. . . . *Perhaps Mr. Raikes's frequent visits to the*

Castle suggested to him this plan as the best means of preventing youth from coming there."

Here is the secret and sustaining motive of Mr. Raikes's Sunday school work. He may himself have revealed it to Howard. In any case, it is a most suggestive and valuable sentence, and it at once places Mr. Raikes apart from all others who, at various times, gave Sunday instruction to children, either contemporaneously with or before him.

The printing and newspaper business was carried on from 1757 to 1802, when it was transferred to Mr. David Walker, the former printer of the *Hereford Times*, a part of the consideration being an annuity on the joint lives of Mr. and Mrs. Raikes. The value of the business was estimated at £1,500 per annum. The sum paid for the copyright is not known. The annuity was £500, being estimated at one-third of the net profit, and it was paid down to 1828.

The honorary freedom of the city was presented to Mr. Raikes in 1804; and with this exception, from the date of his retirement from business the whole of his life is a blank to us, except for the impressions upon the minds of the aged witnesses who have left their testimonies behind them. He was a member of the Stationers' Company, which, since 1556, had exercised extensive powers and privileges; but as his interest was a mere money investment, this did not occupy his time, and he was not a member of any of the literary or scientific societies of his day. Not a scrap of paper written on by him after his retirement has been preserved. When he retired from business his life was finished but for his own family, and the little children whom he had watched grow in obedience and love towards him, and exhibit to all mankind the divine image which before seemed to have been hopelessly overlaid with ignorance and filth. The reforms having been carried out at the County Prison and Bridewell, his attention was mostly devoted to the Sunday schools, and he showed an increased and increasing fondness for having the children around him in his house and on his grounds in Bell Lane.

And when the end came, it came suddenly. His daughter says he was alarmingly ill for only half an hour. He may have had premonitory warnings, for he sometimes told his "children" that one day he must leave them, and, in his own language, made them sorry. In the evening of the fatal day he was in his "study," and had been reading. When he was removed his spectacles[*] were lying upon some papers, just as though they had fallen from his hand. He was found sitting at his desk by a member of the household, into whose possession the spectacles afterwards passed as a remembrance. This was Mrs. James, the housekeeper (distantly connected with their present possessor); but she kept no account of the last moments of Mr. Raikes, probably knowing no

---

[*] These spectacles are still in existence, and in the possession of Mr. Richings, of Gloucester, who showed them to the Editor in November, 1898. They are one of the few, very few, genuine Raikes relics in the city. The glasses are small pebbles, thick tortoise-shell rims, and short side clips, about 3 inches long, with perforated ends. The hinges and mounts are of silver.

more than that there was a sudden illness followed by a sudden death.

His will was not made until about two years before death, and there are no specific bequests to servants or institutions. His family knew his wishes and he trusted them to act loyally. He remembered his "children," and wished them to attend his funeral and be made happy (even at the parting) with a shilling and cake apiece. They had never had such a foster-father, and when they went out into the world and met men who frowned on them, the remembrance of Raikes grew fresh again; and so it was that in 1863, when the Author visited those who had been Raikes's "children," their aged hearts grew young and soft when his name was mentioned.

The personal devotion which Mr. Raikes took in his own schools and school children renders it unnecessary to do more than mention the statement made again and again, and with much confidence, by the Rev. John Adey, an Independent Minister, who died at Bexley Heath, Kent, in 1869. He was a Gloucester man, and in his lifetime wrote and stated that in Mr. Raikes's lifetime *Sunday schools were extinct in Gloucester*, and that he and others resurrectionised them. The "Memorial Adey Schools Fund" was got up in 1870 by way of recognition of his invaluable services in re-establishing Sunday schools in Gloucester.

The statement has been so often repeated, that, as a matter of history, we give the personal narrative of one of the young men who were associated with Mr. Adey in establishing new and entirely independent Sunday schools in the city:—

Mr. Samuel Pitt* said: "When I was about seventeen years of age I used to act as deputy-clerk at St. Mary de Crypt, where Mr. Raikes used to attend. . . . I used to attend the church of St. Mary de Crypt on Sundays, Wednesdays, and Fridays in each week. Mr. Raikes used to come to church on every one of those days. I never saw the school children at church on weekdays. . . . I knew Mrs. Critchley and her daughter, Mrs. Packer, and I think I knew the man Cox.† . . . *Mr. Raikes's Sunday schools were never extinct in Gloucester* during his lifetime, and Mr. Adey must be under a mistake. I knew Mr. Adey, Mr. Curtis, Mr. Sims, Mr. Taylor, and the rest, who, *with myself*, joined in getting up a Sunday school in Gloucester. We subscribed 2s. 6d. each to buy books, &c. Our schools were held in Leather Bottle Lane and the Island, and the children were taken to the Lady Huntingdon's Chapel. We started several schools. Mr. Curtis came from Worcester, and was full of zeal. Mr. Raikes's schools were in excellent condition when we started ours. . . . Mr. Adey is mistaken about his 'resurrection' of Sunday schools in Gloucester. *We started new schools*, and did not interfere with the old ones. Mr. Adey has confused my name with that of Mr. Thomas, because I was an apprentice with a man named

---

* *See* Chapter III., on Punishment in Sunday Schools.

† Charles Cox, the Soot Alley schoolboy. *See* Chapter II.

Thomas at that time. He calls me Thomas, and I explained this to him some time ago when he was here. I know Sunday schools were not extinct at the time, nor looking sickly, because every Sunday evening, when we were trying to get a Dissenters' school up, I used to see the children marching to the church headed by a man named Fream—Daniel Fream, I think. I was never one of Mr. Raikes's schoolboys. I recollect going to Mr. King (who was the master of a school started by Mr. Raikes, I think), and asking him, out of a bit of fun, to let me come, and he said: 'No; the school is not for such ones as you. Your parents can get you taught.'"

That there was a failure in the historical continuity of Sunday schools in Gloucester, by whomever founded, in the lifetime of Mr. Raikes is not true. He took care of that so far as what he called his own schools were concerned, and the city has been spared an indignity which the Christian world would not hesitate to associate with disgrace.

When the time came for Robert Raikes to die the event caused no unusual stir in the city. The only narrative which we have with the touch of authenticity about it is that of his daughter's, Mrs. Ladbroke. The Sunday school children who were his "own," alone followed the coffin and sang over it whilst it was being removed from the house into Crypt Alley, and sang over it as it was carried, shoulder high, into the church. It was only for a few yards that this unique procession followed their benefactor, but it now posseses an historical interest. The pulse of the citizens was not stirred; only Mr. Eycott, a furniture broker, remembered that "there was a many and a respectable lot of people at the funeral." He was about 10 years old at the time, and received his shilling and piece of cake after all was over, like the rest.

No funeral sermon was preached. Mr. Hanson, an old citizen, was of opinion that "funeral sermons were not much in fashion then in Gloucester"; that the people of Gloucester did not understand what Sunday schools had done for, and meant to, the world; and that they certainly did not understand and appreciate the man who was, in some respects, their greatest citizen. William Whitehead remembered that the general feeling was "that Gloucester had lost a good man!"

The obituary notice which appeared in the *Journal* is very short, and, in one particular, wrong. It is as follows:

"Died on Friday* evening, April 5 [1811], suddenly, at his house in this city, Robert Raikes, Esq., aged 75, who in the year 1783 first instituted Sunday schools, and by his philanthropic exertions contributed to the adoption of them in different parts of the kingdom."

* This mention of Friday enables us to test the accuracy of the statement made by Anne Hannam in 1862, who said that Mr. Raikes's funeral was on a Saturday morning. This is quite true. Mr. Raikes was buried on the Saturday week following his decease. According to modern practice, this seems an unusually long time; but it appears to have been customary in his family to keep the body above ground until the eighth day. Mrs. Raikes (his widow) died March 9th, and was buried March 17th, 1828—also eight days after death. Miss Hannam was 73 when she made her statement. *See* Chapter II.—" Human Documents."

No wonder that so many people laid claim to having priority over Robert Raikes in the matter of teaching children on Sundays, when the published date was some three years after the opening of the schools in Sooty Alley, and elsewhere, in the city of Gloucester.

After the funeral Mrs. Raikes removed to the "Spa," London Road. Although she was a nervous and delicate woman, she attained her 85th year, and the immediate cause of death was severe shock to the system when it was discovered that burglars were in the house. Mrs. Raikes was a lady with a slight touch of disdain in her manner for the lower orders. She was always called "Madam," the same as "Madam" Pitt, the wife of Mr. Samuel Pitt, at one time M.P. for the city. She was in the habit of riding in a Sedan chair, of which Mr. Eycott (above quoted) was one of the bearers. He says of her that she was "a kind-hearted and charitable woman, but did not like being imposed on." The *Gloucester Journal* says, in an obituary notice, that she was "a lady of pious and benevolent disposition, with an active and well-cultivated mind, and a heart ever open as day to melting charity."

The immediate connection of the Raikes family with the Cathedral city was now practically closed, but the name remains an imperishable inheritance.

NOTE.—For the Raikes' Jubilee year in 1831 numerous hymns for Sunday school children were written and composed. Mr. John Holland, the literary executor of James Montgomery, whose Jubilee hymns were sung in every clime, informed the Author that no letter from Raikes was in the Poet's possession, nor was there any specific allusion to him in any of the

Poet's papers. The poor of Gloucester, however, had their poem long before, and were accustomed to hear it sung in their villages and in the streets of their market towns on Saturday nights. The composer, "George Stone, the celebrated poet of Bristol," even for a ballad writer was not very particular about his feet, or his rhymes or his dates, for he made Mr. Raikes 106 years old! He, however, knew his audience and the string to play on. The copies of the "poem" are scarce now, and so we reproduce it :—

"VERSES ON ROBERT RAIKES OF GLO'STER CITY.

Composed by George Stone, the Celebrated Poet of Bristol.

" A man Robert Raikes up in Gloucestershire dwelt,
And for the dear souls of young children he felt
 When they did in ignorance lie ;
And there he did form out those wonderful rules
To build in the city some good Sunday schools
 That children might know God on high.

" His heart was the temple of mercy and love,
For he praised God for his mercies above,
 And done good for children also ;
And if he once found their parents in want,
Then to their mothers and fathers would grant
 Some money and clothing below.

" He was the first founder of schools in this land,
And to this grand cause he put forth his hand,
 And hope God his labours would bless ;
So now in this nation his name will be dear,
Because he did help the poor when he was here
 And beg God to bless their distress.

" He was born in seventeen hundred and five,
For there up in Glo'ster for years he did thrive,
 And was a great help to the poor ;
While he up in Glo'ster was living long there,
He kept a few schools open for children where
 The Gospel of Christ was taught pure.

" But when the dear Saviour saw fit he should die
A great many schools he did quickly supply
 With money and clothing and food ;
And when he departed this life full of years,
The people then shed a few penitent tears,
 In wishing him back to do good."

This brother of Robert's passed through life without calling forth either the envy or the antagonism of men. The gentle and refined nature he possessed was singularly out of touch with the pushing combativeness of the Raikes of Hull, of his own father, and of his brother Robert, whose look of prosperity sometimes gave offence as he walked along the streets.

The Rev. Richard Raikes, M.A.

He may not have been more charitable in deeds and opinions than his brother, but he had none of the arts of the man who had his way to make in the world, and none of the swagger of the man who knew himself to be successful. The one name for Richard Raikes is that of Christian gentleman.

He was a St. John's College, Cambridge, man, and after taking orders he returned to Gloucester, and was appointed tutor to the daughters of Lady Guise. In 1793 he was appointed to the Perpetual Curacy of Maisemore, and the reputation he left behind him is that of a learned but simple-hearted gentleman, full of sympathy and good desires, and untouched by personal vanity. Maisemore was a village, and he did not reside there but in the city; and it is in the city that his deeds of charity were, forty-four years after his death, well remembered.* He rode over to Maisemore on a little pony, and when he could no longer ride he emancipated it, leaving it in the care of a gentleman at Maisemore Lodge, and in the enjoyment of perpetual freedom.

Sixty years of his life were passed in much suffering and bodily weakness, and so when he saw suffering in others he knew it well, and approached the sick and poor and abandoned with almost feminine gentleness. The streets of the city were either not lighted, or only badly lighted occasionally, and many tales were treasured up in the hearts of the aged about "Parzun Reekes" and his horn lantern, seeking in the dark and worst quarters of the city whom he could comfort and rescue. "He was like a glow-worm of charity," said one.

"He married," says Canon Samuel Lysons, "a lady named Mee,† a cousin of my great-grandmother, and also a cousin of the late Lord Palmerston's mother." He died without issue on September 5th, 1823, in the 80th year of his age; and on the south wall of the chancel

* This is equally true to-day. There is much confusion now about the two brothers, and even at the Centenary in 1880 old scholars talked about Robert when they meant the parson. It is also said and believed that many good things attributed to Robert belong by rights to Richard. —EDITOR.

† This lady's name was Anne, sister to Thomas Mee, twice Mayor of Gloucester, in 1793 and 1804. It was during his mayoralty in 1804 that the freedom of the city was presented to Robert Raikes. She died in 1812, aged 66 years. This is the lady whose family resided in the Palace Yard, wherein it has erroneously been stated that Robert Raikes was born!—*See ante.*

of Maisemore Church is an In Memoriam tablet, on which it is said of him:

"Pious and benevolent, learned and meek, he here laboured almost thirty years as a faithful minister of the Church of Christ. Through sixty years of peculiar suffering and bodily weakness, he manifested to all who knew him the power of faith by the cheerfulness and diligence with which he fulfilled his duties, rejoicing to prove his love for the Redeemer whose mercy he adored, and on whose merits alone he relied for salvation, by entire submission and devotion to His holy will.

"Reader, whosoever thou art, profit by this memorial of one whose delight and enjoyment consisted in doing good to others."

On a tablet in the Cathedral it is said of him, that "he was eminent from his youth as a scholar, but still more eminent as a Christian."

The promise of his youth at St. John's, Cambridge, where he obtained Latin Alcaics in the Cambridge verses, published in 1763—as already stated—was not belied in maturer years; but it is the fact, that if he published any books or sermons, copies of them are not to be found in the Cathedral library at Gloucester. In 1797 he was appointed Treasurer, and afterwards Canon, of St. David's.

His name does not appear in any document or newspaper in connection with the founding and maintenance of Sunday schools. His brother, Robert, never spoke of him by name in any private letters which we have had the privilege of copying, but it may be that he is included in the reference—made more than once—to the "two clergymen" in the city who gave the movement their active support. It has been suggested, and with every probability, that the Rev. Thomas Stock is the other. At present there is nothing enabling us to identify the two clergymen—his brother certainly must be one; but, then, it is difficult to understand Robert, when he complains to Mr. Lewelyn, by letter, that he is "walking alone in the city!" He must mean that he is "walking alone" in his own parish.

The Rev. Richard Raikes took a great personal interest in Sunday schools, and it must have been his own desire that his name was never mentioned. He seems to have been a constant visitor at all schools established in the city, and it is to him that the schools started by the Rev. Thomas Stock mainly owed their existence after the rev. gentleman's death. He was also in advance of his time in respect of popular education, and commenced building a day school, for the education of the poor, in Lower Northgate Street, in the year 1810. The schools were opened in 1813, when Mr. Thomas Holmes was appointed master, as appears on the fly-leaf of the *Teachers' Assistant*, by Mrs. Trimmer, given to him by the rev. gentleman.* The British and Foreign Bible Society was established in 1805, and the Rev. Richard Raikes was among its earliest promoters,

---

* The Author had an interview with Mr. Holmes, who showed him the book. He said he believed "Richard Raikes was an evangelical clergyman, and of his piety no man doubted."

subscribed to it annually, and acted as Secretary to the Gloucester Branch. His more wealthy brother, Thomas, was an annual donor of £50. Scores of Bibles given away by Richard were, in the course of years, attributed to Robert. So far back as 1862, the Author could not find any person in Gloucester possessing a Bible on the fly-leaf of which Robert Raikes had written. To have believed report, these Bibles and Testaments were quite plentiful in districts such as Leather Bottle Lane, but not a single one was found. The handwriting of Richard Raikes on Bibles and other books was fairly common then, but became much less so after the Centenary.

Mr. Raikes Currie, writing to the Author in 1870, says: "The Rev. Richard Raikes, whom I personally knew when a boy, was the perfect model of a Christian gentleman."*

And this is the highest type of man! This chapter contains more than one of the same family answering to this description, and it can nowhere close more satisfactorily than where showing that over a period of three centuries the evolution of this English family has been steadily towards an ideal, possible, though difficult, of attainment.

* " We have no conception of the true grandeur of his life or character. The language of eulogy, of reverence and admiration, would exhaust itself in the following short and simple sentence: He was a true Christian."
—H. Y. J. TAYLOR.

NOTE.—There is some character in the following entries by the Rev. Richard Raikes in the Parish Register of Maisemore, supplied to the Editor by Mr. Conway Dighton :—

1795. Burials.—Sep. 5. Joseph Smith, aged 51. Fractured leg and amputation.
    Oct. 25. John, son of Thos. and Sarah White, a youth ætat 13. Fall from a tree.
1797. April 14. William Clark, an alien, aged 20. Fever.
    April 27. Emma Wadley, aged 20. Consumption. From London.
    May 14. Richard Townsend, a poor traveller from Ross, aged 49.
1812. G. C., a stranger taken up drowned in Severn, aged about 35.

These and all the other entries show the direct personal interest taken in the affairs of his parishioners.

The Rev. Richard Raikes was buried with his wife in a vault in the churchyard of St. Mary de Lode. Mr. Taylor says: "The tomb is in a sad state, the grass is growing over and is corroding or obliterating the inscription on it." With reference to the monument in the Cathedral, Mr. Taylor says: "It is becoming faint and partially obliterated." *See* next chapter for remarks on the tombs of Robert Raikes and the Rev. Thomas Stock.

CHAPTER XVIII.

LAST WORDS.

"Very little is actually known of Raikes's life and character."—MAYOR OF GLOUCESTER, 1880.

"No new thing has been known about Raikes for fifty years."—W. H. GROSER, 1898.

"We are deeply interested in any investigation which can throw more light on his ever blessed career."—PRESIDENT OF WESLEYAN CONFERENCE, 1898.

A REVIEW of all the facts and probabilities leads to the conclusion that the true birth of Sunday schools was not until November 3rd, 1783. All that went before was tentative and experimental; and what was done by others than Raikes, either contemporaneously or before him, seems lacking in the purpose and design of growth and continuity. Unless we go back to the sainted Archbishop of Milan, there is an entire absence of design except so far as it is immediate and personal.

With Robert Raikes, all the evidence points to a slowly maturing purpose, tending towards popular national education. He proceeded by steps. First, the awakening of a spiritual life by discipline. To bring the unruly "savage" elements under control was the first step. The second was to provide elementary education on Sundays, which should (third) merge into a more complete system of national education in day and industrial schools by voluntary effort. His horizon did not extend beyond, but it did extend so far as this. His ideas were somewhat cramped by the prevailing notion that the education of the masses must be done by charity. He worked on this line. For years Sunday schools were charities, and in his own school the girls wore white bonnets and tippets when they went to church, and were as distinguishable as "Raikes's children" as in the neighbouring city of Bristol were "Colston's children." Limited as we now know his ideas were, he was far in advance of his time in his application of them. Pausing here, we may see for ourselves the tremendous distance travelled in little more than a century.

It is not claimed by the most earnest supporters of any layman or divine, preceding or contemporaneous with Mr. Raikes, that they had any set purpose beyond the present, or idea that Sunday schools might merge into, or lead up to, the establishment of something urgently demanded and national. For the scholarly Mr. Stock it is not claimed that he saw beyond the present, nor is it even suggested that his experiences eminently fitted him for working out the evolution of a new race from the lees of Society.

Mr. Raikes always treated 1783 as the birth of the movement. He was like a modern inventor who does not take into account all the time taken up with his experiments, but dates the birth of his invention from the day whereon he files "his complete and final specification." So far as the world is concerned, what has gone before is of little account. In Mr. Raikes's case, he had consumed his time in proving that by discipline and education a "new life" leaped into existence in the souls of the ragged, filthy, badger loving, cursing infants whom he selected from the mass. This was his problem —the creation of a new life, and the Sunday school was his invention, sealed and dated November 3rd, 1783. Writing to Mrs. Harris, of Chelsea, he once makes a reference which points to 1781 as the date when he first put his ideas into operation. This was a friendly, chatty letter, and too much importance should not be attached to it. He says: "Within this month [November, 1787], the minister of my parish has condescended to give me assistance in the laborious work which I have now carried on for six years alone, with little or no support." There is a looseness in Mr. Raikes's composition in the sixty odd original letters which came into the Author's possession, which precludes the idea that he wrote them with any intention of their preservation, or of their ever being appealed to on matters of history. He is very elliptical; so also is he in his newspaper, where space was precious, and his punctuation often leaves very much to be desired.

The absence of certainty when the experiment was first begun destroys, to some extent, the interest which has attached to certain kitchens and dwelling-houses in the city of Gloucester in which "the very first Sunday school in England was started." Within certain radii these "very first Schools" sprang up in the city with the demand for them. There were more at the "Centenary" than in 1863, and in 1863 than at the Jubilee in 1831. From henceforth there is not likely to be any increase, and it is even now difficult to say when the legend that the first Sunday school was opened in the month of July, 1780, became current. It is said that Mr. Raikes gave James King a Bible in July, 1780, and wrote his name and the date of the gift on the fly-leaf; and because Mrs. King was at some time engaged "to mind the children" on Sundays, it is assumed that the date of the gift and the opening of the school are identical. It was not, however, until after the Jubilee, in 1831, that the year 1780, instead of 1781, was adopted, with-

Mrs. King's School.

out sufficient regard to positive testimony. The utmost which can now be said is that Raikes employed Mrs. Meredith to open a "school" (if such it can be called) in Sooty Alley, and Stock employed Mrs. Roberts to open a "school" at a house 103 Northgate Street, and that Mrs. James King was employed about the same time by Raikes or Stock, or by them conjointly. About this last schoolmistress, it must not be forgotten that she was the wife of James King, the steward to "Madam" Pitt, wife of the local Member of Parliament.* It is hardly credible that she and her husband would consent to receive into their dwelling the fine collection of filthy young savages which Raikes first tried his hand on in Sooty Alley. Other "schools" ruled over by respectable women were opened by Stock and Raikes, either separately or conjointly; and some of the large rooms now shown in antiquated houses in the city lanes were the places of schools, but no further interest attaches to them.

Mr. Raikes did open several schools—he speaks of four,—but he took particular interest in *one*, and *one* set of children. The editing and printing of his newspaper did not leave him too much time on Sundays, and he devoted what he had to one set of children, whom he grew accustomed to call "my" children, and these were assembled at Mrs. Critchley's, in the Grey Fryars, about a good stone's throw from his editor's den, in Bolt Lane.

* In St. Catherine's Church, Gloucester, is a monument, now scarcely legible, bearing the following inscription : "Sacred to the memory of James King, of this parish, gent., who died February 27th, 1832, aged 79. Also of Anne King, wife of the above. She died March 7th, 1824, aged 72." In 1780, Mr. King and his wife would be respectively 27 and 26 years of age, and although they do not answer the description of persons paid two shillings per week for their services, they certainly were amongst the first Sunday school teachers in Gloucester. Mr. King was personally very charitable to the poor, and this decaying tombstone may in future be an object of interest to lovers of Sunday schools and those who helped to establish them.

This school was almost opposite the south porch of St. Mary de Crypt Church. There was a great advantage in the situation, which Mr. Raikes could not have been slow to appreciate. It was so near to the church, that if the boys commenced sticking pins into each other, swearing and fighting, or were inclined to run, he would not be for any length of time subjected to the cross-fire of unkind criticism and easy banter, cutting to the soul of a vain but earnest man. Unless things were very bad indeed, the jeer of "Bobby Wild Goose" would scarcely reach him before his "ragged regiment"—some with logs trailing from their legs, perhaps—would be within the south porch of the church. In these early days the situation was admirable. Mrs. Bradburn's story, so far as it relates to the ridicule of the populace when the children were marching from school to church, points to the fact that the school was, at the time she refers to, at some distance. Had it been in the Grey Fryars, there would have been but little opportunity for jeers and laughter, *and her description would not have been accurate.* Mrs. Bradburn (Sophia Cooke) had been accustomed to ridicule, and so may be taken as a trustworthy witness on this point.

There is a sufficient motive in the desire to escape too much popular attention of this sort, to account for the abandonment of the Sooty Alley premises for those in Grey Fryars; and so this building, still in splendid preservation, may fairly be looked at by strangers to the city as the cradle of Robert Raikes's Sunday school. For this reason we give a reproduction from a sketch in the possession of Mr. Taylor.

One good and sufficient reason for associating this dwelling with the early history of the Sunday school movement is, that it was here that Mr. Raikes was in the habit of bringing the illustrious men and women who visited him from all parts to see this "new thing" in operation. Mr. Jonas Hanway, Mr. Fox, Mr. Howard, the Wesleys, Mrs. Hannah More, the French *savants*, Prince William of Gloucester,— all these and more may be reckoned, without undue presumption, to have entered this dwelling.

Mrs. Critchley's School.

When we imagine to ourselves a man daintily clean in his habits, and personally vain of his dress and appearance as Robert Raikes undoubtedly was, we shall commence to understand the depth of his convictions and the tenacity of his purpose. The city of Gloucester was built in the fashion of a cross—the four main streets being joined together by innumerable narrow lanes and alleys, like an immense cobweb in stones and brick. It wanted courage to go into some of the purlieus, and when children were captured the sight was offended, the nostrils were offended, the ears were profaned and the soul was sickened! That Raikes, naturally so clean that he had a crossing made and swept for him between his houses, so vain as to be called "buckish," should have endured a daily martyrdom for fifty years when slumming in Littleworth and the criminal dens of the city, evidences an earnestness and depth of character which has been sometimes overlooked, and sometimes flatly denied. One object of this book has been to show the man as he was, and the work which he assuredly did accomplish.

It is, however, the truth, and it would not be right to pass it by, that evil days fell like a blight upon the two historical schools in the city, drying up the living sap and leaving them withering. It is no part of the design of this book to account for the phenomenon. Both schools were attacked, and Robert Raikes's was nearly destroyed. For fifty years the sinister epidemic was warded off, but it fell surely, and almost with equal virulence upon Mr. Stock's. A gentleman, writing with all the weight of responsibility and the authority of knowledge, says: "From 1854 to 1881 the less said about this unfortunate parish the better." After the Centenary the outside influences made themselves felt and things began to improve, and are now, as compared with the description of things on the 11th January, 1863, fairly prosperous—about 150 children out of a parish of 1,200 being on the register. Then comes this sentence: "The old tradition has entirely passed away!" The name of

Stock is preserved in marble in his church and in the Cathedral, but the music and magic of the name have disappeared! The spiritual life of Sunday schools in the Cathedral City is most active amongst Dissenters.

Robert Raikes's school suffered earlier and more severely. After the death of its founder, it was seized by an atrophy and withered. It did not absolutely die, but at times was so like death that people mistook it for death. It was in this state in January, 1863, when the Author of this book visited it, and the Rev. Mr. Sayers was the Rector of St. Mary de Crypt. The present Dean of Gloucester (the Rev. H. D. M. Spence) followed Mr. Sayers, but was preferred to the Deanery before his beneficial influence was well felt. The Rev. Mowbray Trotter followed in 1877, and, during his rectorship, the Old Crypt Grammar School—where Raikes was probably educated — was purchased, became a Church Sunday school and a new centre for parochial and Church life.* The rev. gentleman remained in Gloucester until 1894; and on "the children's day," during the Centenary celebration, the number of children from Raikes's parish marching in the procession was 200, out of a total of 3,500 belonging to the various Sunday schools in the city alone—a vast improvement on the previous state of things. The parish is not large; but under the personal superintendence of the present rector (the Rev. G.

---

* " I have been assured by the granddaughter of Mrs. Critchley that, without any break, our present Sunday school has continued to be held ever since the days of Robert Raikes."—Rev. MOWBRAY TROTTER, *now Vicar of East Farleigh, Maidstone,* 1898.

Milner), Robert Raikes's school is continued in three places—in the body of the church, in the old Crypt school, and, thirdly, the infants assemble in a part of the house in Bell Lane in which Raikes died.* The number of children at present on the register is 264, the average attendance being 197.

These details are given in justice to those who have laboured, and so far successfully, in wiping off the reproach which rested on schools which the whole world calls "historical," and claims to have a direct and permanent interest in. Who would not be saddened, as the Author was, at the exhibition of Sunday, January 11th, 1863? †

But what still strikes a chill to the heart of a stranger glowing with enthusiasm for Raikes, and for Sunday schools, is the atmosphere of indifference in the city itself about the Raikes traditions. In no part of the civilised world are they so weak as here. A stranger comes from America or Australia to the City of Raikes, and asks for his "relics," and all that he finds in the Museum is one metal "composing stick." His household furniture, books, pictures, everything belonging to him, was sold by public auction after Mrs. Raikes's death, and the City purchased—nothing! The Author in 1863 saw his silver-plate and the oil painting, a copy of which forms the frontispiece to this volume, in the possession

* This is only a temporary arrangement, through the courtesy of Mr. Frank Brereton, solicitor, the present owner. The house was empty and for sale in 1898.

† *See* Chapter I.—" Why these Materials were Gathered."

of a private gentleman; and the Editor in 1898 saw and handled the spectacles, which were probably the last thing which he fingered with conscious touch. The Raikes "relics" are truly scarce!

There have been a "Jubilee" and a "Centenary," and at the Centenary the city of Gloucester presented all the appearance of genuine worshippers. The Earl of Shaftesbury, Sir Michael Hicks Beach, Mr. W. H. Smith, Lord Herschell,* Mr. Henry Cecil Raikes were amongst those who spent the week in Gloucester and kindled enthusiasm. Every building echoed with the name. The Earl of Shaftesbury, with the tremulous pathos of tears, unveiled the model of a statue to the memory of Robert Raikes. The philanthropist, with the Bible under his arm, was kindly leading a little child in the right way. This was to have been chiselled in Sicilian marble, and placed in the Cathedral.

After the first flush of enthusiasm the old indifference succeeded. It was found that a statue of a man in wig and knee-breeches would not be in harmony with the Gothic design of the Cathedral! A satirical paper of the day, called the *Gloucestershire Wasp*, reproduced the model, and labelled it "The Raikes Progress." The first breath of opposition killed the project.

The outcome of all the enthusiasm of the Centenary year was the erection of a hall, which is let for lectures on occasion, and is used as a school on Sundays. It is

* His Lordship was a Vice-President of the Sunday School Union, and his lamented death was made known whilst this volume was passing through the press.

called the "Raikes's Memorial Hall," and the head of Raikes appears on the outside as a medallion.

The only thing which the city possesses which has the outward seeming of love and affection is a Memorial Tower, built in 1864 on the grounds of the house in Bell Lane where Mr. Raikes died. It was built by the late Mr. Addison, who was residing there in 1863, when the Author visited him, as stated in Chapter IV. of this book. A stranger is not likely to notice the Tower, which is a pity, as it was built at much personal sacrifice, and bears a tablet, on which is the following inscription:

ROBERTUS RAIKES
SCHOLARUM SABBATICARUM PRIMUS AUCTOR
ÆDES PROXIMUS OLIM HABITABAT
IBIQUE EST MORTUUS MDCCCXI.
CORPUS EJUS IN ECCLESIA
SANCTÆ MARIA DE CRYPTUS
SEPULTUM JACET.
IN MEMORIAM
MDCCCLXIV.

And this is all! Mr. Taylor records that the Dean and Chapter of the Cathedral accepted the offer of Mr. J. D. T. Niblett to place in the Cathedral a stained-glass window in memory of Catharine Boevey, Thomas Stock, and Robert Raikes—three nursing parents of Sunday schools. The window was executed by an eminent foreign artist, and was constructed of "the purest, finest, oldest, and the best old mellow Munich glass." When it arrived it was found that all the suitable vacant windows in the Cathedral had been appropriated. The window found its way into the School of Art.*

The Dean and Chapter of the Cathedral have not yet recognised Robert Raikes's title to honour by placing a memorial tablet within its walls.

At the east end of the south wall of St. Mary de Crypt Church is a mural tablet with a Latin inscription to the Raikeses —father and son. The marble tablet is supposed to be above the vault where their remains rest in peace, *but it is not.*

The Raikes tablet was removed, and a tablet sacred to the members of the Willey family put in its place. Above this tablet, now in the wrong place,

Memorial Tablet.

---

* Mr. Taylor tells an amusing story by way of illustrating the way in which the citizens of Gloucester forget or misunderstand some great men whom the world outside delight to honour. He was making certain inquiries about George Whitefield, and said to a respectable man:

"You know about George Whitefield, don't you?"

"Oh! yes, I know all about him. A terrible blackguard and disturber of the peace. I was forced to have him up once for walloping his wife. He's the worst scamp in the place!"

"I don't believe," said Mr. Taylor in conversation, "that four-fifths of the people in Gloucester know of Robert Raikes except by name, and very few know the difference between the brothers Robert and Richard! Old Sunday scholars speak of Mr. Reekes, meaning the parson, Richard Raikes."

one sees upon the wall the outline of the apex of the tablet originally there—the Raikes tablet. It has been washed over with coloured lime, but the outlines remain as plain as the "handwriting on the wall."

After the Centenary celebration the encaustic tiles over the Raikes vault were removed, and the flat stone with an inscription on it was uncovered. The site of the vault was immediately under the place where the mural tablet with its inscription in Latin was originally fixed. People from America, Australia, and from all parts of the world come to this church and read the inscription on the tablet in the extreme east corner of the south wall, and go away with the belief that they have been standing above the ashes of Robert Raikes. For them the spot is consecrated. As a fact they pass by the tomb of Raikes, and are deceived.

The special correspondent of *The Times* was present with Mr. Taylor when the encaustic tiles were removed, and two recommendations were then made: (1) to restore the Raikes tablet to its proper place; and (2) to inlay a brass plate over the tomb. In November, 1898, when the Editor visited the church neither recommendation had been carried out, and the lines on the wall still spoke reproachfully of the slight to a memory which the world thinks sacred.*

* Mr. Taylor says: "It was during the so-called restoration of the church that this change in the position of the Raikes monument was made. It was done at the instance of the executors of the late James Wood, and for a 'consideration.' The transaction was truly Simonical. I drew the attention of Mr. Nisbet—*The Times'* special

At the Centenary in 1880 there were three very aged women—Mrs. Summerhill, Mrs. Allen, and Mrs. Perks, and one old man—Mr. John Oakley Packer, who recollected Robert Raikes and went to his Sunday school; and it is very much to the credit of these old people that they did not enlarge upon the Raikes traditions. They were courted and feasted, and lionised—the Earl of Shaftesbury drank tea out of a cup having the portrait of Robert Raikes upon it, belonging to one of the three old women. She declared it was given to her on the day of Mr. Raikes's funeral, and prized it highly.* All their statements were taken down in writing, and it is to the credit of all four that no traces of invention are discoverable. Mr. Packer's statement in 1880 ran on all fours with that which he made to the Author in 1863, seventeen years previously. No stronger or better test of absolute sincerity can be applied. With regard to the three women—the oldest being 87—they had no knowledge of the earliest days of Sunday schools—the scholars, the conditions under which they were got together, their

correspondent during the Centenary—to the facts, and he was truly shocked."

It is singular that the mural tablet to the memory of the Rev. Thomas Stock has disappeared from the Church of St. Aldate, where his body lies; that the mural tablet to Robert Raikes in St. Mary de Crypt Church has been removed, and that the tombstone over the remains of the Rev. Richard Raikes is perishing from neglect in the churchyard of St. Mary de Lode. This want of reverence and care, to say the least, must stamp the citizens of Gloucester most unfavourably in the eyes of the Sunday school world. Public opinion will, perhaps, insist on a very different course of conduct in future.

* Mr. Evans, in the Cathedral Choir, now possesses Mrs. Allen's cup.—MR. TAYLOR.

behaviour in school and in church. But for the more aged people, long before dead, whose testimonies are preserved in this book, important parts of the story of the first days of Sunday school work would never be known.

To the old witnesses in 1880, the earliest recollections which they had of Sunday schools were of harmony and love. One said: "I longed for Sunday to come again." The schools had been at work for more than twenty years when she went to one of them; and so we must go back to first scholars, like Charles Cox, who came under the hands of Mrs. Meredith, of Sooty Alley, in order to read aright the first pages of Sunday School History, and to learn what rules and standards to apply to Mr. Raikes, the Thinker and the Worker.

The Editor has completed the task which he set for himself. The Reader, with his knowledge of men, and the motives which actuate them, will determine for himself what position Robert Raikes is entitled to hold in his affections and esteem. The Editor does not presume to do more than focus certain stray, and often weak, rays of light in order to reveal Robert Raikes at work, the nature of his work, and the conditions under which the work was performed. The secret, inspiring, and sustaining principle the Reader must determine for himself, as, indeed, he must if this sketch of a good and benevolent man is to be of any aid to his own spiritual growth. Writing to Mr. Lewelyn, in 1789, on his *Exposition of Genesis and Romans*, Mr. Raikes says:

"Your work is calculated only for minds which have been strongly impressed with the love of God. . . . I question if anyone here would read it but myself. Calvanists and Socinians abound here; but there abound more who consider this world as the only abiding place, and, therefore, give themselves no concern about the preparation for another."

Again, in 1791, he writes to the same gentleman:

"There is some pleasure in printing works that purify and elevate the heart, and fit it for an intercourse with the Mansions of Eternity."

These passages may assist the reader in his conclusions, and he must not overlook the fact that they occur in a business correspondence. They may also help him to decide what value to put upon the opinions of gentlemen of great intellectual capacity, and good social positions, quoted in this book, to the effect that Mr. Raikes's conduct was inspired by a vain but benevolent disposition, and *not by any religious motive*.*

One regret the Editor has; namely, that Josiah Harris (his father) was unable to complete the labour of love he contemplated with a sense of joy. For himself, he only asks it to be believed that he has done his best to make this history "as truthful and profitable as possible."

* *See* chapter IV. Opinions of Mr. Paul Hawkins Fisher, Stroud, and Mr. John J. Powell, Q.C., M.P.

APPENDIX.

A.

CHAPTER V.—ROBERT RAIKES'S OWN STORY TOLD IN THE PRESS.

THE first notice of Sunday schools appeared in the *Gloucester Journal* of November 3rd, 1783, quoted as in Chapter V., and the next appeared the following year, namely, May 24th, 1784, as follows:

"Whilst the public-spirited exertions of the most distinguished characters in our country are meditating a reform in our Police by rendering our prisons, if possible, the reverse of what they have hitherto been, *seminaries of every species of villainy and profligacy*, several of the clergy in the county are setting forward a model of general instruction for the children of the lower class of the people, by establishing schools for their reception on Sundays,—a day upon which they are given up to follow their wild and vicious inclinations free from restraint.

"The promoters of this design seem to concur in the idea that *prevention is better than punishment*, and that an attempt to check the growth of vice at an early period, by an effort to introduce good habits of acting and thinking among the vulgar, is at least an experiment, harmless and innocent, however fruitless it may be in its effect.

"A gentleman who adopted this plan about the month of January last has lately written to a friend on the subject, from whose letter we have been favoured with the following extract."

Mr. Raikes then quotes at some length from the letter, and the quotation rhetorically concludes:

"'View it (the misery around them); view it—the total disregard to morals in the higher orders of Society, and the general depravity and profligacy of the vulgar! Have not causes like these in all ages produced similar effects?'"

Mr. Raikes continued:

"The good effects of Sunday schools established in this city are instanced in the account given by the principal persons in the pin and sack manufactories, wherein great reformation has taken place among the multitudes whom they employ. From being idle, ungovernable, profligate, and filthy in the extreme, they say the boys and girls are become not only cleanly and decent in their appearance, but are greatly humanised in their manners—more orderly, tractable, and attentive to business, and, of course, more serviceable than they ever expected to find them. The cursing and swearing and other vile expressions, which used to form the sum of their conversation, are now rarely heard among them.

"Such, we are well assured, is the fact. The *London Chronicle* of Tuesday last mentions that the plan of Sunday schools is taken up with such general concurrence in Leeds and Yorkshire that the spirited inhabitants of that place have them in all quarters of their populous town, and have already admitted near 2,000 poor children!"

The *Gentleman's Magazine* for June, 1784, contains the following letter, which Mr. Raikes, in the November previous, had written to Col. Townley, then residing at Sheffield. The document made a great demand upon the space of the Magazine; and "Mr. Urban" employed commendatory words having a prophetic ring with them. "It is with pleasure," said he, "we give place to this benevolent plan, which bids fair to transmit the name of Mr. Raikes to latest posterity." The letter reads:

"Gloucester, *November 25th*, 1783.

"Sir,—My friend, the Mayor [Mr. Colborne] has just communicated to me the letter which you have honoured him with, enquiring into the nature of Sunday schools. The beginning of this scheme was entirely owing to accident. Some business leading me one morning into the suburbs of the city, where the lowest of the people (who are principally employed in the pin manufactory) chiefly reside, I was struck with concern at seeing a group of children, wretchedly ragged, at play in the streets. I asked an inhabitant whether those children belonged to that part of the town, and lamented their misery and idleness. 'Ah! sir,' said the woman to whom I was speaking, 'could you take a view of this part of the town on a Sunday, you would be shocked indeed; for then the street is filled with multitudes of these wretches, who, released on that day from employment, spend their time in noise and riot, playing at "chuck," and cursing and swearing in a manner so horrid as to convey to any serious mind an idea of hell rather than any other place. We have a worthy clergyman (said she) curate of our parish, who has put some of them to school; but upon the Sabbath they are all given up to follow their own inclinations without restraint, as their parents, totally abandoned themselves, have no idea of instilling into the minds of their children principles to which they themselves are entire strangers.'

"This conversation suggested to me that it would be at least a harmless attempt, if it were productive of no good, should some little plan be formed to check the deplorable profanation of the Sabbath. I then enquired of the woman, if there were any decent well-disposed women in the neighbourhood who kept schools for teaching to read. I presently was directed to four: to these I applied, and made an agreement with to receive as many children as I should send upon the Sunday, whom they were to instruct in reading and in the Church Catechism. For this I engaged to pay them each a shilling for their day's employment. The women seemed pleased with the proposal. I then waited on the clergyman before mentioned, and imparted to him my plan; he was so much satisfied with the idea, that he engaged to lend his assistance, by going round to the schools on a Sunday afternoon, to examine the progress that was made, and to enforce order and decorum among such a set of little heathens.

"This, sir, was the commencement of the plan. It is now about three years since we began, and I could wish you were here to make enquiry into the effect. A woman who lives in a lane where I had fixed a school told me some time ago, that the place was quite a heaven upon Sundays, compared to what it used to be. The numbers who have learned to read and say their Catechism are so great that I am astonished at it. Upon the Sunday afternoon the mistresses take their scholars to church, a place into which neither they nor their ancestors had ever before entered, with a view to the glory of God. But what is yet more extraordinary, within this month these little ragamuffins have in great numbers taken it into their heads to frequent the early morning prayers, which are held every morning at the Cathedral at seven o'clock. I believe there were nearly fifty this morning. They assemble at the house of one of the mistresses, and walk before her to church, two and two, in as much order as a company of soldiers. I am generally at church, and after service they all come round me to make their bow; and, if any animosities have arisen, to make their complaints. The great principle I inculcate is, to be kind and good natured to each other; not to provoke one another; to be dutiful to their parents; not to offend God by cursing and swearing; and such little plain precepts as all may comprehend. As my profession is that of a printer, I have printed a little book, which I gave amongst them; and some friends of mine, subscribers to the Society for Promoting Christian Knowledge, sometimes make me a present of a parcel of Bibles, Testaments, &c., which I distribute as rewards to the deserving. The success that has attended this scheme has induced one or two of my friends to adopt the plan, and set up Sunday schools in other parts of the city, and now a whole parish has taken up the object; so that I flatter myself in time the good effects will appear so conspicuous as to become generally adopted. The number of children at present thus engaged on the Sabbath are between two and three hundred, and they are increasing every week, as the benefit is universally seen. I have endeavoured to engage the clergy of my acquaintance that reside in their parishes; one has entered into the scheme with great fervour, and it was in order to excite others to follow the example that I inserted in my paper the paragraph which I suppose you saw copied into the London papers.

"I cannot express to you the pleasure I often receive in discovering genius, and innate good dispositions, among this little multitude. It is botanizing in human nature. I have often, too, the satisfaction of receiving thanks from parents, for the reformation they perceive in their children. Often I have given them kind admonitions, which I always do in the mildest and gentlest manner. The going amongst them, doing them little kindnesses, distributing trifling rewards, and ingratiating myself with them, I hear, have given me an ascendancy greater than I ever could have imagined; for I am told by their mistresses that they are very much afraid of my displeasure. If you ever pass through Gloucester, I shall be happy to pay my respects to you, and to show you the effects of this effort at civilization. If the glory of God be promoted in any, even the smallest degree, society must reap some benefit. If good seed be sown in the mind at an early period of human life, though it shows itself not again for many years, it may please God, at some future period, to cause it to spring up, and to bring forth a plentiful harvest. With regard to the rules adopted, I only require that they may come to the school on Sunday as clean as possible. Many were at first deterred because they wanted decent clothing, but I could not undertake to supply this defect. I argue, therefore, if you can loiter about without shoes, and in a ragged coat, you may as well come to school and learn what may tend to your good in that garb. I reject none on that footing. All that I require are clean hands, clean face, and their hair combed; if you have no clean shirt, come in that you have on.

"The want of decent apparel at first kept great numbers at a distance, but they now begin to grow wiser, and all pressing to learn. I have had the good luck to procure places for some that were deserving, which has been of great use. You will understand that these children are from six years old to twelve or fourteen. Boys and girls above this age, who have been totally undisciplined, are generally too refractory for this government. A reformation in society seems to me to be only practicable by establishing notions of duty, and practical habits of order and decorum, at an early age. But whither am I running? I am ashamed to see how much I have trespassed on your patience; but I thought the most complete idea of Sunday schools was to be conveyed to you by telling what first suggested the thought. The same sentiments would have arisen in your mind, had they happened to have been called forth as they were suggested to me. I have no doubt that you will find great improvement to be made on this plan. The minds of men have taken great hold on that prejudice, that we are to do nothing on the Sabbath day which may be deemed labour, and therefore we are to be excused from all application of minds as well as body. The rooting out of this prejudice is the point I aim at as my favourite object. Our Saviour takes particular pains to manifest, that whatever tended to promote the health and happiness of our fellow creatures, were sacrifices peculiarly acceptable on that day. I do not think I have written so long a letter for some years. But you will excuse me—my heart is warm in the cause. I think this is the kind of reformation most requisite in this kingdom. Let our patriots employ themselves in rescuing their countrymen from that despotism which tyrannical passions and vicious inclinations exercise over them, and they will find that true liberty and national welfare are more essentially promoted than by any reform in Parliament.

"As often as I have attempted to conclude, some new idea has arisen. This is strange, as I am writing to a person whom I never have, and, perhaps, never may see—but I have felt that we think alike. I shall, therefore, only add my ardent wishes, that your views of promoting the happiness of society may be attended with every possible success, conscious that your own internal enjoyment will thereby be considerably advanced.

"I have the honour to be, Sir, yours, &c.,
"R. RAIKES."

In reply to an enquiry from Bradford, Yorkshire, Mr. Raikes wrote, June 5th, 1784, recapitulating in substance what he had already informed Colonel Townley, and then he says of the children:

"They are frequently admonished to refrain from swearing, and certain boys who are distinguished by their decent behaviour are appointed to superintend the conduct of the rest, and make report of those that swear, call names, and interrupt the comfort of the other boys in their neighbourhood. When quarrels have arisen, the aggressor is compelled to ask pardon, and the offended is enjoined to forgive. The happiness that must arise to all from a kind, good-natured behaviour is often inculcated.

"This mode of treatment has produced a wonderful

change in the manners of these little savages. I cannot give a more striking instance than I received the other day from Mr. Church, a considerable manufacturer of hemp and flax, who employs great numbers of these children. I asked him if he perceived any alteration in the poor children he employed. 'Sir,' says he, 'the change could not have been more extraordinary, in my opinion, had they been transformed from the shape of wolves and tigers to that of men. In temper, disposition, and manners, they could hardly be said to differ from the brute creation; but since the establishment of Sunday schools, they have seemed anxious to show that they are not the ignorant, illiterate creatures they were before. When they have seen a superior come and kindly instruct and admonish them, and sometimes reward their good behaviour, they are anxious to gain his friendship and good opinion. They are also become more tractable and obedient, and less quarrelsome and revengeful. In short, I never conceived that a reformation so singular could have been effected amongst the set of untutored beings I employed.'

"From this little sketch of the reformation which has taken place, there is reason to hope that a general establishment of Sunday schools would, in time, make some change in the morals of the lower class. At least, it might in some measure prevent them from growing worse, which, at present, seems but too apparent.

"I am, Sir, &c.,
"R. Raikes.

"P.S.—The parish of St. Nicholas has lately established two schools, and some gentlemen of this city [Gloucester] have also set up others. *To some of the schoolmistresses I give 2s. a week extra to take the children when they come from work and during the week days.*"

Replying to Mr. William Fox, formerly a merchant of London, and afterwards a resident at Lechdale, in Gloucestershire, Mr. Raikes says, June 20th, 1785:

"With respect to the possibility of teaching children by the attendance they give upon the Sunday, I thought with you, at the first, that little was to be gained, but I now find it has suggested to the parents that the little progress we made on the Sundays might be improved, and they have therefore engaged to give a teacher a penny a week to admit children once or twice a day during the recess from work, at dinner-time, or evening, to take a lesson every day in the week."

In a second letter to Mr. William Fox, with reference to the formation of the Sunday School Society, Mr. Raikes gives an account of the endeavour to civilise the young savages at Mitchel-Dean, on the borders of the Forest of Dean. After a year's trial, he says:

"The promoters of the undertaking did me the honour to invite me to dine with them on their anniversary, to witness the progress that had been made in this effort at civilisation. The children, though many of them in apparel very ragged, were extremely clean. They walked in great order two and two to the church, where they were placed in the gallery, exposed to the view of the whole congregation; their behaviour during the service was perfectly silent and becoming. In the repetition of the Lord's Prayer they all joined, and formed a charm that made every heart dilate with joy.

"After church the children were conducted to the inn, where an examination took place of the progress made in reading. I was highly pleased to see the proficiency some of them had made. Several could read in the New Testament, and I found among them two or three with extraordinary memories. They have learned to repeat several chapters.

" Near fifty of them were perfect in their Catechism, and all could repeat some of Dr. Watts's hymns. The children were so much pleased with these pieces, that two or three of them could repeat the whole book. But what pleased me most of all was the result of my enquiry into the effect upon their manners. 'That boy,' said one of the gentlemen (pointing to a very ill-looking lad, about thirteen), 'was the most profligate little boy in this neighbourhood. He was the leader of every kind of mischief and wickedness. He never opened his lips without a profane or indecent expression. And now he is become orderly and good natured, and, in his conversation, quite left off profaneness.'

"After dinner the gentleman called in six boys who had previously been taught a hymn, which I can assure you they sang to admiration. I observed that one of the singers was the boy before mentioned.

"The silence that prevailed among these children was remarkable; their benefactors dined in a room adjoining, but were not disturbed with their talking.

"I have given you this little recital, and if it tends to prove the practicability of doing good to our fellow-creatures, I hope it may prove an incitement to the work you are bringing forward.

"I am, with great respect, Sir,
 "Your most obedient Servant,
  "R. RAIKES.

"Gloucester, *Monday, August* 29*th*, 1785."

On the 2nd September, 1785, Mr. W. Fox, writing with reference to his efforts and those of Mr. Jonas Hanway—the Persian traveller—to form the Sunday School Society, made use of these words:

"The fire which you have had the honour to light up in Gloucester having now reached the Metropolis, will, I trust, never be extinguished but with the ignorance of every individual throughout the kingdom."

The letter from Mr. Raikes to the Sunday School Society, of which he was elected an hon. member in 1785, is in one sense historical. The Mr. Webb mentioned is the Mr. Samuel Webb briefly noticed in Chapter XII., and the date of the first Sunday school in Painswick is definitely fixed as in the summer of 1784. This letter was published in the *Gentleman's Magazine*, January, 1787, vol. lvii. It, however, bears date October 7th, 1786:

"The parish of Painswick exhibited on Sunday, the 24th ult,, a specimen of the reform which the establishment of Sunday schools is likely to introduce.

"An annual festival has from time immemorial been held on that day: a festival that would have disgraced the most heathenish nations. Drunkenness and every species of clamour, riot, and disorder formerly filled the town upon this occasion. Mr. Webb, a gentleman who has exerted the utmost assiduity in the conduct of the Sunday schools in Painswick, was lamenting to me the sad effects that might be naturally expected to arise from this feast. It occurred to us that an attempt to divert the attention of the vulgar from their brutal prostitution of the Lord's Day, by exhibiting to their view a striking picture of the superior enjoyment to be derived from quietness, good order, and the exercise of the benevolence which Christianity peculiarly recommends, was an experiment worth hazarding. We thought it could do no mischief—it would not increase the evil. It was immediately determined to invite the gentlemen and people of the adjacent parishes to view the children of the Sunday schools, to mark their improvement in cleanliness and behaviour, and to observe the practicability of reducing to a quiet, peaceful demeanour the most neglected part of the community, those who form the great bulk of the people.

"In the parish of Painswick are several gentlemen who have a taste for music, they immediately offered to give every assistance in a church service, and my benevolent friend, the Reverend Dr. Glasse, complied with our entreaty to favour us with a sermon. Mr. Campbell, a very active Justice of the Peace, Mr. Townsend, Mr. Sheppard, Mr. Webb, of Ebworth, and several other gentlemen engaged to give their countenance: We were highly gratified, too, with Mr. Boddington's company, who kindly came from Cheltenham to take a view of this progress of civilisation; he is one of your vice-presidents, and from his report you will receive a far more perfect idea than my pen can give. On this Sunday afternoon the town was filled with the usual crowd who attended the feast; but instead of repairing to the alehouses, as heretofore, they all hastened to the church, which was filled in such a manner as I never remember to have seen any church in this country before; the galleries, the aisles were thronged like a playhouse. Drawn up in a rank around the churchyard appeared the children belonging to the different schools to the number of 331. The gentlemen walked round to view them—it was a sight interesting and truly affecting; young people lately more neglected than the cattle in the field, ignorant, profane, filthy, clamorous, impatient of every restraint, were here seen cleanly, quiet, observant of order, submissive, courteous in behaviour, and, in conversation, free from that vileness which marks our wretched vulgar. The inhabitants of the town bear testimony to this change in their manners. The appearance of decency might be assumed for a day, but the people among whom they live are ready to declare that this is a character fairly stated.

"After the public service a collection for the benefit of the institution was made at the doors of the church. When I considered that the bulk of the congregation were persons of the middling rank, husbandmen and other inhabitants of the adjacent villages, I concluded that the collection, if it amounted to £24 or £25, might be deemed a good one. My astonishment was great indeed when I found that the sum was not less than £57! This may be accounted for from the security which the establishment of Sunday schools has given to the property of every individual in the neighbourhood: the farmers, &c., declare that they and their families can now leave their houses and gardens, &c., and frequent the public worship, without danger of depredation: formerly they were under the necessity of leaving their servants, or staying at home themselves, as a guard; and this was insufficient, the most vigilant were sometimes plundered. It is not, then, to be wondered at that a spirit of liberality was excited on this occasion. A carpenter put a guinea in the plate, and afterwards brought four more to Mr. Webb. 'It was my fixed design,' says he, 'to devote the sum that I received for a certain job of work to the support of Sunday schools. I received five guineas, one only I put in the plate; it did not become me to put more, it would have looked like

ostentation, but here are the other four,' giving them to
Mr. Webb. Another instance of spirit occurred in a man
upwards of 80 years of age, who seemed about the rank
of the yeomanry. 'Oh! that I should live,' said he, 'to
see this day, when poor children are thus befriended,
and taught the road to peace and comfort here, and
happiness and heaven hereafter.' The old man gave a
guinea, and said he would leave another in the hands of
a friend, if he should die before the next anniversary.
When the matter of the collection was settled, we went
to the schools to hear what progress was made in
reading, &c. The emulation to show their acquirements
was so very great, that it would have taken up a day to
have gratified all the children. In the meantime the
town was remarkably free from those pastimes which used
to disgrace it; wrestling, quarrelling, fighting were totally
banished; all was peace and tranquility. I fear I have
been too prolix, but I could not convey the complete idea
that I was desirous of imparting to the generous promoters
of Sunday schools, without writing these particulars.

"I forgot to mention that Mr. Fox, one of the worthy
members of your Committee, was present with us at Painswick. *The Sunday schools were first established at Painswick
in the summer of the year* 1784. The children had been bred
up in total ignorance. Of the number that attend the
school 230 can read, 80 can read in the *Sunday Scholars'
Companion*, and about 21 are in the alphabet. *These children
had no teaching but on the Sunday;* what they learn in the
leisure hours in the week is the effect of their own desire

to improve; many have their books at their looms, to seize any vacant minute when their work is retarded by the breaking of threads.

"To relieve the parish of the burden of clothing these poor creatures, Mr. Webb proposed that such children as by increase of industry would bring a penny each Sunday towards their clothing, should be assisted by having that penny doubled: this has had an admirable effect; the children now regularly bring their pence every Sunday; many of them have been clothed, and the good consequences of laying up a little are powerfully enforced. It is pretty evident that were every parish in this kingdom blessed with a man or two of Mr. Webb's active turn of and benevolent mind, the lower class of the people in a few years would exhibit a material change of character, and justify that superior policy which tends to prevent crimes rather than to punish them.

"The liberality with which the members of your Society have stood forth in this attempt to introduce a degree of civilisation and good order among the lowest ranks, entitles them to the thanks of the community, and particularly of an individual who will be ever proud to subscribe himself, &c.,

"R. RAIKES.

"P.S.—The gentlemen of Painswick intend making a request to Dr. Glasse to publish his sermon.

"The happy choice of the text had a remarkable effect in commanding the attention of the audience. The Scriptures could not have furnished a passage more literally applicable to the subject. It was taken from Deuteronomy xxxi., verses 12 and 13: 'Gather the people together, men, and women, and children, and thy stranger that is within thy gates, that they may hear, and that they may learn, and fear the Lord your God, and observe to do all the words of this Law; and that their children *which have not known anything* may hear, and learn to fear the Lord your God as long as ye live.'"

In another letter to Mr. William Fox, July 12th, 1787, Mr. Raikes says:

"I regret that the variety of my business and my engagements, when I was last in town, prevented me from devoting an afternoon to the enjoyment of your company.

"The loss was mine, for I find few pleasures equal to those which arise from the conversation of men who are endeavouring to promote the glory of the Creator and the good of their fellow-creatures.

"I consider you, too, with the greater respect, as I believe you were one of the first of my encouragers at the outset of the little plan I was the humble instrument of suggesting to the world.

"I thank you, my good friend, for communicating the pleasing recital from Colchester. What a wide and extensive field of rational enjoyment opens to our view, could we allow the improvement of human nature to become the source of pleasure.

"Instead of training horses to the course, and viewing

with delight their exertions at Newmarket, let our men of fortune turn their eyes to an exhibition like that at Colchester. Impart to them a small portion of that solid enjoyment which a mind like yours must receive from the glorious sight. Children more neglected than the beast of the field, now taught to relish the comfort of decency and good order, and to know that their own happiness greatly depends on promoting the happiness of others. When the community begins to reap the benefits of these principles, let us hope that the nation will manifest to the world the blessed effects of a general diffusion of Christianity. The great Reformers of past times have only been removing obstructions in our way. Let us hope that the day is approaching when 'The knowledge of the Lord shall cover the earth as the waters cover the sea.' The number of children admitted into a state of culture in this short period seems to me little less miraculous than the draught of fishes, and would incline [one] to think that the prophecy above quoted is advancing to its completion.

"Some French gentlemen, members of the Academy at Paris, were with me last week, and were so strongly impressed with this scheme of civilisation, that they have taken all the pieces I have printed on the subject, and intend proposing establishments of a similar nature in some of their parishes in the provinces by way of experiment. We have seen the rapid progress of Christianity. Dr. Adam Smith, who has so ably written in the *Wealth of Nations*, says: 'No plan has promised to effect a change of manners with equal ease and simplicity since the days of the Apostles.'

"I have sent you my paper of this week, that you may see we are extending towards Wales, with the improvement of a School of Industry.

"I have only room to add that I am, dear Sir,

"Your sincere Friend and Servant,

"R. RAIKES.

"*July 12th*, 1787."

The *Teacher's Magazine*, October, 1831, New Series, vol. ii., published a letter to Mrs. Harris, Chelsea, dated November 5th, 1787. The original of this letter is understood to be in the possession of the Committee of the Sunday School Union:

"MY DEAR MADAM,—Amongst the numerous correspondents which my little project for civilising the rising generation of the poor has led me to address, I have to no one taken up my pen with more pleasure than to you, my old friend, with whom I formerly passed so many cheerful hours.

"I am rejoiced to find that the people in your neighbourhood are thus ready to listen to that strong and pathetic injunction given by our Saviour a little before His resurrection—'Feed my lambs'; and if it were possible for me to afford any hints that might be useful, great would be the pleasure I should receive.

"In answer to your queries, I shall as concisely as possible state that I endeavour to assemble the children as early as is consistent with their perfect cleanliness—an indispensable rule. The hour prescribed in our rules is eight o'clock, but it is usually half after eight before our flock is collected. Twenty is the number allotted to each teacher; the sexes kept separate. The twenty are divided into four classes; the children who show any superiority in attainments are placed as leaders of the several classes, and are employed in teaching the others their letters, or in hearing them read in a low whisper, which may be done without interrupting the master or mistress in their business, and will keep the attention of the children engaged, that they do not play or make a noise. Their attending the service of the Church once a day has to me seemed sufficient; for their time may be spent more profitably, perhaps, in receiving instruction than in being present at a long discourse, which their minds are not yet able to comprehend; but people may think differently on this point. Within this month the minister of my parish has, at last, condescended to give me assistance in this laborious work, which I have carried on six years with little or no support. He chooses that the children should come to Church both morning and afternoon. I brought them to Church only in the afternoon. If this should answer better than my plan, on some future occasion I will let you or Mr. H. know it.

"The stipend to the teachers here is a shilling each Sunday; but we find them firing, and bestow gratuities as rewards of diligence, which may make it worth sixpence more.

"But the success of the whole depends on the attention paid by people of condition. If persons of some consequence will condescend to officiate as visitors, and by kind words encourage the good among these hitherto despised and neglected creatures, and give gentle reproof to those who sway from their duty, a wonderful effect will in a few months be discoverable. Were I among you, I would call forth the gentlemen to visit the boys, and the ladies to superintend the girls. 'Go to Brentford, and learn of Mrs. Trimmer!' This is what I should say to the ladies of Chelsea. I would beg leave to recommend the perusal of Mrs. Trimmer's *Œconomy of Charity*. It may be had at Johnson's, in St. Paul's Churchyard.

"It had been sometimes a difficult task to keep the children in proper order when they were all assembled at Church; but I now sit very near them myself, which has had the effect of preserving the most perfect decorum. After the sermon in the morning they return home to dinner, and meet at the schools at half-past one, and are dismissed at five, with strict injunctions to observe a quiet behaviour, free from all noise and clamour. Before the business is begun in the morning, they all kneel down while a prayer is read, and the same before dismission in the evening.

"To those children who distinguish themselves as examples of diligence, quietness in behaviour, observance of order, kindness to their companions, &c., &c., I give some little token of my regard, as a pair of shoes, if they are barefooted, and some who are very bare of apparel I clothe. This I have been enabled to do, in many instances, through the liberal support given me by my brothers in the city. By these means I have acquired considerable ascendance over the minds of the children. Besides, I frequently go round to their habitations to enquire into their behaviour at home and into the conduct of the parents, to whom I give some little hints now and then, as well as to the children.

"I was taking a woman to task one day, before her husband, because the house was not so clean as it ought. 'Troth, sir,' said the man, 'I wish you would come a little oftener; we should be all the better.' The people tell me they keep their children in more order by the threat of telling Mr. R. than they could formerly by the most severe stripes.

"It is that part of our Saviour's character which I aim at imitating: '*He went about doing good.*' No one can form an idea what benefits he is capable of rendering to the community by the condescension of visiting the dwellings of the poor. You may remember the place without the Southgate called Littleworth; it used to be the St. Giles of Gloucester. By going amongst the people I have totally changed their manners. They avow at this time that the place is quite a heaven to what it used to be. Some of the vilest of the boys are now so exemplary in behaviour, that I have taken one into my own service.

"I mention this as an evidence of what may be done. But I fear I am growing too prolix, and that I shall cause you to repent the opening a correspondence with your old acquaintance.

"I must now tell you that I am now blessed with six excellent girls and two lovely boys. My eldest boy was born the very day that I made public to the world the scheme of Sunday schools in my paper of November 3rd, 1783. In four years' time it has extended so rapidly as now to include 250,000 children; it is increasing more and more. It reminds me of the grain of mustard seed.

"Remember me in kindest terms to Mr. Harris, and believe me, dear Madam,

"Both his and your most obedient Servant,

"R. RAIKES."

B.

CHAPTER VI.—SUNDAY SCHOOLS IN FRANCE.

Mr. Raikes states that he was visited by members of the French Academy, Paris; but it does not appear that Sunday schools were established as the result of that visit.

M. le Pasteur Henry-Paumier, Société des Ecoles du Dimanche, Paris, in the course of a letter to the Author, says: "Our Sunday school work here in France may be said to be both very ancient and very new—very ancient, for our French Reformers made it a point of duty for all our churches to teach even the youngest children, and elementary catechisms were established [sic] in the churches, the schools, and the families by order of the Synods or ecclesiastical authorities; very new, if you look to the particular mode of teaching as it is now arranged in Sunday schools (groups, teachers, &c.).

"The first school of the kind was created at Bordeaux about the time of the restoration of the public worship, both for the Catholic and the Protestant, by Napoleon I., about the year 1800. The only thing that I have been able to discover is from one of our members, belonging to the Wesleyan Church, the fact that some English members belonging to the Wesleyan denomination settled, he thinks, in Paris about the year you mention (1790), and may, perhaps, have written to Robert Raikes to help them."

The Rev. Jean Paul Cook, son of the Dr. Cook whom D'Aubigné called the "Wesley of France," in an interview with Mr. Harris at St. Helier's, Jersey, said a Sunday school was founded in Paris in 1815 by the Rev. Mr. Martin. Mr. Jean Paul Cook was born in the South of France, and took an active part in founding and organising Sunday schools in the South of France, in Normandy, and in Paris. He started and edited *Les Magasin des Ecoles du Dimanche* and *l'Evangeliste*. At one time he had a special mission to visit all the Protestant churches in France. The mission occupied two years. He said he travelled 12,000 miles, preached in 300 pulpits, and organised or re-organised about 100 Sunday schools. All his expenses were paid by Mr. Woodruffe, salt merchant, Brooklyn, U.S., and a member of the New York Union.

He also said: "The influence of Sunday schools in France is very small among us as a nation. Future generations may feel the benefit of them. There are no Sunday schools attached to the Roman Catholic communion. As to political influence, Sunday schools in France possess none."

C.

"THE SUNDAY SCHOLAR'S COMPANION."

This little book was printed by R. Raikes, and was in use in 1785. The edition quoted in his volume was published in 1794, and its full title is: "*The Sunday Scholar's Companion;* Consisting of Scripture Sentences, disposed in such order, As will quickly ground Young Learners in the Fundamental Doctrines of our most Holy Religion; And at the same time Lead them Pleasantly on from Simple and Easy to Compound and Difficult Words. Gloucester: Printed by R. Raikes; and sold by Messrs. Rivington, St. Paul's Churchyard, and J. Evans, Paternoster Row, London; J. Washbourn, Gloucester; and T. Stevens, Cirencester. MDCCXCIV."

This little book, admirably adapted for its purpose, probably owes its origin to the Rev. C. Moore, Vicar of Boughton Blaen, Kent, who, having formed the nucleus of a Sunday school in 1785, "stuck a printed paper on the church doors and dispersed it about," as follows:

"Sunday schools supported by voluntary subscriptions in the parish of Boughton Blaen, in Kent, 1785:

"The points aimed at in the introduction of Sunday schools, are—to furnish opportunities of instruction to the children of the poorer part of the parish, *without interfering with any industry of the week days;* and to inure children to early habits of going to church, and of spending the leisure hours on *Sunday* decently and virtuously.

"The children are to be taught to read and to be instructed in the plain duties of the Christian religion, with a particular view to their good and industrious behaviour in their future character of labourers and servants.

"The extent of the plan must be guided by the subscription that may be raised; and all persons willing to encourage the same, even by the smallest donations, are desired to apply to the Rev. C. Moore, Vicar."

This very judicious notice was calculated to allay the fear of parents that they might be robbed of the earnings of their children; and of employers, that education would unfit children becoming labourers and servants in that state of life to which it had pleased God to call them!

D.

BREACHES OF PRIVILEGE OF PARLIAMENT.

The following is the full story told by the newspaper reports of the day and the Journals of the House:—

March 28th, 1722.—Robert Raikes, printer, at Gloucester, and J. Wilson, bookseller, at Bristol, attending according to order, the former was called to the Bar of the Commons, where he confessed the printing the pamphlet above mentioned, and said he had his intelligence relating to the proceedings of the House from Edward Cave, of the Post Office, London, and that J. Wilson was not concerned in the printing thereof. Then he withdrew, and the Commons resolved that Robert Raikes was guilty of a breach of the privilege of the House, and ordered: (1) That the said Robert Raikes be, for his said breach of privilege, taken into the custody of the Sergeant-at-Arms attending the House; (2) That the said J. Wilson be discharged from his further attendance upon the House; (3) That Edward Cave, of the Post Office, London, do attend the House upon Saturday next.

March 30th.—Edward Cave attending according to order, he was called in and examined at the Bar of the House of Commons touching his sending to Robert Raikes the intelligence before-mentioned. He owned that he had sent him several written News Letters which he said he received from William Wye, John Stanley, John Willys, and Elias Delpench, containing likewise intelligence relating to the proceedings of the House. Being withdrawn, the *Journal* of the 23rd of January, 1722, was read, upon which it was resolved that Edward Cave having presumed to disperse written News Letters containing accounts of the proceedings of the House is guilty of a breach of privilege of the House, and he was ordered to be taken into custody of the Sergeant-at-Arms. And William Wye, John Stanley, John Willys, and Elias Delpench were ordered to attend the House on the 2nd April.

April 3rd.—William Wye, John Stanley, John Willys, and Elias Delpench attending at the door were severally called in and examined. Whereupon it was resolved that they were guilty of a breach of the privilege of the House, and they were ordered to be taken into the custody of the Sergeant-at-Arms.

April 8th.—Robert Raikes, printer at Gloucester, was brought to the Bar of the House, where, upon his knees, having received a reprimand from Mr. Speaker, he was ordered to be discharged, paying his fees.

Upon the humble petition of John Stanley, William Wye, Edward Cave, and Elias Delpench, the Commons ordered that they be brought to the Bar on Wednesday following, in order to be discharged.

April 10th.—John Stanley, William Wye, Edward Cave, and Elias Delpench were brought to the Bar of the

Commons, where, having upon their knees, received a reprimand from Mr. Speaker, they were ordered out of custody, paying their fees.

After Mr. Raikes's second offence, in February, 1728 (when it was disclosed that Mr. Gythins was the sender of the news letter), and after, on his petition, he was excused attendance at Westminster, the following entry appears in the Journal of the House of Commons:

"*Resolved, nemine contradicente*, That it is an indignity to and a breach of the privilege of this House for any persons to presume to give, in written or printed newspapers, any account or minutes of the debates or other proceedings of this House, or of any Committee thereof. *Resolved, nemine contradicente*, That upon discovery of the authors, printers, or publishers of any such written or printed newspapers, this House will proceed against the offenders with the utmost severity."

E.

A ROYAL ANECDOTE.

The *Gentleman's Magazine*, 1788, contains the following:

"A great female personage hearing lately that Mr. Raikes, of Gloucester, was at Windsor on a visit to one of his relations, sent for him to the Lodge, and expressed a desire to know by what accident a thought which promised so much benefit to the lower order of the people, as the institution of Sunday schools, was suggested to his mind, and what effects were observed in consequence on the manners of the poor. In the conversation, which lasted more than an hour, her Majesty most graciously said that she envied those who had the power of doing good by thus personally promoting the welfare of society in giving instruction and morality to the general mass of the common people, a pleasure from which, by her station, she was debarred. What a glorious sentiment is this for a Queen! Were this known among the ladies of the British nation, it would serve to animate them with zeal to follow the example which the Queen is desirous to set before them."

F.

SIR THOMAS B. THOMPSON.

Nelson's Despatches, vol. iii., p. 51, contains the following, written by Captain Sir Edward Berry: "Captain Thompson, of the *Leander*, of 50 guns, with a degree of skill and intrepidity highly honourable to his professional character, advanced towards the enemy's line on the outside, and most judiciously dropped his anchor athwart the hawse of *Le Franklin*, raking her with great success, the shot from the *Leander's* broadside, which passed that ship, all striking *L'Orient*, the flagship of the French Commander-in-Chief."

Again, p. 90, same vol.: "Captain Thomas Boulden Thompson, of the *Leander*, distinguished himself by his 'gallant and almost unprecedented defence of that ship against *Le Genéreux*, of 74 guns, on the 18th August, 1799,' when he was severely wounded and made prisoner."

He was knighted in 1799; lost a leg in command of the *Bellona*, 74, at Copenhagen, in 1801; was made a baronet in December, 1806, a K.C.B. in 1815, and a Knight Grand Cross in 1822. He died on the 3rd March, 1828, being then a Vice-Admiral of the Red and Treasurer of Greenwich Hospital.

THE END.

www.ingramcontent.com/pod-product-compliance
Lightning Source LLC
Chambersburg PA
CBHW020317240426
43673CB00039B/836